D0872272

The Map of Time

The Map of Time

Seventeenth-Century English Literature
and Ideas of Pattern in History

ACHSAH GUIBBORY

University of Illinois Press

Urbana and Chicago

Publication of this work was supported in part by grants from
the Andrew W. Mellon Foundation and the Campus Research Board,
University of Illinois–Urbana-Champaign.

© 1986 by the Board of Trustees of the University of Illinois
Manufactured in the United States of America
C   5   4   3   2   1

This book is printed on acid-free paper.

Library of Congress Cataloging-in-Publication Data

Guibbory, Achsah, 1945–
     The map of time.

     Bibliography: p.
     Includes index.
     1. English literature—Early modern, 1500–1700—
History and criticism.   2. Literature and history.
I. Title.
PR439.H56G8   1986   820'.9004   85–8729
ISBN 0–252–01264–X (alk. paper)

PR
439
.H56
G8
1986

For Tony, Gabriel, and my mother
and
in memory of my father

600937

600037

Contents

Acknowledgments

In writing this book, I have incurred a number of debts that I would like to acknowledge. I am grateful to my colleagues who have been generous with their help, especially Melissa Cain, Thomas Clayton, Margaret Dickie, Anthony Kaufman, David Kay, Earl Miner, and Brian Wilkie. Arnold Stein read the entire manuscript and offered invaluable advice at a crucial time. The staffs of the William Andrews Clark Library and the Rare Book Room of the University of Illinois Library have provided not only books but also congenial environments in which to work. At an early stage of my research, an appointment to the University of Illinois Center for Advanced Study gave me the necessary time and freedom to envision the whole project. My thanks also go to Ann Lowry Weir and Susan L. Patterson of the University of Illinois Press for the careful attention that they have given my manuscript. Some of the material in chapters 2 and 7 and a small section of chapter 3 appeared in earlier, different versions in the *Journal of English and Germanic Philology, Philological Quarterly,* and the *Huntington Library Quarterly,* respectively, and I appreciate permission to use this material. The one debt that I cannot adequately repay is to my husband, for his compassion and selfless generosity.

CHAPTER I

Introduction

W HEN ARCHBISHOP JAMES USSHER began his *Annals of the World* (1658) with the confident announcement that history began with Creation on Sunday "the twenty third day of *Octob.* in the year of the Julian Calendar, 710," 4,004 years before Christ,[1] he assumed, like many writers in the seventeenth century, that temporal experience had shape and order, that history revealed a pattern that human beings could comprehend. With its providentially fixed beginning at Creation and its end at the Last Judgment, history had a definite, limited shape. The order was there; it had only to be discovered and charted.

Not all shared Ussher's confidence that we could precisely date the beginning of history. His contemporary, Sir Thomas Browne, for example, believed that God had wrapped these matters in obscurity: "Concerning the World and its temporal circumscriptions, who ever shall strictly examine both extreams, will easily perceive there is not only obscurity in its end, but its beginning; that as its period is inscrutable, so is its nativity indeterminable."[2] Moreover, there seems to have been in the late sixteenth and the seventeenth centuries a growing sense that human history was larger, more vast than had earlier been believed. The older, "universal" histories of the world were going out of fashion (though some historians still attempted them) as writers focused their histories more narrowly on particular nations, periods, principalities, cities, or even important individuals. Such trends in historiography suggest a recognition that there was a great deal more to know about the past than medieval historians had assumed. Although Sir Walter Raleigh's *History of the World* (1614) and Ussher's *Annals* aspired to universal history, neither writer was able to complete his projected design.

Nevertheless, despite the practical impossibility of writing a complete history of the world, people still believed that it was theoretically possible to comprehend much of the whole. And so we

1

find numerous writers praising the virtue of having a comprehensive view of history. Thomas Fuller gave a delightfully witty turn to this commonplace as he introduced his *Historie of the Holy Warre* (1639): "What a pitie is it to see a proper Gentleman to have such a crick in his neck that he cannot look backward! yet no better is he who cannot see behind him the actions which were long since performed. History maketh a young man to be old, without either wrinkles or gray hairs; priviledging him with the experience of age, without either the infirmities or inconveniences thereof."[3] Even late in the seventeenth century the belief in the importance of comprehending the entire past remained strong. Justifying the importance of writing and reading histories, Richard Baxter explained: "Every one should desire to know as much of the *whole*, as he is capable, and as tendeth to his duty and delight. And how small a parcel of *Time*, or *Men*, or *Actions* are present in our daies? How little knoweth he that knoweth no more than he hath lived to see?"[4]

Discovering the order of history could give a sense of security, sometimes a sense of power. In *An Apologie of the Power and Providence of God in the Government of the World* (1627), George Hakewill insisted that if one looked at the large pattern of time rather than simply the particular events of the present, he would discover a reassuring order in human history. Trying to gain such a comprehensive view, Hakewill "abstracted and raised [his] thoughts to a higher pitch, and as from a vantage ground tooke a larger view"; he saw that "what was lost to one part, was gained to another; and what was lost in one time, was to the same part recouered in another."[5] Seeing what Browne aptly called the "Map of Time"[6] could give man a special wisdom, even a kind of transcendence. History was to be studied for its usefulness as a store of past experience and examples that give "necessarie light to the Present in matter of state, law, historie."[7] It also appealed to the human desire for immortality. Raleigh observed that history

hath triumphed over time, which besides it, nothing but eternity hath triumphed ouer: for it hath carried our knowledge ouer the vast & deuouring space of so many thousands of yeares, and giuen so faire and peircing eies to our minde; that we plainely behould liuing now, as if we had liued then, that great World . . . as it was then, when but new to it selfe. . . . And it is not the least debt which we owe unto History, that it hath made vs acquainted with our dead Ancestors; and, out of the depth and darkenesse of the earth, deliuered us their memory and fame.[8]

Raleigh's words suggest not only that history gives immortal fame to the people whose deeds it records, but also that the study of history can compensate for our short span of life. As John Selden said when dedicating his *Historie of Tithes* (1618) to his friend Robert Cotton, "The many ages of former Experience and Observation . . . may so accumulat yeers to us as if we had liud even from the beginning of Time."[9]

But it was not only historians who hoped to possess a comprehensive vision of time. F. J. Levy has shown that interest in history had become widespread by the end of Queen Elizabeth I's reign: "From about the middle of the 1580's a typical Englishman must have found it more and more difficult to avoid having any knowledge of the past. Regardless of his purse, his background, or his tastes, sooner or later he was bound to be exposed to history."[10] In the second half of the sixteenth century there had been a remarkable increase in history writing. Translations of classical histories and more recent Continental ones, English historical chronicles, church history writing spawned by the Protestant Reformation, and historical poetry — the proliferation of all these forms of historical writing reflected the demand for histories and pointed to the conclusion that "this was a most historically-minded age."[11]

The concern with history could hardly be said to have diminished in the seventeenth century. Translations of classical historians into English continued to appear. To name but a few, there were Thomas Heywood's Sallust (1608), Thomas May's Lucan (1627), Thomas Hobbes's Thucydides (1629), as well as numerous editions of Thomas North's sixteenth-century translation of Plutarch and of Sir Henry Savile's Tacitus, first published in 1591. The seventeenth century produced histories of Britain, antiquarian histories of feudalism and tithes, yet more histories of the English church, and historical controversies about episcopacy and church government. Historians were even more concerned than they had been in the sixteenth century with accuracy and the reliability of their sources; some of them, like Gilbert Burnet in his *History of the Reformation of the Church of England* (published 1679–1715), even printed the written documents that were the primary sources. Especially during the Civil War period and the Restoration, there was a notable interest in writing the histories of the times one was living in, rather than histories of a distant past. Though Fuller was aware of "how dangerous it is to follow Truth too nere to the heels," he included in his *Church-History of Britain* (1655) an account of the period of James I and Charles I because "the most *informative Histories* to *Posterity,* and such as are most *highly prized* by the *judicious,* are such as were *written* by the *Eye-witnesses* thereof."[12] The earl of Clarendon (supporter of monarchy) and John Rushworth (supporter of Parliament), both of whom were immediately and intimately involved in the events they recorded, wrote accounts of the Civil War period, though Clarendon, sensitive to the dangers of printing his "open" history while the participants were still alive, refrained from publishing it in his lifetime and passed it on instead to his posterity. This interest in writing contemporary history continued after the Restoration. After his banishment from England, Clarendon extended his history to encompass the years from the Restoration of Charles II in 1660 until Clarendon's own exile in 1667. Burnet's *History of his Own Time* covered the period from 1660 to the treaty of peace at Utrecht in the reign of Queen Anne.[13]

As in the sixteenth century, the interest in history was by no means limited to historians. Many writers had not just a curiosity about the past or an interest in contemporary events of moment, but a comprehensive view of history, a sense of the shape of time. The purpose of this book is to explore some of the important ways in which seventeenth-century English literature reflects a pervasive, deep concern with the pattern or shape of history. I am not attempting a history of seventeenth-century historiography or of seventeenth-century historical thought — though these subjects deserve studies of their own. Rather, in my concern with the relationship between literature and ideas of history, the focus will be primarily on literature. Concentrating on six authors — Sir Francis Bacon (1561–1626), John Donne (1572–1631), Ben Jonson (1572/3–1637), Robert Herrick (1591–1674), John Milton (1608–74), and John Dryden (1631–1700) — the following chapters will show how radically seventeenth-century literature reflects ideas of history's pattern. Few of these writers can actually be considered historians. Only Bacon, Milton, and Dryden wrote histories per se, and indeed these histories constitute only a small part of their literary achievements. However, all of these writers had clearly defined views of history. And their ideas of history affected the nature, scope, and purposes of their works in personal, often unique ways.

Before exploring the importance of ideas of history in these six writers, it is necessary to discuss the major views of history's pattern that were current during this period. In the seventeenth century there were three major conceptions of the shape of history: the idea of decay; the cyclical view of history; and the idea of progress. In order to provide a necessary context for the chapters that follow, the rest of this chapter will define briefly these three views of history, indicate their prevalence, and suggest some of their important assumptions. Although historians defined and debated these various conceptions of history, they were not the exclusive possession of historians. These ideas of the shape of history, often tacitly assumed rather than explicitly stated, underlie poetry, drama, scientific and religious prose, as well as histories and works on historiography.[14] Because these ideas of history were of such pervasive currency and importance, I will draw on a variety of writers, not just historians, to define them. I do not wish to argue that the historians influenced these other writers, but rather to suggest that the three basic ideas of history were quite common and were held by writers of widely varying interests and talents.

The three views of history are in themselves simple, indeed reductive, though they could be put to complex uses. They provided rather limited explanations of history, since they reduced its complexity to clear, simple paradigms. Nevertheless, they were extremely powerful: they could be used to account for and order a wide range of events; they molded a person's interpretation of temporal experience; and they could either encourage or limit his sense of the individual's ability to affect the course of the present and future.

The idea of decay was perhaps the most limited and limiting view of history in the seventeenth century. According to this view, the world has been declining since the Fall of Adam and Eve. With the passing of every year, indeed every minute, the world is approaching its final dissolution.

> For as the World by time still more declines,
> Both from the truth, and wisedome of Creation:

> So at the truth she more and more repines,
> As making hast to her last declination.

> Fulke Greville, "A Treatie of Humane Learning," st. 63[15]

Because the process of time is a process of decay, all nature tends to corruption. Evidence that the sun's heat was not as strong as it had been, discoveries of mutability in the heavens, and even accounts that suggested that giants had existed in the distant past provided many people with confirmation of their fears that the world was decaying. Thus Henry Reynolds began *Mythomystes* (1632) with this grim remark: "I haue thought vpon the times wee liue in, and am forced to affirme the world is decrepit, and, out of its age & doating estate, subiect to all the imperfections that are inseparable from that wracke and maime of Nature."[16] Like everything in it, the world is mortal and thus subject to corruption like man.[17]

Corruption is progressive, inevitable. It is both physical and moral: the world as it ages has become weaker and less fruitful, and people are more vicious now than in the past. As Browne laments, in "our present Degeneration . . . how widely we are fallen from the pure Exemplar and Idea of our Nature: for after this corruptive Elongation from a primitive and pure Creation, we are almost lost in Degeneration; and Adam hath not only fallen from his Creator, but we our selves from Adam, our Tycho and primary Generator."[18] Such a view tends to idealize the past as the time of greatest virtue and wisdom. Thus the idea of decay is often associated with a reverence for antiquity and for the achievement of the ancients. After indicting the general loss of truth and wisdom, Fulke Greville insists:

> . . . they that Arts first began,
> Pierc'd further, than succeeding ages can.

> Since how should Water rise aboue her fountaine?

> "A Treatie of Humane Learning," st. 75–76

Like Greville, Reynolds's observations about the world's decay lead to his insistence that "awefull reuerence [is] due" to "the neuerenough honoured Auncients."[19]

In his *Methodus* (1566) Jean Bodin, the most important French historian in the sixteenth century, attributed the idea of decay to the influence of the classical myth of the four ages: the first age was the golden, and man subsequently degenerated through the silver, brass, and iron ages.[20] But people could find biblical as well as classical sanctions for their belief in decay, as Bodin well observed when he linked the conception of the four ages not only to the ancient poets' fables but also to interpretations of the vision in Daniel (2:31–45) of a figure, representing four monarchies, whose head was gold, chest and arms silver, legs iron, and feet clay.[21] Moreover, the Judaeo-Christian conception of the Fall from innocent bliss merged nicely with the classical idea of the golden age, and the Fall could be interpreted as occurring throughout history: man and nature have continuously moved further away from their early perfection. As biblical confirmation of the theory of decay, Reynolds cites the apocryphal second book of Esdras where God tells Ezra to put his house in order: "For the world has lost its youth, and the times are beginning to grow old. . . . For worse evils are still to come than those you have seen happen. For the more the world grows weak with age, the more evils will increase upon those who live in it. Truth will more and more retire, and falsehood draw near" (2 Esd. 14:10, 16–18).

This view of history as a process of continual, irreversible decay was widespread enough in late sixteenth-century Europe for Bodin to devote the major part of chapter seven of his *Methodus* to refuting it, but the idea of decay was probably strongest in England during the first quarter of the seventeenth century. Bacon complained of the popularity of this view of history, which he believed was one of the most insidious obstacles to the advancement of learning. The most exhaustive statement of the idea of universal decay is Godfrey Goodman's *The Fall of Man, or the Corruption of Nature* (1616), whose very title suggests the religious context that was frequently invoked to explain the world's degeneration. But Goodman's treatise is itself indebted to Donne's *First Anniversary* on the death of Elizabeth Drury, and it is Donne's works that best reveal the complex, fascinating ways in which the idea of decay could shape a person's thought and writing.

Despite its currency, this view of history came under increasing attack. Bodin was one of its early critics in the sixteenth century, and he was enormously influential in England as well as Europe. Bodin was cited by so many English writers in the late sixteenth and early seventeenth centuries that Leonard Dean has concluded that *Methodus* "was probably read by most serious English students

7

of history between 1580 and 1625."[22] It was not only Bodin's ideas about history writing and his insistence on the historian's need for objectivity that were influential, but also his attack on the decay theory. To cite merely one example, Gabriel Harvey, writing to Edmund Spenser, invoked Bodin as his authority for rejecting the idea of decay: "You suppose the first age was the goulde age. It is nothinge soe. Bodin defendith the goulde age to flourishe nowe, and our first Grandfathers to have rubbid thorowghe in the iron and brasen age, at the beginninge when all things were rude and unperfitt in comparison of the exquisite finesse and delicacye, that we ar growen unto at these dayes."[23] Bodin boldly suggested that the ancient Romans were far more vicious than his own contemporaries. Instead of glorifying the first age as the most perfect and virtuous — the standard against which all subsequent ages were to be measured — he insisted that men were actually bestial and barbaric in the so-called golden and silver ages when they "were scattered like beasts" and sustained themselves "by force and crime."[24] This rejection of the golden age myth surfaces again in Hakewill's *Apology of the Power and Providence of God,* written to refute Goodman. Hakewill's *Apology* enjoyed considerable popularity, as evidenced by the fact that after the first edition in 1627, it went through two more editions by 1635. Like Bodin, he denied that decay is either "perpetuall" or "universall," arguing instead that there is a "certaine wheeling about of all things," a cyclical "vicissitude" that "will neuer cease as long as the world lasts."[25] Time manifests a cyclical rather than a degenerative pattern.

In refuting the idea of decay many writers asserted the cyclical view of history, which was the dominant theory of history in the sixteenth and seventeenth centuries and which continued to influence historical thinking well into the eighteenth century.[26] With the Renaissance revival and recovery of the classics, and the numerous English translations of classical historians in the late sixteenth and early seventeenth centuries, came renewed interest in the cyclical theory of history defined by ancient historians such as Tacitus and Polybius. The classical view of history included two related concepts: nature is always the same, and history is a series of repetitive cycles. Machiavelli invokes this first commonplace when he remarks in his *Discourses upon the first Decade of T. Livius* that "in all cities and all peoples there are now the same desires and the same humors, there were always."[27] Because of the uniformity of nature and the revolution of time, events and people find their parallels in different ages. Fuller well expresses the major assumptions of this view of history as he praises the importance of knowing the past: "Yea, it not onely maketh things past, present; but inableth one to make a rationall conjecture of things to come. For this world affordeth no new accidents, but in the same sense wherein we call it *a new Moon*, which is the old one in another shape, and yet no other then what hath been formerly. Old actions return again, furbished over with some new and different circumstances."[28] Few people thought that the cycles were exactly or completely repetitive. Nevertheless, the basic patterns were believed to be constant, unchanging, and thus history provided examples from which humanity could learn. Because of the essential sameness of human experience, Samuel Daniel could even suggest that knowledge of only "a few ages" is "sufficient" for our "instruction": "For had we the particular occurrents of all ages, and all nations, it might more stuffe, but not better our vnderstanding. We shall finde still the same correspondencies to hold in the actions of men: Vertues, and Vices the same . . . the causes of the ruines, and mutations of States to be alike."[29]

That the same patterns were repeated throughout history allowed the prudent observer to draw lessons about the present and sometimes even to give warnings about the future. As Machiavelli said, "It is very easy for him that examines with diligence the things that are past, to foresee the future in any Commonwealth."[30] Historians like Bodin and Raleigh concluded from their study of the past that cities, states, and empires rise to a certain height but then "decline, and fall," and Bodin gloomily predicted that his country, too, though now enjoying glory and prosperity, must eventually decay. "By some eternal law of nature the path of change seems to go in a circle."[31] Machiavelli discerned a similar pattern in history: "All Countries in their alterations, doo most commonly chaunge from order to disorder, and from disorder to order againe. For nature having made all worldly thinges variable, so soone as they haue atteined their vttermost perfection and height, doo of force descend: and being come downe so low, as lower they cannot, of necessitie must ascend. So that from good they descended to euill, and from euill ascend to good."[32]

Such conclusions suggest an inevitability that tends to discourage human effort. The cycles seem inescapable. But many historians retained a faith that despite the generally repetitive pattern of history, people could learn to avoid the errors of the past. Rushworth insisted that though all *"Empires* and *Kingdoms . . .* have their *Periods,"* "the *Pilot"* of the ship of state can learn to "escape" disaster once he has "discovered those Shelves and Rocks, upon which others have been split."[33] That the historian strove to be objective and unbiased in his pursuit of truth did not prevent him from offering lessons that were at times rather pointed. John Hayward's *Lives of the III Normans, Kings of England* (1613) showed that disorder and "tragical events" follow when the eldest son's right of succession is violated.[34] Hayward dedicated the book to Charles, Prince of Wales and heir apparent to the throne, hoping to insure England's political stability. Even Rushworth, whose *Historical Collections* studiously avoided personal intrusions and commentary, saw his history as providing lessons. Addressing the first volume to Richard Cromwell in 1658, Rushworth explicitly warned him not to make the mistake of Charles I, but rather to respect the laws and Parliament.[35]

The classical historians were important in transmitting a cyclical view of history to the Renaissance, but people did not have to go to the ancient historians to discover that time is cyclical. They could find evidence in the rotation of the sun, in the seasons of the year, or in the biological cycle—all of which provided metaphors or analogies for the history of kingdoms, states, and individuals. Browne found in the sun's pattern of ascent and descent the paradigm for the shape of history: "the lives not onely of men, but of Commonweales, and the whole world, run . . . on a Circle, where, arriving to their Meridian, they decline in obscurity, and fall under the Horizon againe."[36] Because of the correspondence between the microcosm and the larger world, the history of the body politic parallels the life of the individual. Thus biological and seasonal metaphors could be seen as appropriate images for the history of kingdoms:

> *States haue degrees, as humane bodies haue*
> *Springs, Summer, Autumne, Winter and the graue.*
>
> Fulke Greville, "A Treatie of Warres," st. 42

Many writers assumed that history is not radically separated from nature but rather obeys the same laws. As Bodin remarked, "There

10

is a change in human affairs similar to that in the nature of all things."[37] In his important *De la Vicissitude* (1576), which was translated into English in 1594 and approvingly cited in Hakewill's *Apology*, Louis Le Roy placed an even greater emphasis on the close relationship between the order of history and the order of nature as he traced the cycles in which arms and arts have flourished and decayed in different countries in successive ages. Le Roy explained that history shows the same pattern of "successiue alteration" or "vicissitude" that the entire universe does. The rise and fall of kingdoms is like the alternation of day and night or the rotation of the seasons from spring and summer to fall and winter.[38] Similarly, Hakewill insisted that all things under the moon "haue a time of *groweth* and increase, of *ripenesse* and perfection, and then of *declination* and decrease, which brings them at last to a finall and totall *dissolution*."[39] It is precisely this assumption that the history of human institutions partakes of the cyclical pattern of all natural things that allowed the republican James Harrington to proclaim during the Interregnum that "the *dissolution* of the late *Monarchy was as natural as the death of a man*"—an assertion that would surely have shocked Royalists who believed in the divine right of kings. Because "the *corruption of one Government (as in natural bodies) is the generation of another,*" Harrington believed that England, having witnessed what he thought was the end of monarchy, was now prepared for the "generation" of a commonwealth form of government.[40]

But perhaps the recurring image of the commonwealth or kingdom as plant most suggestively reveals the intimate relationship between the cycles of history and those of nature. Bodin describes how first the commonwealth is "rooted and grounded"; gradually it "groweth vp vntill it be come to the full perfection of it selfe"; finally it falls either by its own weight or "by the enemies violence" or "by the wrath of God."[41] Like plants, nations go through cycles of growth and decay. Raleigh's eloquent description of the fate of Rome develops this analogy even more fully. His *History of the World* ends with Rome almost at her height: "We haue left it flourishing in the middle of the field; hauing rooted vp, or cut down, all [the other kingdoms] that kept it from the eyes and admiration of the world. But after some continuance, it shall begin to lose the beauty it had; the stormes of ambition shal beat her great boughes and branches one against another; her leaues shall fall off, her limbes wither, and a rabble of barbarous Nations enter the field, and cut her downe."[42] Like plants and beautiful women, kingdoms are mortal, and Raleigh's language emphasizes their transience and fragility. For all their show of magnificence, bravery, wealth, and power, ultimately they must yield to the same fate as plants, animals, and people.

Scholars have argued that the cyclical view of history is essentially a Greco-Roman interpretation of time, which contrasts with the Judaeo-Christian belief that history is linear, nonrepetitive, and eschatologically oriented, always moving toward the Apocalypse and the Day of Judgment, which will signal the end of historical time.[43] But recently this dichotomy between cyclical and Christian linear views has been challenged.[44] The Jews had a strong sense of the cyclical aspect of time, for their holy days and festivals, such as Shvuoth and Sukkoth, were closely tied to the cycle of the season. For Christians, too, the liturgical calendar fostered a deep feeling for the yearly cycles. Moreover, typology tended to combine the cyclical view of history with a linear, eschatological one. Initially a Christian way of interpreting the Old Testament, typology finds that a specific historical person or event in the Old Testament prefigures Christ or an event in the New Testament; the later figure or event is the fulfillment or perfection of the promise contained in the earlier. While denying that history is entirely repetitive and thus directionless, typology does assume that there are parallels between people or events in different times. This sense that there is a sameness, a pattern that is repeated in history albeit with variations, was further reinforced by the later Protestant extension of typology into a way of interpreting the life of every Christian,[45] whose sufferings could parallel David's or Job's or Christ's. Clearly Christianity could and did assimilate the cyclical view of history, one of whose most important virtues lies in its ability to organize all temporal experience into a pattern that allows people in the present to feel an intimate connection with the past.

For many sixteenth- and seventeenth-century writers, the cyclical view of history seemed sanctioned by God. Insisting that he is vindicating God's glory by attacking the idea of decay and asserting that history and all nature reflect a cyclical order, Hakewill invoked Solomon in support of the cyclical view: "how often doth he beat vpon the *circulation* and *running round of all things as it were in a ring.*"[46] For Browne, the cyclical pattern of history, with its suggestions of circularity, reflected the perfection of God, the great circle whose center is everywhere and circumference nowhere.[47] Though Raleigh found more to mourn than to celebrate in such cyclical vicissitudes, he, too, discerned the hand of Providence in the cycles of history. He saw in the cyclical decline of the great kingdoms of the world—Babylon, Persia, Egypt, Syria, Macedon, Carthage, Rome—the record of "GODS judgments vpon the greater and greatest."[48] This tendency to see Divine Providence in the cycles of history persisted, despite the increased secular emphasis of seventeenth-century thought. As late as 1680 Burnet could preach that "there is nothing in which the overruling Force of divine Providence shows it self more than in the rising and Falling of Empires."[49]

The cyclical view of history was probably both a cause and a result of the way in which the Renaissance saw its own achievements. The rediscovery of ancient learning and languages and the subsequent development of knowledge and eloquence on the Continent and in England were believed to be the beginning of a new cycle in history. Bodin observed that the recent revival of learning occurred "after a long eclipse of letters throughout almost the entire world." With the dawn of this new day, the sun that had set with the fall of Rome was rising again. Le Roy, too, celebrated the recovery of learning after it had "long time remained in a manner extinguished." Bacon, writing in England in the early seventeenth century, similarly noted that there had been a renovation of knowledge among the nations of Western Europe.[50] The sense of cyclical renewal clearly worked against the idea that decline was continuous and irreversible. Participating in this renewal, historians held up the great Greek and Latin histories as models for imitation. William Camden, for example, wrote his *Annales* (1615) consciously imitating Tacitus. John Speed in his own *History of Great Britaine* (1611) praised Camden, who had earlier published *Britannia*, as "another *Polybius,* & no way his inferior."[51] The hope was for England to produce historians to rival the great classical ones. England was as worthy of good histories as Greece or Rome had been.

Much as these writers believed that there had been a renewal of learning, so too poets like Sir Philip Sidney and Edmund Spenser felt themselves participating in (or at least they hoped for) a renaissance in English letters. When Sidney in his *Defence of Poetry* (1595) praised the virtues of the English language, he did so in the faith that England was capable of producing poetry comparable to that of ancient Greece and Rome.[52] Indeed, the ideal of imitating the classics, with its aim of creating a wisdom, eloquence, and literature that could rival those of the ancients, implicitly assumed a cyclical interpretation of history. Such a historical perspective was suggested when Jonson in his poem "To the Memory of My Beloved, the Author Mr. William Shakespeare" praised the great English dramatist as the peer of the great classical tragedians.

Even the reforms of the Protestant Reformation were seen in essentially cyclical terms. The religious aim to revive the perfection of an earlier period paralleled the more secular, humanist desire to regain the wisdom of the ancients. Sixteenth-century defenders of the English church typically offered a cyclical reading of church history: after a long period of decay the church was being restored to the purity of primitive Christianity. In *Actes and Monumentes* (1563) John Foxe placed the English Reformation within the larger context of the history of the "universal church": first there was "the suffering time of the Church, which continued from the Apostles age about 300 yeares. Secondly . . . the flourishyng tyme of the churche, which lasted another 300 yeares." Then came a long period during which the church was continually "declinyng or backeslidying." Now finally has come the "reformation and purging of the Church of God." Foxe insisted that the English Reformation was not an innovation but a return to an earlier perfection, declaring that "this our church reformed now, not to be the begynnyng of any new Churche of our owne, but to be the renewynge of the old auncient Church of Christ." Indeed it was Rome that was guilty of innovation.[53] Apologists for the Anglican church in the early seventeenth century continued to insist on its antiquity and to charge the Roman Catholic church with "Noveltie."[54] Although most Protestant reformers recognized that the church would be "reborn into a quite different historical scene and under a different dispensation,"[55] nevertheless the assumptions were essentially cyclical. At the end of the seventeenth century, when the Church of England existed in a quite different situation than it had in the mid-sixteenth century and faced very different threats, Burnet's *History of the Reformation* could still invoke the cyclical paradigm. Though Burnet clearly saw the reformation of the Church of England as an ongoing, lengthy process that was far from complete in his own day, his cyclical view of the Reformation's aim was much like Foxe's: "The design of the *Reformation,* was to restore Christianity to what it was at first, and to purge it of those Corruptions, with which it was over-run in the later and darker Ages." Despite the defects and abuses in the Anglican church that still needed to be reformed, Burnet concluded that "our Doctrine is pure and uncorrupted; that our Worship is . . . freed from Idolatry and Superstition; and that the main Lines of our Church Government agree to the First Constitution of the Churches by the Apostles."[56] In religion as in learning and literature, many believed that they had in large part regained the perfection of the past.

Cyclical interpretations of history persisted throughout the seventeenth century. Perhaps one reason for their popularity was the adaptability of the cyclical paradigm: it could account for prosperity or adversity, peace or war. As the popular motif of the return of the golden age suggests, Englishmen often saw the advent of prosperity or peace in essentially retrospective, cyclical terms. At the end of the sixteenth century, Daniel in his *Civil Wars* declared that though England had been ravaged by the disastrous wars between the houses of Lancaster and York, peace was restored with Henry VII and England was now witnessing a glorious rebirth.[57] With Queen Elizabeth I's reign, England has reached "that glorie, which few Times could ever showe" (*Civil Wars,* Bk. I, st. 3, l. 8). Poets who praised Elizabeth as England's *Astraea* also implied a cyclical reading of history: the golden age had returned.[58] More than half a century later, the myth of the golden age restored was again invoked as Dryden and Abraham Cowley celebrated the restoration of Charles II: *Astraea Redux.* For these poets, the Interregnum was the iron age. If Queen Elizabeth to her times seemed to signal the return of an age of justice, peace, and happiness, so, too, could Charles. The terms might change, but the paradigm remained the same.

The cyclical view of history was also useful in explaining times of adversity, endowing them with a certain orderliness. Moreover, it could accommodate and subsume a sense of decay since the growth to maturity was followed by decline or weakening of power. After Queen Elizabeth's death, many people felt that England had declined from her former greatness.[59] While for some this decline seemed to support the idea of universal decay, others saw it as part of the cyclical pattern of history. Although Daniel had begun his *Civil Wars* in the belief that England's glory had been recovered after the disorder and bloodshed of the War of the Roses, by 1609, when he published his final version of the long historical poem, he saw that England's history had taken a turn for the worse. The final book opens with a clear sense that England in the reign of James I has fallen from the glory of Elizabeth's time, when poet-historians received more favor and encouragement:

> On yet, sad Verse: though those bright starres from whence
> Thou hadst thy light, are set for euermore;
> And that these times do not like grace dispense
> To our indeuours, as those did before. . . .
>
> (Bk. VIII, st. 1, ll. 1–4)

Still another cycle was discerned by Royalists in the mid-seventeenth century. For them the Civil War showed that England, after the summer of her glory, was now precipitously declining. Some of Cowley's poems from the 1650s reveal that he saw the revolution as part of a larger cyclical pattern in which "in time each great imperial race / Degenerates, and gives some new one place."[60] For Peter Heylyn, only a recognition of the essentially cyclical nature of history could make sense of the catastrophic, seemingly chaotic events of his day. As he worked on *Cosmographie* (1652), a revised and enlarged version of his earlier *Microcosmos* (1621), Heylyn's review of history—"the fall of so many great and puissant Empires" and "the desolation of so many flourishing *Christian* Churches"— helped him put England's present calamities in perspective. "For is there any of these *things,* whereof it may be said, Ecce hoc est novum. . . . Have they not been already in the times before us?"[61] Clarendon, too, sought to find an order in the "total and prodigious alteration and confusion over the whole kingdom." In the part of his *History of the Rebellion and Civil Wars in England* written during 1646–48, he suggested that the turmoils of the age signaled the decline of England, which had its parallel in the history of other kingdoms. The diligent observer "will find all this bulk of misery to have proceeded, and to have been brought upon us, from the same natural causes and means which have usually attended kingdoms swoln with long plenty, pride, and excess towards some signal mortification, and castigation of Heaven." Locating the apex of England's felicity in the early years of Charles I's reign, when "this kingdom, and all his majesty's dominions . . . enjoyed the greatest calm and the fullest measure of felicity that any people in any age for so long time together, have been blessed with," Clarendon found that even in the height of the cycle the seeds of decay were present.[62]

The important question, of course, was whether each country had only one cycle allotted to it. Perhaps England's glorious days could never be recovered. Heylyn thought that with the advent of the Civil War, England was going the way of all "the greatest Monarchies of the World, the *Babylonian, Persian, Grecian, Roman* [that] have all had their *periods,* nothing remaining of them now but the name and memory."[63] But the cyclical view could sometimes provide hope, as we shall see especially in the case of Herrick. Perhaps in the circular revolution of time winter would give way to spring, peace to war, and the Royalist cause would prevail. When the Restoration actually came about, it was greeted by supporters of the monarchy as a cyclical renewal that gave England a second chance. Despite Heylyn's pessimism in the early 1650s, he observed in a sermon preached on the first anniversary of Charles II's restoration that though England "had attained to that height of wretchedness; that Loyalty must pass for Treason . . . as in the worst and most deplorable condition of the *Roman* Empire," she now with the return of Charles II had regained her former "peace and happiness." Apparently, England, unlike Rome, had survived its decline and was to be blessed with yet another period of prosperity.[64]

As should be apparent by now, writers could share a generally cyclical view of history and yet differ in their attitudes toward the pattern they saw. Hakewill and Herrick were reassured that the orderliness of cyclical change was evidence of God's providence and gave promise of renewal. Few in the seventeenth century, however, could contemplate the cyclical vicissitudes of time with such optimism. Jonson, seeing vicissitude as a threat to stability and order, hoped to transcend the cycles through a Stoic virtue that would remain unaffected by time. Many writers felt that the cycles, though orderly, were constricting, destructive of human potential. Raleigh looked at the process in which "all that the hand of man can make, is either ouerturnd by the hand of man, or at length by standing and continuing consumed." Overwhelmed by a depressing sense of futility, he concluded with Solomon that *"all is vanitie and vexation of spirit,"* though no one "beleeues it, till Death tells [him]."[65]

But quite another attitude was developing during this period. Convinced that the course of history could be changed, Bacon and Milton hoped that people would end the repetitive, cyclical pattern and progress in the future. Both writers, and Dryden as well, were attracted by a different sense of history—the idea of progress.

Although for a long time it was assumed that the idea of progress did not emerge until the eighteenth and nineteenth centuries, more recent scholarship has suggested that a distinct idea of progress was even held by some of the ancient classical writers. Robert Nisbet in his important *History of the Idea of Progress* has argued that "no single idea has been more important than, perhaps as important as, the idea of progress in Western civilization for nearly three thousand years," and he traces the idea of progress from the Greeks, through the early church fathers such as St. Augustine, and up to the twentieth century.[66] Nisbet spends little time on the Renaissance, since he believes that during this period the idea of progress essentially disappeared—largely because of "the almost total domination of ideas of cyclical recurrence in Renaissance thought."[67] I would suggest, however, that we do not need to wait until the mid-seventeenth century to see the renewal of an idea of progress. There were indeed a number of writers during the late sixteenth century and the early seventeenth who suggested that history might reveal a pattern of progress rather than decay or mere cyclical change. The idea of progress we find during this period is, of course, not the same one that came to dominate nineteenth-century thought, in which progress was assumed to be universal, inevitable, and unlimited. Nevertheless, some of the historians who asserted the cyclical view of history found themselves at times tentatively approaching a concept of history that allowed for progress.

The idea of progress depends on a disposition to see change as positive and good. As long as stasis is the ideal, change is associated with mutability, decay, mortality, and imperfection. The Aristotelian/Ptolemaic cosmology, which was dominant down through the sixteenth century and persisted in some quarters even into the eighteenth, probably did much to encourage this view that change is the condition of imperfection. In what Thomas Kuhn calls the traditional "two-sphere" Aristotelian cosmology, the immutable, unchanging, and therefore perfect heavens contrasted with the terrestrial sphere, the realm of mutability, change, and decay. But whereas this traditional cosmology reinforced the association of change with decay and imperfection, the revolutions in astronomy during the late sixteenth and the early seventeenth centuries could foster a different, more positive attitude toward change.[68] As the distinction between the imperfect, mutable earth and the perfect, unchanging heavens was eventually destroyed, the universe was discovered to be larger (perhaps infinitely so) than had been previously believed. There were novas (Tycho Brahe's in 1572 and Johann Kepler's in 1604), believed to be new stars that if some saw as signs that the universe was falling apart, others viewed as evidence of God's continuing creativity. The same scientific discoveries that caused Donne to fear that the universe was decaying, losing its old order, made others excited at the growth of knowledge and the expansion of the universe. Although it is not possible to explore the topic fully here, it seems likely that the changes in astronomy during this period (what has been called the Copernican revolution) were closely linked with the emerging disposition to see change as positive.

Giordano Bruno was an eloquent spokesman for this positive view of change. Believing that the universe was continually changing, he asserted unequivocally that change is a sign of perfection. He proclaimed in his *De l'infinito universo et mondi* that "an immutable universe would be a dead universe," rejoicing not only in the infinitude of the universe but also in its disposition to change.[69] The extent of Bruno's influence in England is uncertain, though he lived there from 1583–85 and three of his most important works on cosmology (including *De l'infinito universo*) were published in England during these years.[70] But Bruno was not alone in rethinking the conventional negative attitude toward change and mutability. We also see in Galileo, who was the most important scientist of the early seventeenth century to argue for the new Copernican astronomy, the insistence that change is not inevitably "corruption," a mark of imperfection. Though Galileo, unlike Bruno, assumed the sun-centered universe was limited and finite, in his third letter on the sunspots that he had seen through his telescope (1612) he attacked the negative view of change, which he associated with the old Aristotelian cosmology. These Aristotelians, he wrote, wish

to keep the heavens free from even the tiniest alteration of material. Well, if alteration were annihilation, the Peripatetics would have some reason for concern; but since it is nothing but mutation, there is no reason for such bitter hostility to it. It seems to me unreasonable to call "corruption" in an egg that which produces a chicken. Besides, if "corruption" and "generation" are discovered in the moon, why deny them to the sky? If the earth's small mutations do not threaten its existence (if, indeed, they are ornaments rather than imperfections in it), why deprive the other planets of them? Why fear so much for the dissolution of the sky as a result of alterations no more inimical than these?[71]

"Mutations" can be "ornaments," marks of beauty and even possible perfection, not harbingers of "annihilation."

Galileo's discoveries and works were well known in England. But what I wish to suggest here is not that Bruno or Galileo necessarily influenced the English writers who saw change as positive, but rather that similar ideas about mutability were occurring to a number of people during this period who were questioning what they saw as the traditionally negative view of change.[72] By the late sixteenth century and the seventeenth, there were a number of writers (scientists, historians, and literary men) interested in the idea that change might be for the better. This positive attitude toward change, which is essential to a belief in progress, we will see in Bacon, Dryden, and especially Milton, who in their various ways were committed to an ideal of progress.

It was not only the new astronomy that offered a different view of change. That the modern age had made discoveries that were unknown to the ancients itself encouraged a sense that change could be for the better. Though Bodin was far from embracing the new astronomy (he was a firm believer in old forms of superstition that were being questioned and was obsessed with numerological calculations), he was keenly aware that his age had made remarkable advances in geography and medicine. Bodin boasts, "Printing alone can easily vie with all the discoveries of all the ancients." Such statements reflect his sense that we are not only equal to the ancients but in some ways greater than they were. Still, he concludes his praise of modern accomplishments by asserting that ultimately the "path of change" is cyclical: "vices press upon virtues, ignorance upon knowledge, base upon honourable, and darkness upon light."[73]

In Le Roy, too, the cyclical view of history seems at times on the verge of yielding to a progressive one. The Renaissance has not only "restored" the language, learning, and writings of the ancients but has also "newly inuented" many things.[74] Near the end of his book, Le Roy questions whether we can avoid repeating the cyclical pattern of the past in which the height of achievement was followed by decline. He fears that all our power and wisdom, "being come to so great excellencie," will "fall againe, as they have done in the times past, and come to decay"; he foresees that Europe, like Rome before her, will suffer a barbarian invasion in which temples, cities, and libraries will be destroyed. Like so many others of his age, Le Roy suspects that the pattern of history is fixed; the cycles of growth and decay are always repeated. Nevertheless, he holds out the possibility that God might avert this decay. No matter how tentatively, Le Roy has introduced the possibility that the future might not be doomed to repeat the pattern of the past. Moreover, even if Europe's cyclical decay is inevitable, some future state will advance beyond our present knowledge. "That which is now hidden, with time will come to light, and our successours will wonder that wee were ignorant of them."[75]

We see as early as Bodin and Le Roy that the cyclical idea of history is beginning to be modified by a conception of progress. Neither historian believed that progress had been steady, or had occurred in all areas of human endeavor, and neither believed that it was inevitable. But both suggested that some progress was possible and, in fact, had already been achieved.

Indeed, Bodin had a strong sense of the historical process in which civilization develops gradually.[76] Rejecting the idea that the first age was the golden and that subsequent ages fell further away from this early perfection, Bodin insisted instead that people in these earliest ages were actually rude and barbaric, living like beasts. Only "gradually" were they "reclaimed from that ferocity and barbarity to the refinement of customs and the law-abiding society which we see about us."[77] These changes are clearly an advancement. Bodin's comments interestingly anticipate Hobbes's argument in *Leviathan* (1651) that the state of nature which preceded the formulation of society was warlike and brutal. But much earlier than Hobbes, we find a number of English historians taking a position much like Bodin's. As early as 1586, Camden in his *Britannia* explained that the early histories of nations are obscure because "the first inhabitants of countries had other cares and thoughts, than the transmitting their several originals to posterity. . . . For their life was altogether uncivilized, perfectly rude, and wholly taken up in wars; so that they were a long time without learning; which, as it is the effect of a civilized life, of peace, and leisure, so is it the only sure and certain means of preserving and transmitting to posterity the memory of things past."[78] Speed's *History of Great Britaine,* which was indebted to Camden and frequently cited Bodin with approval, similarly emphasized the rude beginnings and the gradual growth of civilization, as it vividly described the ancient people of Britain as barbarous, illiterate, and naked, adorned only with pictures painted or engraved on their bodies. Careful to defend England's honor, which might be thought tainted by such rude beginnings, Speed insisted that all nations have similar origins:

In the relations of these things, let no man thinke, that the glory of these ancient and warlike nation of *Britains,* is any waies disparaged, or made inferior to them that would be more famous, whose beginning have been as meane, and state as rude, if not more. For let vs consider the *Romans* so lavish in their owne worths and greatnesse; who notwithstanding, bring their name and originall from *Romulus,* a bastard by birth, nourished by a beast, educated among a sort of rusticke shepheards: . . . he became ringleader of a damned crue, that liued by robberies and without lawes. . . . And, to let passe many others, the like may be said of the beginners of the *Scythian* and *Turkish* Empires.[79]

Like Bodin, Speed vacillated between a sense of progress and a cyclical view of history. If pressed, Speed would probably have said that the growing civility of a nation is actually part of a cycle that will eventually lead to decline.[80] Nevertheless, the overall effect of his patriotic history is to reveal the growth of civilization in England.

Elsewhere, too, we find the cyclical idea of history yielding to a sense of progress. The Renaissance ideal of imitating the classics to produce a literature equal to that of Greece and Rome suggested that the greatness of the past could be revived in the present. But this cyclical ideal gradually gave way to patriotic hopes of outdoing the ancients. In his *Defence of Ryme* Daniel suggested that perhaps the English language might be capable of "greater and worthier" poetry than either Latin or Greek.[81] Jonson praised Shakespeare for creating better and more enduring comedies than the ancients did. Just as in knowledge, so in literature people hoped that the present might advance beyond the accomplishments of the past.

In religion, too, we see a disposition among some writers to acknowledge the possibility of progress. To some extent, perhaps the Christian typological view of the New Testament as a fulfillment and perfection of the Old could foster a sense of history as progress. Moreover, though the Protestant Reformation tended to assume a basically cyclical reading of history (the church was being restored after a long period of degeneration), the idea of reformation could also encourage a sense of progress.[82] When Martin Luther, John Calvin, and especially Calvin's followers who desired a thorough-going reform of the English church insisted that the model was to be found only in Scripture, they were in some sense working against the tendency to idealize the primitive church.[83] If the model for the Christian church was to be found in the words of Scripture rather than in an institution existing in a particular historical period, then perhaps the church had not existed in its perfect form in the early centuries after Christ. Insofar as the emphasis on *sola scriptura* could weaken the idealization of the first age of the church as the best, it allowed for the possibility that a modern reformed church might surpass the perfection of any church institution that had previously existed.

But it is not just in the *sola scriptura* argument that we see assumptions that could be favorable to the emergence of a belief in progress. Indeed, Richard Hooker, the most important Elizabethan defender (and definer) of the Anglican *via media*, rejected the *sola scriptura* position but showed a remarkable inclination to conceive of a church that might grow and progress through time. Hooker was far from being simply a conservative defender of the status quo, of the Anglican church as a fixed and unchanging institution. Indeed, in his *Laws of Ecclesiastical Polity* he presents his opponents (the Calvinists who wanted more extreme reform) as actually reactionary in their idealization of the ancient church. With a keen sense of anachronism, he argues that matters of church polity should not be tied narrowly either to Scripture or to the model of the church as it existed in the time of the apostles. The times have changed. The English church exists, Hooker argues, in different historical circumstances, and thus what was fitting for the discipline of the ancient church is not necessarily suitable for ours.[84] His recognition that the conditions of the present differ from those of the past and his sense of ongoing, continuous change are especially evident throughout the third book of his *Laws of Ecclesiastical Polity*, where he insists that a law "which hath been once most sufficient may wax otherwise by alteration of time and place" (ch. x, p. 331) and that laws of church government "may after they are made be also changed as the difference of times or places shall require" (p. 332). Hooker, interestingly, anticipates the far more radical Milton in recognizing that historical circumstances change and in arguing that the New Testament revelation, which abrogated ceremonies of the Old Testament, teaches us that one should not be tied to past ways of doing things (p. 329). Hooker insists that "change" or "alteration" is not necessarily bad, that Christ has not forbidden change (Bk. III, ch. xi), and paradoxically, that though "God never ordained any thing that could be bettered. Yet many things he hath that have been changed, and that for the better" (p. 332).[85] Of course, Hooker is moderate and restrained in his view of change and innovation. Praising England's gradual reform, he rejects any radical change of church government as dangerous. I would not wish to make Hooker into an advocate of progress, nor to deny the crucial differences that separate the Anglican Hooker from the iconoclastic Milton, who argues against the very church government that Hooker defended, and whose idea of reform is, as we shall see, based on a strong commitment to progress and a far more radical attitude toward tradition. Nevertheless, we see in Hooker's writings the rejection of the idealization of the past, the idea that some innovations may be good, and the sense that change may be for the better. All these positions are important for the emergence of an idea of progress.

For all these sixteenth-century anticipations of an idea of progress, it is Bacon who at the beginning of the seventeenth century clearly defined a firm, consistent idea of progress, predicated on man's ability to shape the course of time. Though he did not believe that the course of human history had in the past been characterized by a pattern of progress, he eloquently celebrated an ideal of progress that was enormously influential. The scientists and writers associated with the Royal Society in the mid-seventeenth century looked back to Bacon as father, mentor, and leader, assimilating his idea of historical progress.[86] But whereas Bacon's main point was that progress was possible, these later writers argued that it was actual as well. Bacon distinguished between the cyclical past and the progress he foresaw in the future, but these writers felt that England's recent history revealed a steady course of progress in scientific knowledge.

Thomas Sprat's *History of the Royal Society* (1667) asserts that this age "doth far exceed" the previous ones in the "extent" of its learning, "there being a much larger plot of ground, sown with Arts, and civility at this time." With the establishment of the Royal Society, England has "set on foot, a *new* way of improvement of Arts."[87] For those who believed in universal decay or equated change with imperfection and mutability, anything new was suspect. For them innovation was a term of disapprobation. But Sprat reflects a quite different attitude when he argues against those who are frightened by the idea of change: "For if all things that are *new* be *destructive,* all the several means, and degrees, by which Mankind has risen to this perfection of *Arts,* were to be condemn'd. If to be the *Author* of *new things,* be a crime; how will the first Civilizers of *Men,* and makers of *Laws,* and Founders of *Governments* escape?"[88] Essential to the idea of progress is this idea that the new may be good, indeed better than the old. This assumption may seem simple and quite unexceptional to those living in the twentieth century, but it was by no means universally accepted in the seventeenth.

In Robert Boyle, one of the most energetic and prolific members of the Royal Society, we also see this new attitude toward change. Whereas the idea of universal decay typically assumed that God had created nature perfect and that it had declined since Creation, Boyle sees the changes in nature since Adam's time as evidence of a progress dependent upon man's scientific arts: "if *Adam* were now alive, and should survey that great variety of man's productions, that is to be found in the shops of artificers, the laboratories of chymists, and other well furnished magazines of art, he would admire to see what a new world, as it were, or set of things has been added to the primitive creatures by the industry of his posterity."[89] For Bacon, as we shall see, the goal of the progress of learning was to restore the perfect knowledge of nature that Adam had before the Fall. Thus, for him progress was, paradoxically, a restoration of an early, original perfection. By Boyle's time, however, it is possible to believe that mankind can progress to levels of perfection never achieved in any age. As the passage from Boyle indicates, he is far from idealizing the earliest age as the most perfect. Rather than seeing nature as complete at Creation, Boyle finds it continually in the process of growth. His comments reflect his dispositon to see change, the addition of new things, as exciting and good. "It is observable, that so many excellent trees, shrubs, and an innumerable company of herbs, some few excepted, should all appear so unlike the vegetables of the antiently known world, both in figure, leaf, and fruits: and the same observation is made of birds, beasts and fishes; and of insects."[90] The scientist, with his knowledge of natural philosophy, can improve nature, achieving the dominion and power that Bacon had defined as one of science's goals. As with many other scientists of his time, Boyle's awareness of the many recent discoveries leads to an expanded sense of possibility. The universe is "teeming with profitable inventions, and may . . . by human skill or industry, be made the fruitful mother of divers things useful."[91]

Like Boyle, Joseph Glanvill praises the many recent inventions (the microscope, telescope, barometer, and airpump), and feels that the universe he lives in is infinitely rich: "There is an *inexhaustible variety* of *Treasure*, which Providence hath lodged in Things, that to the Worlds end will afford *Fresh Discoveries*."[92] Because these treasures are "inexhaustible," progress is possible until the final apocalyptic end of the world. Like most people during this time, Glanvill assumes that the world will have an end just as it had a beginning, but he apparently does not fear that this end is imminent. "We must *seek* and *gather, observe* and *examine*, and *lay up* in Bank for the Ages that come after."[93] But not everyone who believed in progress shared Glanvill's sense that it could proceed indefinitely. Sprat thought that man would reach a perfection in knowledge beyond which he could not advance. He confidently announced that "the absolute perfection of the *True Philosophy*" was "not now far off."[94]

The idea of progress became increasingly influential during the seventeenth century. By the 1660s it had found strong advocates in the field of science, and growing numbers of writers were proclaiming that England's language and literature had also advanced. Edward Phillips observed that "nothing, it seems, relishes so well as what is written in the smooth style of our present language, taken to be of late so much refined."[95] Dryden similarly insisted that, though England's language was rough and unpolished at the beginning of the century, it had now become civilized, graceful, and urbane. The idea of progress even shaped the interpretation of literary history, as Sprat's *Life of Cowley* reveals. Sprat noted that his age had improved both the art of translation and the genre of the familiar letter, and he praised Cowley's imitations of Pindar as "rather a new sort of Writing than a restoring of an Ancient."[96]

26

In his Latin poems, Cowley has surpassed any single poet that Rome can boast: "he has expressed to admiration all the Numbers of Verse and Figures of Poesie that are scattered up and down amongst the Ancients. . . . This is the more extraordinary in that it was never yet performed by any single Poet of the Antient Romans themselves. . . . it was their constant Custom to confine all their thoughts and practice to one or two ways of Writing, as despairing ever to compass all together."[97] Cowley himself in his poem "To Sir *William Davenant,* Upon his two first Books of *Gondibert* . . ." praised Davenant for reforming *"Heroick Poesie"* and surpassing his classical predecessors: "ancient *Rome* / May blush no less to see her *Wit o'recome."* Disdaining servile imitation of the ancients, Davenant has forged a new path:

> Thou in those beaten pathes disdain'st to tread,
> And scorn'st to *Live* by robbing of the *Dead.*
> Since Time does all things change, thou think'st not fit
> This latter *Age* should see *all New but Wit.*

Cowley's and Sprat's views of England's literary achievements reflect the earlier Renaissance ideal of imitating the classics to produce an English literature that would rival that of Greece and Rome, but we can see here how the ideal of progress has modified the essentially cyclical view that England might be able to match Rome's glory.

But despite its growing influence, the idea of progress was by no means universally accepted in the late seventeenth century. Both the cyclical and decay theories persisted throughout the century. The battle of the ancients and moderns shows particularly well that the older interpretations of history's pattern continued despite the emergence of the idea of progress. Reaching its climax in the late seventeenth century, this battle reflected a conflict between competing views of history. While the advocates of the moderns assumed a progressive interpretation of history, defenders of the ancients upheld either cyclical or decay theories. But the very attack on the idea of progress indicated that it was an important, influential view that had to be contended with. And though the idea of decay could be presented as an argument against progress, it no longer had the force or scope that it had had earlier in the century.

Sir William Temple attacked the idea of progress by reviving the idea of decay. Like Reynolds long before him, he argues that the ancients "made the greatest Progress in the Search and Discoveries of the vast Region of Truth and Nature."[98] But whereas Reynolds insisted that decline was continuous, Temple admits that the course of learning and literature has not been unrelievedly degenerative. Though Homer and Virgil are the rulers of the empire of poetry which has decayed since the fall of Rome, in dramatic comedy the English have "excelled both the Modern and the Antient" writers."[99] Moreover, like Le Roy, Temple notes that "Science and Arts have run their circles, and had their periods in the Several Parts of the World." After having been "buried" with the Roman empire, they have "sprung up again" in Europe.[100] In the last 150 years there has been tremendous progress in learning, though the progress really shows how low learning had fallen. The idea of decay merges with a cyclical sense of history, as Temple speculates that perhaps "the Growth of [learning], as well of Natural Bodies" has "short Periods beyond which it [can]not reach, and after which it must begin to decay. It falls in one Country or one Age, and rises again in others but never beyond a certain Pitch. One Man or one Country at a certain Time runs a great Length in some certain Kinds of Knowledge, but lose as much Ground in others that were perhaps as useful and as valuable. There is a certain Degree of Capacity in the greatest Vessel."[101] Ultimately Temple has a rather depressing sense that man's achievements are necessarily limited, that once they reach a certain height they will inevitably decay. Nevertheless, his argument reveals how the idea of decay has been modified by a cyclical view of history.

Others who believed that the modern age had degenerated from the glory of the past admitted that the pattern of decay was neither inevitable nor irreversible. Thomas Rymer, that inveterate defender of Aristotle's rules, thought that poetry and drama had declined since the ancients, but his insistence that the English should follow "the rules" is founded on the belief that the English *might* surpass the literature of the ancients. They have the *"genius"* and *"language"* to produce great tragedy. "Had our Authors begun with Tragedy as *Sophocles* and *Euripides* left it, had they either built on the same foundation or after their *model*, we might e're this day have seen Poetry in greater perfection, and boasted such *Monuments* of wit as *Greece* or *Rome* never knew in all their glory."[102] If English writers adhere to the rules, they may be able to reverse the degenerative trend of England's literary history. Even Rymer was affected by the idea of progress. By the end of the seventeenth century it was difficult to retain the old view of universal, inevitable decay.

These three ideas of history—decay, cycles, and progress—are the basic shapes that the seventeenth century assumed history could take. In defining them, I have had to treat them as discrete, quite different theories. In actuality, however, they sometimes overlap—the cyclical view of history can emphasize either the process of decay or that of growth—and frequently writers combine several ideas of history. Greville and Temple mingle cyclical and decay theories. Both Bodin and Le Roy lean toward the idea of progress despite their essentially cyclical points of view.

There is, however, another conception of history that must be mentioned, since it often colors these three views. The seventeenth century inherited the providential interpretation of history along with the secular Greco-Roman cyclical view. I have not discussed this view as a separate idea of history's pattern because, although it assumes that time has shape and direction, it does not define a distinct shape of history as the cyclical, progressive, or decay theories do. Deriving ultimately from the Old Testament and strongly influencing Christianity from St. Augustine through the seventeenth century, the providential view insists that the course of history is eschatological, teleologically oriented, unfolding under the direction of God, whose hand in man's affairs is responsible for its outcome.[103] History begins with Creation and the Fall and moves steadily toward the Apocalypse—the Second Coming of Christ, the Day of Judgment, and the destruction of the world that will be accompanied by the creation of a new heaven and earth.

It has been argued that the idea of Providence diminished in importance during the seventeenth century. Historians turned to natural, secondary causes to explain events.[104] Clarendon, for example, was not satisfied with explaining the "prodigious" calamities of the Civil War period as simply the result of "a universal corruption of the hearts of the whole nation" or with attributing these calamities to "Providence, and the instances of divine displeasure."[105] Instead throughout his *History* Clarendon painstakingly analyzed the natural, secondary, very specific causes, emphasizing the responsibility of individual persons. Though he astutely recognized that it might be safer simply to take refuge in the providential explanation or to stick to "a bare relation of what was done," Clarendon could not resist "prying . . . strictly into the causes," and he found that "those lamentable effects . . . proceeded only from the folly and the frowardness [sic], from the weakness and the wilfulness, the pride and the passion of particular persons."[106] Indeed, Clarendon's critical focus on individuals, with their specific flaws, their often unique combination of virtues and weaknesses, tends to undermine any simple, paradigmatic explanations of history. Nevertheless, the example of Clarendon is also witness to the persistence of the providential interpretation of history. For all his insistence on secondary causes—and his recognition that providential explanations can be a refuge for historians who fear openly affixing blame on individuals—Clarendon finds there is finally something mysterious, inexplicable about history, which perhaps can only be attributed to God's providence. In the later books of the *History* and in his *Life* (both of which were written after his banishment) are numerous and far from perfuntory references to Providence and "the immediate hand of God." Despite the increasing secularization that scholars have observed in this period, the providential view of history remained influential. Milton and Dryden offer some of the fullest statements of the idea of Providence, and the Christian sense that history is bounded by Creation and Judgment was assumed by such notoriously secular writers as Hobbes and the earl of Rochester.[107]

As an attitude that found a divine plan in the course of time, the providential view of history could be incorporated into any of the three shapes of history, even the cyclical one that derived from classical, pagan writers. Goodman and Reynolds found Providence behind the process of decay, and, as we have already noted, the idea of universal decay frequently gained its force from the apocalyptic sense that the world was rapidly approaching its end. Hakewill, Browne, and Herrick insisted that the cycles declared the wisdom of God, and Raleigh saw the punitive hand of God in the cycles of retribution. Even the idea of progress could find divine sanction. Bacon believed that the advancement of knowledge had been reserved for this last age of the world, and Milton thought that God was offering England a special opportunity for progress.

The following chapters focus on six writers whose works were radically shaped by these views of history: Bacon, father of modern science and influential proponent of the idea of progress; Donne, the foremost, most varied, and most complex Metaphysical poet and also the seventeenth-century writer most deeply affected by the idea of decay; Jonson and Herrick, two poets who share a basically cyclical view of history but whose attitudes toward time are nonetheless quite different; Milton, who, though he has been seen as the culmination of Renaissance humanism, embodies a radically progressive view of history; and Dryden, the most important literary figure of the Restoration, who assimilated many of the ideas of history that his predecessors held. My concern is not only to define these six writers' ideas of history—the various combinations and permutations of the three views of history—but also to show the fundamental, often intricate ways in which these views affect their writing. Although explicit statements about history are important, deeply ingrained attitudes toward history are also reflected in these writers' observations about art, love, science, and religion—indeed, even (or rather, especially) in their characteristic images and their preferences for certain kinds of metaphors or allusions. Attempting to combine literary analysis and the history of ideas, my interest is not in the so-called idea-content of literature but in language, metaphor, and patterns of imagery, for I believe that a writer's view of time and history is more truly and interestingly revealed by his characteristic modes of expression than by his explicit statements about history.

Rather than offering a survey of ideas of history during this period, I want to explore the complex interrelationships that can exist between a writer's conception of the pattern of time and the literature he creates. These are by no means the only seventeenth-century writers whose works were shaped by ideas of history, but I have chosen to concentrate on some of the greatest, most influential writers. With the exception of Herrick, all are major figures, undisputed giants of the century. Despite the large amount of scholarship and criticism on them, their views of history have never been fully defined, nor has it been recognized how deeply and subtly their views of history affected their work. I am including Herrick in part as a contrast to his poetic "father," Jonson, and in part because of all seventeenth-century poets Herrick would seem one of the least likely to be concerned with ideas of history. In showing that Herrick's poetry is fundamentally shaped by his historical perspectives, I make my case for the importance of ideas of history in seventeenth-century literature even stronger.

To understand as completely as possible any writer's view of history, it is necessary to consider all of his writing. Not only can his view change over time, but also his historical perspectives lend a distinctive quality to his whole work. Thus I have not limited my discussion to, say, Donne's prose or Milton's major poems. Because my concern is to define the way views of history shape a writer's entire work, I have not always been able to address fully the literary complexity and uniqueness of every poem, prose piece, or play. Not that matters of form, genre, occasion, or style that distinguish individual works are unimportant. Indeed, it is possible that the genre of a particular work might to some extent explain why a particular pattern of history is implied in a text. One might expect, for example, to find in satire an emphasis on the decay of civilization. Nevertheless, genre does not in itself provide a sufficient explanation for whatever historical patterns are implicit in a writer's text. After all, a writer chooses to work in certain genres that he feels are congenial, and he might very well find satire congenial *because* he believes in historical degeneration. Donne writes *Anniversaries* and satires; Milton, revolutionary pamphlets. Such choices reflect these two writers' radically different historical perspectives. Throughout the following chapters my primary emphasis will be on the historical perspectives and attitudes that transcend distinctions of genre, occasion, and style and that give a coherence, a characteristic shape to the whole.

Because I am interested in defining each writer's all-encompassing view of history, I have discussed each writer's work synchronically rather than diachronically. In the chapters on Milton and Dryden, however, a somewhat different approach was necessary. With Bacon, Donne, Jonson, and Herrick, there is an essential consistency in each writer's view of history. For all the variety and complexity of Donne, the view of history as degenerative runs throughout his writing. Though Jonson and Bacon late in their careers experienced personal or professional disappointments or reversals, their views of and attitudes toward history remained basically unchanged. For Herrick, we have only the *Hesperides,* and since we cannot accurately date all the poems within this text, it is impossible to chart changes in his historical perspectives, despite the fact that his attitude toward history seems very much affected by his political experiences. In contrast to these four writers, however, Milton's and Dryden's views of history underwent important, discernible changes, and consequently in both chapters I have discussed these changes.

The group of writers I have selected is admittedly varied. It includes Puritan, Anglican, Catholic; a royalist supporter of Charles I, a propagandist for the Puritan Revolution, and a defender of the reestablished monarchical order under Charles II — writers in what Earl Miner has called the private, social, and public modes.[108] Thus in a sense this group of writers mirrors the various, often conflicting concerns, religious/political affiliations, and literary interests of this most various, complex century. Despite their differences, however, all of these writers were concerned with understanding the large pattern of time and history, and their writings are responses to the patterns of time that they perceived. Spanning the entire century, these men reveal not only the importance of the three basic views of the shape of history but also the range of diverse attitudes toward history during this period — the desire to find in history a comforting order, the impulse to withdraw from its threatening flux, the attempt in some way to undo or reverse what was seen as its dangerous or destructive effects, and finally the hope to change it for the better.

Notes

1. James Ussher, *The Annals of the World* (London, 1658), p. 1.
2. Thomas Browne, *Pseudodoxia Epidemica*, Bk. VI, in *The Works of Sir Thomas Browne*, ed. Geoffrey Keynes, 4 vols. (Chicago: University of Chicago Press, 1964), 2:398.
3. Thomas Fuller, *The Historie of the Holy Warre* (Cambridge, 1639), "The epistle Dedicatorie."
4. Richard Baxter, *Church-History of the Government of Bishops and Their Councils* (London, 1680), preface, sig. A2v.
5. George Hakewill, *An Apologie of the Power and Providence of God in the Government of the World* (Oxford, 1627), sig. C1v–C2r.
6. Browne, *Christian Morals*, in *Works*, 1:284.
7. John Selden, *The Historie of Tithes* (London, 1618), dedication to Robert Cotton. Cf. Hobbes's comment that Thucydides best performs "the principal and proper work of history [which is] to instruct and enable men, by the knowledge of actions past, to bear themselves prudently in the present and providently towards the future" (*The English Works of*

Thomas Hobbes, ed. Sir William Molesworth, 8 [London: John Bohn, 1843], p. vii).

8. Sir Walter Raleigh, *The History of the World* (London, 1614), sig. A2r–A2v.

9. Selden, *Historie of Tithes*, dedication. See also, e.g., John Hayward, *Lives of the III Normans, Kings of England* (London, 1613), "Dedicatorie."

10. F. J. Levy, *Tudor Historical Thought* (San Marino: Huntington Library, 1967), p. 234.

11. Ibid., p. 235. Levy's book provides an excellent discussion of historiography and the interest in history in Tudor England.

12. Thomas Fuller, *The Church-History of Britain*, 4 pts. in one vol., with separate pagination (London, 1655), pt. III, p. 232, and "The Epistle Dedicatory to . . . Robert Lord Bruce," which begins Fuller's account of the seventeenth century (pt. IV). Hobbes, too, suggested that the best histories are of one's own time when he praised Thucydides: "He overtasked not himself by undertaking an history of things done long before his time, and of which he was not able to inform himself" (see "Of the Life and History of Thucydides," which introduces Hobbes's translation of the *History*, in *English Works*, 8:xx).

13. See Edward Hyde, first earl of Clarendon, *History of the Rebellion and Civil Wars in England*, ed. W. Dunn Macray, 6 vols. (Oxford: Clarendon Press, 1888); John Rushworth, *Historical Collections*, 8 vols. (London, 1659–1701); Clarendon, *The Life of Edward Earl of Clarendon*, 3 vols. (1759; 3d ed., Oxford: Clarendon Printing-House, 1761); and Gilbert Burnet, *History of his Own Time* (London, 1734).

14. Arthur B. Ferguson, in *Clio Unbound: Perception of the Social and Cultural Past in Renaissance England* (Durham, N.C.: Duke University Press, 1979), has well observed that it is important to look at "writings not in themselves primarily historical rather than [at] the political narratives then customarily designated as 'histories'" in order to discover Renaissance historical perspectives (p. x).

15. *Poems and Dramas of Fulke Greville, First Lord Brooke*, ed. Geoffrey Bullough, 1 (Edinburgh: Oliver and Boyd, 1938), p. 169.

16. Henry Reynolds, *Mythomystes*, in *Critical Essays of the Seventeenth Century*, ed. J. E. Spingarn, 3 vols. (Bloomington: Indiana University Press, 1963), 1:144.

17. Marjorie Hope Nicolson, *The Breaking of the Circle* (New York: Columbia University Press, 1960), p. 45, has suggested that the sense of historical decay was probably linked to the belief in the correspondence between the microcosm and the geocosm: men saw their own mortality reflected in the larger world. On the preoccupation with decay in the late sixteenth and early seventeenth centuries, see also George Williamson, "Mutability, Decay, and Seventeenth-Century Melancholy," *ELH* 2 (1935), 121–50; Don Cameron Allen, "The Degeneration of Man and Renaissance Pessimism," *SP* 35 (1938), 202–27; and Victor Harris, *All Coherence Gone* (Chicago: University of Chicago Press, 1949).

18. Browne, *Christian Morals*, in *Works*, 1:255.

19. Reynolds, *Mythomystes*, in Spingarn, ed., *Critical Essays*, 1:149.

20. Jean Bodin, *Method for the Easy Comprehension of History*, trans. Beatrice Reynolds (New York: Columbia University Press, 1945), pp. 296–98.

21. Ibid., pp. 291–96.

22. Leonard F. Dean, "Bodin's *Methodus* in England before 1625," *SP* 39 (1942), 160–66; quotation appears on p. 166. Beatrice Reynolds cites thirteen Latin editions of the *Methodus* between 1566 and 1650 in the introduction to her translation (p. x). Thomas Heywood translated ch. 4 of the *Methodus* as a preface to his translation of Sallust (1608). On the importance of Bodin in England, see also Levy, *Tudor Historical Thought*, pp. 247–48.

23. *The Works of Gabriel Harvey*, ed. Alexander B. Grosart, 3 vols. (London: Hazell, Watson, and Viney, 1884–85), 1:146.

24. Bodin, *Method*, p. 298.

25. Hakewill, *Apologie*, title page and pp. 35, 37; on his rejection of the golden age myth, see pp. 22–23 and esp. p. 33, where he quotes Bodin.

26. On the Renaissance interest in the cyclical view of history, see Frank E. Manuel, *Shapes of Philosophical History* (Stanford: Stanford University Press, 1965), pp. 46–69; Herschel Baker, *The Race of Time: Three Lectures on Renaissance Historiography* (Toronto: Univ. of Toronto Press, 1967), pp. 59–65; Herbert Weisinger, "Ideas of History during the Renaissance," in *Renaissance Essays from the "Journal of the History of Ideas*,*"* ed. Paul Oskar Kristeller and Philip P. Wiener (New York: Harper and Row, 1968), pp. 74–94; and Robert Nisbet, *History of the Idea of Progress* (New York: Basic Books, 1980), ch. 4.

27. Niccolò Machiavelli, *Discourses upon the first Decade of T. Livius*, trans. E[dward] D[acres] (London, 1636), ch. 39, p. 162.

28. Fuller, *Historie of the Holy Warre*, "The epistle Dedicatorie."

29. Samuel Daniel, *The Collection of the History of England* (London, 1621), p. 1.

30. Machiavelli, *Discourses*, ch. 39, p. 162.

31. Bodin, *Method*, pp. 153, 302; cf. Hakewill, *Apologie*, p. 37.

32. Niccolò Machiavelli, *Florentine Historie*, trans. T. B. (London, 1595), p. 111. For a similar sense of mutability as the operative principle in worldly affairs, see the other great sixteenth-century Italian historian, Francesco Guicciardini, *The Historie of Guicciardin, Conteining the Warres of Italie and Other Partes*, trans. Geffray Fenton (London, 1579), pp. 1, 22, 353. Levy, *Tudor Historical Thought*, pp. 239–40, has suggested that Guicciardini's influence in Tudor England was actually greater than Machiavelli's.

33. Rushworth, *Historical Collections*, 1:"Preface" and "The Epistle Dedicatory."

34. Hayward, *Lives of the III Normans*, esp. pp. 147–52.

35. Rushworth, *Historical Collections*, 1:"The Epistle Dedicatorie."

36. Browne, *Religio Medici*, in *Works*, 1:27.

37. Bodin, *Method*, p. 296.

38. Louis Le Roy, *Of the Interchangeable course, or variety of things in the whole world*, trans. Robert Ashley (London, 1594), pp. 2r–5r. *De la Vicissitude* went through three editions in France by 1584. The popularity of Le Roy as well as Bodin in England during the late sixteenth century is attested to by Gabriel Harvey's remark in a letter to Edmund Spenser: "You can not stepp into a schollars studye but (ten to on [*sic*]) you shall litely [*sic*] finde open either Bodin de Republica or Le Royes Exposition vppon Aristotles Politiques or sum other like Frenche or Italian Politique Discourses" (*Works of Gabriel Harvey*, 1:137–38).

39. Hakewill, *Apologie*, p. 27.

40. John Harrington, *The Common-wealth of Oceana* (London, 1658), pp. 46, 45.

41. Jean Bodin, *Six Bookes of a Commonweale*, trans. Richard Knolles (London, 1606), p. 406.

42. Raleigh, *History of the World*, p. 775.

43. See, e.g., Karl Löwith, *Meaning in History* (Chicago: University of Chicago Press, 1949), pp. 4–9, and C. A. Patrides, *The Phoenix and the Ladder: The Rise and Decline of the Christian View of History* (Berkeley: University of California Press, 1964), pp. 46–52, and esp. Patrides, *The Grand Design of God: The Literary Form of the Christian View of History* (London: Routledge and Kegan Paul; Toronto: University of Toronto Press, 1972), which updates, enlarges, and revises the earlier study.

44. See, e.g., Manuel, *Shapes of Philosophical History*, pp. 11–13, and G. W. Trompf, *The Idea of Historical Recurrence in Western Thought: From Antiquity to the Reformation* (Berkeley: University of California Press, 1979), esp. ch. 3. Trompf argues not only that the New Testament reveals a sense of cyclical recurrence patterns, but also that "the whole history of recurrence ideas from the first century to the early Renaissance saw the withering away of a linear-cyclical, or better still, a linear-recurrence dichotomy" (p. 309). Nevertheless, the conviction persists that the Judaeo-Christian view of history opposes a cyclical interpretation of time. See, e.g., Northrop Frye's argument that typology and the Old and New Testaments are radically anticyclical in their vision of history (*The Great Code: The Bible and Literature* [New York: Harcourt, Brace, Jovanovich, 1981], pp. 68–72, and ch. 4).

45. See Barbara K. Lewalski, "Typology and Poetry: A Consideration of Herbert, Vaughan, and Marvell," in *Illustrious Evidence: Approaches to English Literature of the Early Seventeenth Century*, ed. Earl Miner (Berkeley: University of California Press, 1975), pp. 41–43; and Lewalski, *Protestant Poetics and the Seventeenth-Century Religious Lyric* (Princeton: Princeton University Press, 1979), ch. 4.

46. Hakewill, *Apologie*, "The Epistle Dedicatory" and p. 45.

47. Browne, *Religio Medici*, in *Works*, 1:19.

48. Raleigh, *History of the World*, sig. A2v. Cf. Raphael Holinshed, comp., *Chronicles of England, Scotlande, and Ireland*, 2 vols. (London, 1577), "The Preface to the Reader."

49. Gilbert Burnet, *A Sermon Preached before . . . the Lord-Mayor and Al-*

dermen of the city of London, September 2, 1680 (London, 1680), p. 29. See also, e.g., Burnet's *History of the Reformation of the Church of England,* 3 vols. (London, 1679–1715), vol. 3, esp. the introduction, and Peter Heylyn, *Cosmographie in foure Bookes Contayning the Chorographie and Historie of the Whole World* (1652; 3d ed. London, 1665), "To the Reader."

50. Bodin, *Method,* p. 300; Le Roy, *Of the Interchangeable course,* pp. 107r-107v; Bacon, *Novum Organum,* in *The Works of Francis Bacon,* ed. James Spedding, R. L. Ellis, and D. D. Heath, 15 vols. (Boston: Houghton Mifflin, 1861), 8:110.

51. William Camden, *Annales: The True and Royall History of the famous Empresse Elizabeth. Queene of England* [trans. Abraham Darcie?] (London, 1625), "The Author to the Reader"; John Speed, *The History of Great Britaine* (London, 1611), p. 168.

52. "Defence of Poetry," in *Sir Philip Sidney: Selected Prose and Poetry,* ed. Robert Kimbrough, 2d ed. (Madison: University of Wisconsin Press, 1983), pp. 154–56.

53. John Foxe, *Actes and Monumentes* (London, 1563), pp. 1–2. Levy, *Tudor Historical Thought,* has argued that the "primary issue" for Tudor writers who sought to justify the Reformation of the English church was "the denial of innovation" (p. 79).

54. See, e.g., Joseph Hall, *The Olde Religion* (London, 1628), and James Ussher, *An Answer to a Challenge made by a Jesuite in Ireland. Wherein the Iudgement of Antiquitie in the points questioned is truely delivered, and the Noveltie of the now Romish doctrine plainly discovered* (Dublin, 1624).

55. Trompf, *Idea of Historical Recurrence,* p. 303. He has a valuable discussion of the variety of historical views that were held by the Protestant reformers (pp. 297–309).

56. Burnet, *History of the Reformation,* 1:"Epistle Dedicatorie"; and 3:331. Useful discussions of the Reformation include George H. Tavard, *Holy Writ or Holy Church: The Crisis of the Protestant Reformation* (New York: Harper, 1959); John R. H. Moorman, *A History of the Church in England* (London: Adam and Charles Black, 1953); Norman Sykes, *Man as Churchman* (Cambridge: Cambridge University Press, 1960); Sir Maurice Powicke, *The Reformation in England* (1941; rpt. London: Oxford University Press, 1961); and Charles H. and Katherine George, *The Protestant Mind of the English Reformation, 1570–1640* (Princeton: Princeton University Press, 1961).

57. Samuel Daniel, *The Civil Wars,* ed. Laurence Michel (New Haven: Yale University Press, 1958), Bk. I, st. 3–8; cf. also Bk. VI, st. 30–47. The first four books of Daniel's *Civil Wars* were published in 1595.

58. See Frances A. Yates, "Queen Elizabeth as Astraea," *JWCI* 10 (1947), 27–82. On the idealization of the queen, see also Roy Strong, *The Cult of Elizabeth: Elizabethan Portraiture and Pageantry* (London: Thames and Hudson, 1977).

59. See, e.g., the poem "Englands Eliza," bound with *A Mirour for Magistrates . . . Newly Enlarged* (London, 1610), p. 787, and Speed, *History of Great Britaine,* pp. 880–81.

60. See Cowley's "To Sir *William Davenant*" and "To Mr. *Hobs*," in *The Works of Abraham Cowley* (London, 1668). The quotation is from "To Mr. *Hobs*," st. 2.

61. Heylyn, *Cosmographie*, "To the Reader."

62. Clarendon, *History of the Rebellion*, 1:1, 2, 93. On the composition and dating of the *History*, see Charles Firth's three-part article, "Clarendon's 'History of the Rebellion,'" *English Historical Review* 19 (1904), 26–54, 246–62, 464–83.

63. Heylyn, *Cosmographie*, "To the Reader."

64. Heylyn, *A Sermon Preached in the Collegiate Church of St. Peter in Westminster on Wednesday May 29th 1661* (London, 1661), pp. 28, 34. Cf. Thomas Hobbes, *Behemoth; The History of the Causes of the Civil. Wars of England* (London, 1682), p. 338, and Clarendon, *History of the Rebellion* (Bk. XVI), 6:98–234, for other examples of the interpretation of the restoration as a cyclical renewal. Clarendon called the restoration of Charles II "such a prodigious act of Providence as [God] hath scarce vouchsafed to any nation, since he led his own chosen people through the Red Sea" (6:143). But as his autobiography written after his banishment in 1667 makes abundantly clear, Clarendon came to feel that England never regained the peace and prosperity she had known in the early years of Charles I's reign (see *Life*, 2:2–3).

65. Raleigh, *History of the World*, sig. A3r, p. 776.

66. Nisbet, *History of the Idea of Progress;* the quotation is from p. 4. See also Ludwig Edelstein, *The Idea of Progress in Classical Antiquity* (Baltimore: Johns Hopkins University Press, 1967). For the older view that the idea of progress is a relatively late development, see J. B. Bury, *The Idea of Progress: An Inquiry into Its Origin and Growth* (1932; rpt. New York: Dover, 1955); Weisinger, "Ideas of History," pp. 75–83; and F. Smith Fussner, *The Historical Revolution: English Historical Writing and Thought, 1580–1640* (New York: Columbia University Press, 1962), p. 299 and passim.

67. Nisbet, *History of the Idea of Progress*, p. 103.

68. On the revolutions in cosmology and astronomy during this period, see Thomas S. Kuhn, *The Copernican Revolution: Planetary Astronomy in the Development of Western Thought* (Cambridge, Mass.: Harvard University Press, 1957), and Alexander Koyrè, *From the Closed World to the Infinite Universe* (Baltimore: Johns Hopkins University Press, 1957).

69. See Giordano Bruno, *On the Infinite Universe and Worlds* (1584), trans. Dorothea Waley Singer, in her *Giordano Bruno: His Life and Thought* (New York: Henry Schuman, 1950), pp. 243–45. I am here quoting Koyrè's summary of Bruno's position (p. 44).

70. See Singer, *Giordano Bruno*, pp. 26–45.

71. *Discoveries and Opinions of Galileo*, trans. with intro. Stillman Drake (Garden City, N.Y.: Doubleday, 1957), p. 142.

72. See, e.g., Edmund Spenser's "Two Cantos of Mutabilitie," which focus on the problem of whether change is evil and destructive, or whether it is associated with beauty and perfection (*The Poetical Works of Edmund Spenser*, ed. J. C. Smith and E. De Selincourt [1911; rpt. London: Oxford

University Press, 1959]). The figure of Mutabilitie, who threatens to take over the universe, at first is linked with the Fall, universal decay, and mortality, but later appears in a more attractive light. The dual view of mutability that the poem offers is only in part resolved by Nature's pronouncement at the end:

> . . . all things steadfastnes doe hate
> And changed be: yet being rightly wayd
> They are not changed from their first estate;
> But by their change their being doe dilate:
> And turning to themselues at length againe,
> Doe worke their own perfection so by fate: . . . (VII. 58. 2–7)

73. Bodin, *Method,* p. 302.

74. Le Roy, *Of the Interchangeable course,* p. 107v.

75. Ibid., pp. 126r–126v, 127v.

76. Nisbet, *History of the Idea of Progress,* pp. 119–24, sees Bodin as the single remarkable exception to his view that there is no idea of progress during the Renaissance.

77. Bodin, *Method,* p. 298.

78. William Camden, *Britannia,* trans. Edmund Gibson, 2 vols. (London, 1772), p. 3. *Britannia* was originally published in Latin in 1586.

79. Speed, *History of Great Britaine,* p. 170.

80. The example of Rome suggests that all empires "end and perish" ("The Proeme" to Speed's *History of Great Britaine*). For a similar mixture of cyclical and progressive views, see Samuel Daniel, who has a basically cyclical view of history but insists that the beginnings of all nations are rude (*Collection of the History of England,* p. 2).

81. Samuel Daniel, "A Defence of Ryme," in *Poems and A Defence of Ryme,* ed. Arthur Colby Sprague (Cambridge, Mass.: Harvard University Press, 1930), pp. 129–58; quotation is from p. 138.

82. On the link between the idea of progress and the Reformation, especially Puritanism, see Ernest Lee Tuveson, *Millennium and Utopia: A Study in the Background of the Idea of Progress* (1949; rpt. New York: Harper and Row, 1964); and Nisbet, *History of the Idea of Progress,* pp. 124–39. Ferguson has observed that "the position of early Protestantism, although purporting to be a return to a primitive Christianity, in fact left more room for originality than the Catholic" (*Clio Unbound,* p. 133).

83. See Levy, *Tudor Historical Thought,* pp. 80–81; Tavard, *Holy Writ or Holy Church;* and John M. Headley, *Luther's View of Church History* (New Haven: Yale University Press, 1963), esp. ch. 2. Headley argues that although Luther saw church history as degenerating from the early period of the church, he did not idealize the early historical period but rather rejected the idea that any historical period was "normative."

84. Richard Hooker, *Of the Laws of Ecclesiastical Polity,* 2 vols. (New York: Dutton, 1965), 1:328–35 (Bk. III, ch. x).

85. Henry Spelman, a seventeenth-century Anglican apologist, takes a similar position in his support of maintaining tithes for the clergy. Insisting

that many things in the gospel were conditioned by historical circumstances, he rejects the idea that the early times of the primitive church should provide the pattern for everything (see *The Larger Treatise Concerning Tithes* [London, 1647], esp. pp. 50, 56).

86. On the influence of Bacon, see Richard Foster Jones, *Ancients and Moderns: A Study of the Rise of the Scientific Movement in Seventeenth-Century England* (rev. ed. 1961; rpt. New York: Dover, 1982).

87. Thomas Sprat, *The History of the Royal-Society of London, for the Improving of Natural Knowledge* (London, 1667), pp. 22, 3.

88. Ibid., pp. 321–22.

89. *The Works of the Honorable Robert Boyle,* 6 vols. (London, 1772), 2:14.

90. Ibid., p. 27; he is here translating a passage from Gulielmus Piso's *Medicina Brasiliensis* (1648).

91. Boyle, *Works,* 3:423.

92. Joseph Glanvill, *Plus Ultra: or, The Progress and Advancement of Knowledge Since the Days of Aristotle* (London, 1668), p. 7.

93. Ibid., p. 91.

94. Sprat, *History,* p. 29.

95. Edward Phillips, preface to *Theatrum Poetarum,* in Spingarn, ed., *Critical Essays,* 2:263.

96. Thomas Sprat, *An Account of the Life and Writings of Mr. Abraham Cowley,* in Spingarn, ed., *Critical Essays,* 2:132. Sir William Davenant similarly sees himself as writing a new kind of epic. Rather than following Homer as "a Guide," he will "venture beyond the track of others" and try "a new and remote way of thinking" (Preface to *Gondibert,* in ibid., 2:2).

97. Sprat, *An Account,* in ibid., 2:134–35.

98. Sir William Temple, *An Essay upon the Ancient and Modern Learning,* in ibid., 3:36.

99. Ibid., p. 103.

100. Ibid., pp. 50, 52.

101. Ibid., p. 60.

102. Thomas Rymer, *The Tragedies of the Last Age,* in ibid., 2:186–87.

103. See Manuel, *Shapes of Philosophical History,* p. 48; Patrides, *Grand Design of God,* esp. pp. 1–9; R. G. Collingwood, *The Idea of History* (Oxford: Clarendon Press, 1946), pp. 46–52; and Frye, *Great Code.*

104. See Patrides, *Grand Design of God,* pp. 58–59, 124. Fussner, *Historical Revolution,* argues that humanism helped to emancipate historiography from its preoccupation with discovering the hand of God in human affairs, because it dismissed as "irrelevant" the Augustinian belief that "secular history could have no ultimate meaning without reference to divine providence" (p. 11).

105. Clarendon, *History* (Bk. IX), 4:2–3.

106. Ibid.

107. In *An Approach to Congreve* (New Haven: Yale University Press, 1979), Aubrey L. Williams has gone against the prevailing critical opinion to argue for the continued importance of the Christian providential "vi-

sion of human existence" (p. x) in the later seventeenth century and, more specifically, in the plays of William Congreve.

108. See Earl Miner's *The Metaphysical Mode from Donne to Cowley* (Princeton: Princeton University Press, 1969), *The Cavalier Mode from Jonson to Cotton* (Princeton: Princeton University Press, 1971), and *The Restoration Mode from Milton to Dryden* (Princeton: Princeton University Press, 1974).

CHAPTER II

Francis Bacon: The Cycles of Error and the Progress of Truth

Let men therefore cease to wonder that the course of science is not yet wholly run, seeing that they have gone altogether astray; either leaving and abandoning experience entirely, or losing their way in it and wandering round and round as in a labyrinth; whereas a method rightly ordered leads by an unbroken route through the woods of experience to the open ground of axioms.

Novum Organum, I. lxxxii

WRITING AT THE BEGINNING of the century, Sir Francis Bacon looked at the pattern that history had taken and boldly proclaimed that its course in the future could be different. In his preoccupation with the shape of history, Bacon defined what was to be one of the major concerns of seventeenth-century English writers. Not many could find comfort in the pattern history had followed, but a few shared Bacon's belief that people could actually alter its course.

Bacon's interest in history is well known. In the second book of *Advancement of Learning* (1605) he included an important discussion of history as one of the three parts of human learning that correspond to the three faculties of the mind—memory, imagination, and reason. Linking history with memory, he divided it into four categories (natural, civil, ecclesiastical, and literary), which were in turn still further subdivided, and he noted where there were deficiencies. In *De Augmentis Scientiarum* (1623) Bacon expanded his discussion of history writing, this time including ecclesiastical and literary history under the category of civil.[1] Not satisfied with theorizing about historiography, Bacon himself made some additions and corrections to William Camden's *Annales*, wrote a *History of the Reign of King Henry VII*, and began a history of Great Britain, of which we have only the first few pages. But Bacon's concern with

43

history is even more far-reaching than such evidence suggests. The bulk of his writing—from *Advancement of Learning* and *Wisdom of the Ancients* (1609) to *Novum Organum* (1620) and the *New Atlantis* (1627)—reflects his interpretation of the history of philosophy and offers a distinctive vision of history's pattern.

Despite the amount of scholarship on Bacon's interest in history, his actual views of history and the way they inform his work have never been fully explored. Scholars have disagreed about exactly what his view of history is. While Ernest Tuveson, for example, has labeled Bacon's view as essentially cyclical, others have claimed him as a firm believer in the idea of progress.[2] Recently, Robert Nisbet in his important *History of the Idea of Progress* has rejected the idea that Bacon had "a historical philosophy or theory of progress," insisting that he lacked the sense of the past as "indispensable soil that alone makes intelligible the present and any anticipated future."[3] Bacon's irreverent attitude toward tradition disqualifies him from having any idea of progress for Nisbet, who defines "the idea of progress" as holding "that mankind has advanced in the past—from some aboriginal condition of primitiveness, barbarism, or even nullity—is now advancing and will continue to advance through the foreseeable future."[4] Certainly Bacon, as we shall see, did not believe that the history of learning showed this kind of gradual, continual advance. He did not see progress as something inevitable, like a law of nature. But it seems to me wrong to deny him an idea of progress. His idea does not fit Nisbet's definition, but it is an idea of progress nonetheless. Bacon was convinced that progress was something that human beings could make possible, that it could be brought about through human effort, and that through human effort the future *could* be characterized by gradual, continuous progress. His writings are inspired by these convictions, and he expresses his idea of progress in language that influenced the scientists and writers later in the century who believed that progress was actual, already accomplished, as well as possible, though that is the subject for another essay. For now, I am concerned to define Bacon's view of history and the ways that it shapes his work.

Bacon's idea of history is complex and includes both cyclical and progressive views. In order to assess precisely his conception of history's pattern, it is necessary to distinguish between his statements about the past and his predictions for the future.

Changing the Course of History

Bacon's works draw their life from his profound desire to effect a radical change in the shape of mankind's history. He analyzes the history of learning to expose the lack of intellectual progress and to convince people of the need for his new program, which will make the advancement of knowledge possible. Most of his observations concern the past 2,500 years, in which "only three revolutions and periods of learning can properly be reckoned; one among the Greeks, the second among the Romans, and the last among us, that is to say, the nations of Western Europe" (*Novum Organum,* in *Works,* 8:110). Like Louis Le Roy, who traced the various cycles in which learning had flourished and decayed, Bacon finds that intellectual history has assumed the form of cycles, or "revolutions"; each period that has been favorable to the growth of knowledge has been followed by an unprosperous, even barbaric era. Bacon was probably familiar with Le Roy's theory that the fortunes of arms and arts have gone together, for his defense of learning in *Advancement of Learning* echoes Le Roy as he insists that "experience doth warrant that both in persons and times there hath been a meeting and concurrence in learning and arms, flourishing and excelling in the same men and the same ages. . . . For both in Ægypt, Assyria, Persia, Graecia, and Rome, the same times that are most renowned for arms are likewise most admired for learning" (*Works,* 6:99).[5] But Bacon's interpretation of these cycles of learning is much more pessimistic than Le Roy's, for he finds that in each successive cycle the state of knowledge has not advanced over the previous one. "The sciences stand where they did and remain almost in the same condition; receiving no noticeable increase" (*Novum Organum,* in *Works,* 8:106).

Bacon's history of learning, however, covers more than these three periods. He recalls there existed a time before the Greeks, a period that, though rude, had a truer, closer knowledge of nature than the Greeks did. The learning of this period has generally sunk into oblivion, but we still have a partial record of its wisdom in the classical myths. As he suggests in his preface to *Wisdom of the Ancients,* these "fables," older than Homer or Hesiod, embody the wisdom of more ancient nations as it was transmitted in the course of time to the Greeks.[6] In the form of parables, the myths set forth "a doctrine concerning the principles of things and the origins of the world" that is quite similar to the philosophy of Democritus, except that it is "more severe, sober, and pure" (*De Principiis atque Originibus*, in *Works*, 10:344). Scholars have debated whether Bacon actually believed that the classical myths embodied the truths he "discovered" in them as he explicated their hidden meanings in *Wisdom of the Ancients*, or whether he was craftily using these fables for his own rhetorical end of persuading resistant readers to accept his new philosophy of science.[7] Such questions about Bacon's intentions and sincerity can never be resolved. What is clear, however, is that his insistence on the wisdom of the ancient myths certainly accords with the belief expressed elsewhere in his writings that there was in the distant past a more accurate understanding of nature than the Aristotelian one that had dominated science up until Bacon's time. But Bacon insists that even the knowledge of these ancient times was far from perfect, for their theories were developed by men who did not rely constantly on "experience." Only before the Fall was there "that pure and uncorrupted natural knowledge" that enabled Adam to name the creatures correctly (Preface to *Great Instauration*, in *Works*, 8:35).

As this reference to the Fall suggests, religious ideas are far more important in Bacon's thought than has been recognized. Scholars have variously praised and blamed him (according to their biases) for emancipating science from religion, and the sincerity of his religious sentiments has been questioned.[8] Bacon is, indeed, eminently practical and this-worldly, and perhaps to some extent he uses the language of religion to make his radical ideas acceptable to his more conservative contemporaries. Nevertheless, his assumptions are fundamentally religious. His view of past history, his attack on false philosophy, and his proposal for a new philosophy are all firmly based on traditional Judaeo-Christian ideas and values.[9]

The Fall is central to Bacon's thought, because it marks the beginning of the long history of false knowledge. Adam turned away from both nature and God when he aspired to "the proud knowledge" of good and evil, intending to provide his own laws rather than depending on God's (*Advancement of Learning*, in *Works*, 6:92). Once the human mind was focused inward upon itself, it became a "false mirror," filled with idols distorting our knowledge of nature as well as our relationship to God. The Augustinian conception of the basic sin of pride, or self-love, informs Bacon's description in *Novum Organum* of the four idols of the mind that misshape our perceptions "according to the measure of the individual and not according to the measure of the universe" (8:77). In the proud belief that the human mind is the proper "measure" of the world, we have sought to "impress" our "own image" on God's works, instead of discovering in them "the stamp of the Creator himself" (*Historia Naturalis et Experimentalis,* in *Works,* 9:370–71).[10] But the "Idols of the human mind" do not accurately reflect the "Ideas of the divine" (*Novum Organum,* in *Works,* 8:72), and consequently our distorted vision has not led to truth. Throughout history, philosophers have reenacted the Fall by looking inside their own minds rather than by observing and studying nature as she truly is. The schoolmen, for example, "left the oracle of God's works and adored the deceiving and deformed images" that their own minds or a few books presented to them (*Advancement of Learning,* in *Works,* 6:124). By inventing fanciful systems of the universe, philosophers have committed a sin perhaps greater than Adam's: "For we copy the sin of our first parents while we suffer for it. They wished to be like God, but their posterity wish to be even greater. For we create worlds, we direct and domineer over nature, we will have it that all things *are* as in our folly we think they should be, not as seems fittest to the Divine wisdom, or as they are found to be in fact." We lose dominion over the creatures a second time because we insolently desire to be like God in following "the dictates of our own reason" (*Historia Naturalis et Experimentalis,* in *Works,* 9:369–70, 371).

Bacon's recurrent image for the errors of the mind, the false philosophies that have dominated science up until his time, is the circle. Because philosophers have not rested firmly on experience and the close observation of nature, they have wandered aimlessly and have been "carried round in a whirl of arguments" (preface to *Great Instauration,* in *Works,* 8:30–31). The circle symbolizes the futility of their intellectual pursuits. Lacking a settled course, they "fetch a wide circuit and meet with many matters, but make little progress" (*Novum Organum,* in *Works,* 8:100). In its self-centeredness the circle is also an appropriate image of pride. The proud philosophers whom Bacon attacks "have based themselves in everything on the agitation of their own wit, content to circle round and round for ever amid the darkest idols of the mind under the high-sounding name of contemplation."[11]

The circular pattern characterizes not just the intellectual motions of the false philosophers but the entire course of past history. In the various revolutions of learning, the intellectual sciences have not advanced. Le Roy had implied that within the generally cyclical course of history there had been some clearly discernible progress. Bacon, however, insists not only that there has been no real progress, but also that the cycles have even been degenerating. While people have been wandering in the false circles of pride, time has been perpetuating error and obliterating truth. Bacon is usually remembered for calling "truth" the "daughter of time" (*Novum Organum*, in *Works*, 8:117), but his more typical description of the passage of time is far less optimistic: "Time is like a river, which has brought down to us things light and puffed up, while those which are weighty and solid have sunk."[12] Only errors and "puffed up" vanities have been accumulated through "the descent of times" (*Valerius Terminus*, in *Works*, 6:38). Intellectual sciences tend to "flourish most in the hands of the first author, and afterwards degenerate."[13]

Ever since the Fall, intellectual history has followed a degenerative, cyclical course. At first man, though fallen, could have regained his dominion over the creatures if he had humbly dwelt on experience; and the myths, the only records of these earliest post-lapsarian times, are evidence for Bacon that some men retained a fairly accurate understanding of nature. These early observers of nature were succeeded by the pre-Socratic Greek philosophers whose knowledge was less pure, but still not completely corrupt. When the sciences, however, passed into the hands of Plato, Aristotle, and their disciples, learning degenerated much further, for these men left nature to wander in their own minds, in endless disputes, and in circuitous syllogisms. Modern science has merely perpetuated these Greek errors since "the sciences which we possess come for the most part from the Greeks. For what has been added by Roman, Arabic, or later writers . . . is built on the foundation of Greek discoveries" (*Novum Organum*, in *Works*, 8:102). While the philosophy of Aristotle has dominated the science of the two later periods, "time of course alter[s] things to the worse," as Bacon comments in the essay "Of Innovations" (12:160). Greek philosophy, which itself was corrupt, has been further "debased" by "many men's wits spent to deprave the wit of one" (*Valerius Terminus*, in *Works*, 6:40). Men have been content to defend and embellish rather than to improve upon their predecessors, and the use of Aristotelian logic has served only to rigidify the errors (*Novum Organum*, in *Works* 8:69). In the modern period the cycles of learning have, in fact, reached the nadir.[14] Despite Bacon's admiration for some modern achievements, his overall judgment is that his contemporaries fall somewhat below the heights of the two earlier cycles; "the learning of these later times" is still "giving place to the former two periods or returns of learning."[15]

Some of Bacon's predecessors and contemporaries found in the cycles of history a cause for optimism.[16] Jean Bodin, Le Roy, and George Hakewill all argued that the cyclical course of history proves false the popular belief that the world and man have steadily decayed since creation. The cycles gave these writers hope that people could equal the achievements of the ancients. Bodin thus claimed that in his own time "such a wealth of knowledge shone forth, such fertility of talents existed, as no age ever excelled." And Le Roy boasted that "our age may compare with the most learned that ever were."[17] Le Roy and Hakewill even saw in the providentially ordained cycles a reassuring image of perfection.[18]

Bacon, however, has quite a different attitude toward the cycles. Rather than taking consolation in the cyclical course of history, he encourages people to break with the pattern of the past. Like Le Roy and Hakewill, he recognizes that people, in believing that the ancients possessed the greatest wisdom, despair of equaling the achievements of Greece and Rome. But he also sees that despair can result from the belief that the course of history is inevitably cyclical. One of the "greatest obstacle[s] to the progress of science and to the undertaking of new tasks" is the notion that we cannot advance beyond the achievements of previous cycles. Even "wise and serious men" suppose "that in the revolution of time and of the ages of the world the sciences have their ebbs and flows; that at one season they grow and flourish, at another wither and decay, yet in such sort that when they have reached a certain point and condition, they can advance no further" (*Novum Organum*, in *Works*, 8:128). Refuting the idea of decay, writers such as Bodin and Le Roy argued that history always follows a cyclical course, and thus they replaced one obstacle to progress with another.

Bacon, however, is radical in his approach. He does not deny that the course of history has been both cyclical and degenerative. He simply announces that the pattern of history is not fixed and unalterable. The future is not doomed to repeat the errors of the past. It is Bacon's refusal to submit to the notion that the universe is governed by inexorable, unchanging laws that allows him to have faith in progress. His idea of progress, his sense that people can change the course of history, is the counterpart of his belief that man can control nature, have dominion over her, and transform her.[19]

Bacon believes his age has the potential to reach much greater heights than have been attained in the two previous cycles of learning. He praises the advantages of his civilization to inspire people to terminate the degenerating cycles of history:

> when I set before me the condition of these times, in which learning hath made her third visitation or circuit, in all the qualities thereof; as the excellency and vivacity of the wits of this age; the noble helps and lights which we have by the travails of ancient writers; the art of printing, which communicateth books to men of all fortunes; the openness of the world by navigation, which hath disclosed multitudes of experiments, and a mass of natural history; the leisure wherewith these times abound . . . the present disposition of these times at this instant to peace; the consumption of all that ever can be said in controversies of religion, which have so much diverted men from other sciences . . . I cannot but be raised to this persuasion, that this third period of time will far surpass that of the Graecian and Roman learning. (*Advancement of Learning*, in *Works*, 6:391–92)

Bacon's writings reverberate with his apocalyptic announcement that the time for the glorious advancement of knowledge is at hand. This age, which is the true antiquity or old age of the world, is the most fit for wisdom since it has both the accumulated experience of a long history and an extensive knowledge of the world through recent navigational discoveries. The fundamentally religious tone that characterizes his indictment of past philosophies is once again present in his hopes for the future expressed in *Valerius Terminus:* "as all knowledge appeareth to be a plant of God's own planting, so it may seem the spreading and flourishing or at least the bearing and fructifying of this plant, by a providence of God, nay not only by a general providence but by a special prophecy, was appointed to this autumn of the world" (6:32).

As this passage suggests, Bacon's writing reveals strong apocalyptic overtones.[20] He frequently quotes Daniel's prophecy (12:4) "touching the last ages of the world:—'Many shall go to and fro, and knowledge shall be increased.' "[21] This is the "special prophecy" that Bacon believes God has directed to his age. The recent discoveries of new lands are evidence that part of this prophecy has already been fulfilled, and Bacon feels it is now mankind's duty to accomplish the other part, for the exploration of the New World and the advancement of the sciences "are destined by fate, that is, by Divine Providence, to meet in the same age" (*Novum Organum,* in *Works,* 8:130). Like many of his contemporaries, Bacon believes that he is living in the "autumn of the world," that the end of time is approaching. But his sense that the end is not far off leads to a vision of progress, not an obsession with decay. Whereas Henry Reynolds, Sir Thomas Browne, and even Donne tend to dwell on the degeneracy and corruption that Old and New Testament prophecies foretold would characterize the world, Bacon is excited by the prospect of knowledge and discovery. His apocalyptic thought emphasizes not the evils and the cosmic catastrophe that Daniel and St. John the Divine's Revelation saw would precede the millennium, but the fruitfulness and promise of the final age. In quoting Daniel, Bacon carefully omits the first half of the verse, in which God tells Daniel to "shut up the words, and seal the book, even to the time of the end." He seeks instead to inspire men with hope and energy for discovery. Like John Milton after him, Bacon feels that God has given his age a special opportunity for progress.

Just as Christopher Columbus was largely responsible for the geographical discoveries, so Bacon has the providential mission of initiating this new era of scientific discovery. He often compares himself with the great explorer. He feels that by publishing "those conjectures" in the *Novum Organum* which make him hope for progress in science, he is following the example of Columbus, who before his voyage set forth "the reasons for his conviction that new lands and continents might be discovered" (8:129). And in *Advancement of Learning* Bacon actually sets himself the task of exploring the "small Globe of the Intellectual World" (6:412), discovering which parts are cultivated and which lie waste.

Bacon sees himself as an agent of God, not only in his exploration of the present state of knowledge but also in his proposal for the reformation of learning. His writings are filled with "such a passion as we believe God alone inspires" (*Historia Naturalis et Experimentalis,* in *Works,* 9:372), and his *Novum Organum* clearly has its "beginning . . . from God" (8:130). In these "last ages of the world,"

Bacon's divinely appointed task is to change the course of history. His *Great Instauration* is "the true end and termination of infinite error" (preface, in *Works*, 8:37). If philosophers will accept his inspired plan for the advancement of knowledge, the cyclical pattern of the past can be broken.

The future will take a new course of progress once people abandon the false traditions they have inherited and turn to the close observation of nature. Because the existing philosophies are idolatrous, fictitious creations rather than accurate descriptions of God's creation, people must start again from the very beginning. Rather than proudly creating "a dream of our own imagination for a pattern of the world," philosophers must in humility keep "the eye steadily fixed upon the facts of nature" ("Plan of the Work," in *Works*, 8:53). Bacon repeatedly insists that philosophers must have a new "foundation" if they are to avoid continuing the cyclical pattern of error. "We must begin anew from the very foundations, unless we would revolve for ever in a circle with mean and contemptible progress" (*Novum Organum*, in *Works*, 8:74). Thus he proposes a "total reconstruction" of all knowledge. Only in his plan is there "some issue; whereas in what is now done in the matter of science there is only a whirling round about, and perpetual agitation, ending where it began" ("Procemium," in *Works*, 8:18).

Bacon is curiously reminiscent of St. Augustine, who argued against the cyclical theory of history as pagan, suggesting instead that people follow the straight path of Christian truth.[22] When Bacon criticizes the past cyclical course of history, he also associates it with the pagans. Our modern learning revolves in circles precisely because it is based on the philosophy of the pagan Greeks, who proudly turned away from the proper study of God's creation. In *Redargutio Philosophiarum* Bacon most clearly indicates the religious basis of his objections to Greek philosophy: "Let me remind you, in the words of the prophet [Isaiah 51:1] of the rock from which ye were hewn and bid you reflect that the nation whose authority you follow is the Greek."[23]

St. Augustine patently denied the existence of recurring cycles, but Bacon admits that the past course of history has indeed been cyclical. He insists, however, that it is necessary to oppose the current of time. In his essay "Of Fortune," Bacon stresses the importance of the individual's actions, asserting that "the mould of a man's fortune is in his own hands" (12:215). A similar principle holds true in the life of mankind as a whole. It is the duty of human beings to reshape the pattern of history, for "if time of course alter things to the worse, and wisdom and counsel shall not alter them to the better, what shall be the end?" ("Of Innovations," in *Works*, 12:160). Instead of becoming dizzy by gazing too much on the "turning wheels of vicissitude" ("Of Vicissitude of Things," in *Works*, 12:280), people should unite their efforts to alter the course of history.

Whereas time tends to perpetuate error, mankind must work to accumulate truth, to effect a continual augmentation of knowledge. People are not bound to the long "revolution of many ages" (*Novum Organum*, in *Works*, 8:142). By the "association of labors" through "successions of ages" (8:145), they can replace the old cyclical pattern of history with a new pattern of progress. Bacon sees himself fulfilling this ideal of cumulative succession. In his examination of past and present philosophies, his purpose is to "make a justification of that which is good and sound" by weeding out the errors (*Advancement of Learning*, in *Works*, 6:117). He by no means rejects all the past. If he criticizes those who reverence "Antiquity" and believe there can be no "new additions," he also attacks those who would go to the opposite extreme and embrace "Noveltie" (*Advancement of Learning*, in *Works*, 6:129). In fact, he harshly criticizes Aristotle (whom he compares in this respect to "Anti-Christ") for waging "war on all antiquity" in an attempt to "extinguish and obliterate all ancient wisdom" (*De Augmentis*, in *Works*, 8:482–83).

Bacon's explication of the classical myths in *The Wisdom of the Ancients* clearly illustrates his theory that the course of history can be changed only through the accumulation of and addition to the best from the past. He finds in the Orpheus myth (13:113) a description of the cyclical course which the history of learning has taken: the disappearance and reemergence of the Helicon shows that "the works of wisdom . . . have their periods and closes." When a civilization has flourished for a time, people "return to the depraved conditions of their nature," and philosophy is torn in pieces like Orpheus; but after the season of barbarism, the waters of learning "break out and issue forth again" in other nations.[24] Bacon's explication of the Prometheus myth (13:155–56), however, suggests that mankind's cooperative efforts can create a different pattern in the future. The torch races that were anciently held in honor of Prometheus show that "the perfection of the sciences is to be looked for not from the swiftness or ability of any one inquirer, but from a succession." These races, which have not been held for many centuries, should be revived so "that the victory may no longer depend upon . . . each single man." Bacon's actual explanations of the fables typically exemplify his ideal of cumulative wisdom, for he adds his own interpretations to those of earlier mythographers.[25]

In his writings as a whole, Bacon believes he is reviving this lost ideal of succession. He is "willing to go beyond others" and "to have others go beyond me again" (*Advancement of Learning*, in *Works*, 6:412), improving his ideas, discarding his errors. His work in *De Augmentis* has been to tune the instrument of science so that in the future "the strings may be touched by a better hand or a better quill" (9:343). He has followed his own advice to others, "determined to add as much as I could to the inventions of others," but "no less willing that my own inventions should be surpassed by posterity" (9:356). Only when there is this true succession will the cycles and vicissitudes of learning end. Only then will truth become the daughter of time.

The Path of Progress

Bacon's attempt to substitute a future line of progress for the past cyclical movement of history is probably the most pervasive characteristic of his writing. In *Advancement of Learning* he "delivers" learning from "the discredits and disgraces" it has received (6:91). Much of the *Novum Organum* not only provides "grounds . . . for putting away despair" about progress (8:146) but also offers numerous "argument[s] for hope" (e.g., 8:130, 140). Even *Wisdom of the Ancients,* whose title alone would seem to refute the idea of progress, actually seeks to foster advancement. Addressed to those who in their reverence for antiquity stand in the way of progress, Bacon's explications of the classical myths provide a vehicle for his own revolutionary ideas.[26] In the preface he suggests that by combining the original and the traditional, he will advance and point the way toward future achievements: "though the subjects be old, yet the matter is new; while leaving behind us the open and level parts, we bend our way towards the nobler heights that rise beyond" (13:81).

Bacon's language consistently reveals his preference for the linear, the goal-directed, over the circular. The dominant images throughout the *Advancement of Learning* and the *Great Instauration* are those of "discovery," "journey," and "progression."[27] As Bacon embarks on his "voyage" through all fields of knowledge, he assures his readers that they will "not be kept for ever tossing on the waves of experience" ("Plan of the Work," in *Works*, 8:50). In the past science was "more laboured than advanced; the labours spent on it having been rather in a circle, than in progression" (*De Augmentis*, in *Works*, 9:29). His concern, however, is to give the "true direction" to mankind. People should "discover what is the best way" and then "make progression" (*Advancement of Learning*, in *Works*, 6:129–30).

The most important prerequisite for the advancement of knowledge is "the pointing out and setting forth of the straight and ready way to the thing which is to be done," and Bacon accordingly lays out "a road for the human understanding direct from the sense" (*De Augmentis* and *Novum Organum* in *Works*, 8:396, 114). Whereas others pursue labyrinthine courses, he offers a path that "leads by an unbroken route through the woods of experience to the open ground of axioms" (*Novum Organum*, in *Works*, 8:115). He is amazed that no person before him ever attempted "to direct the resources of human wit and intellect towards the arts and sciences and to pave a path towards that goal! To think that this whole endeavour should have been, should still be, left to the obscurity of tradition, the dizzy round of argument, the eddies and whirlpools of chance and mere experience."[28] People need a clear, firm, orderly sense of direction, if they are to win the race and attain the goal of dominion over nature. They should not be distracted, as Atalanta was, from the "true course" and "end" of science by a greedy desire for more immediate profits (*Wisdom of the Ancients*, in *Works*, 13:142–44). Philosophers have not "run a course aright" because the goal itself has not been rightly placed (*Novum Organum*, in *Works*, 8:113) and because they have looked backward to the authority of the past rather than "forward to that part of the race which is still to be run" (*De Augmentis*, in *Works*, 8:398).

Even in the communication of knowledge, philosophers have not been properly concerned with the advancement of learning. Too often they have relied on the magistral method, which merely induces belief, rather than used the initiative method, which, by transmitting knowledge to the true "sons" of science, aims at the "continuation and further progression" of knowledge (*De Augmentis,* in *Works,* 9:122). Bacon prefers aphorisms that go straight to the "pith and heart of sciences," "point to action," and "invite men to enquire farther" over methods that "carry a kind of demonstration in orb or circle, one part illuminating another, and therefore satisfy" (*Advancement of Learning,* in *Works,* 6:291–92).

This radical desire to replace circular with linear movement is similarly reflected in Bacon's description of his "new organon," the inductive method without which, he believed, there could be no important augmentation of knowledge. Bacon's definition of induction actually incorporates his historical ideal of linear progress. Induction begins with the particulars and experience of nature and then moves up "a just scale of ascent, and by successive steps not interrupted or broken, we rise from particulars to lesser axioms; and then to middle axioms, one above the other; and last of all to the most general" (*Novum Organum,* in *Works,* 8:138). This ascending orderly path is the true way for the advancement of learning. The inductive method accumulates empirical truth, whereas the deductive syllogism, like time, tends "to fix and give stability" to errors founded in "commonly received notions" (8:69). Because philosophers have lacked a proper method, they have made no progress. Either they have completely abandoned experience and "gone altogether astray," or they have lost their way in it, "wandering round and round as in a labyrinth" (8:115). The linear direction of induction opposes the circular wanderings of the past, which have resulted in the nonprogressive, degenerative course of history.

In its gradual ascent induction contrasts with the proud philosophies that have disdained to concern themselves with "the senses and particulars" (8:71). Induction is the method of humility. It directs the mind outward to the observation of nature, seeking to regain Adam's close relationship with the creatures. It begins "nearer the source" than people have done in the past and examines those things that are generally taken "on trust" (8:43). Bacon believes that "our chief hope" lies in induction, since only this method can purge the mind of its idols, "the venom which the serpent infused into it, and which makes the mind of man to swell" (8:139, 35).

Like the Protestant reformers of religion, Bacon rejects corrupt human traditions, desiring to seek truth from its source. As a remark in *Advancement of Learning* indicates, Bacon himself was quite aware of the parallel between the two reformations: "in the age of ourselves and our fathers, when it pleased God to call the church of Rome to account for their degenerate manners and ceremonies . . . at one and the same time it was ordained by the Divine Providence that there should attend withal a renovation and new spring of all other knowledges" (6:143).

Other philosophers have been satisfied with the barren fantastic productions of their minds, but Bacon's man of science aims at "the glory of the Creator and the relief of man's estate" (*Advancement of Learning*, in *Works*, 6:134). The true philosopher must be primarily concerned with the common good, for the worthy augmentation of knowledge can be achieved only if men, motivated by charity, actively pursue the fruits and works of learning that benefit mankind, rather than selfishly indulging in the contemplative life.[29] Bacon is here making the Christian distinction between the cardinal sin of pride and the cardinal virtue of charity. One need only examine the lengthy discussion of charity in *De Augmentis* (*Works*, 9:196–227) to see the central part that specifically Christian ideas play in his conviction that scientists must have a charitable concern with the common good. As Bacon insists, knowledge needs the "corrective spice" of charity (*Advancement of Learning*, in *Works*, 6:94). Unlike his predecessors who have generally been absorbed in their own private interests, his "endeavour [is] to advance human interests," for it is better to "raise" something to a "higher nature" than to "preserve" it in its same condition (*De Augmentis*, in *Works*, 9:204).

This new philosophy seeks not only to improve the material condition of human life but also to re-establish the proper relationship with God that was lost when man began to wander in the circles of pride. Although a little exploration in natural philosophy may incline the mind to atheism, a "further proceeding" brings man back to religion (*Valerius Terminus*, in *Works*, 6:33). As philosophers ascend the "pyramid" of knowledge by induction, "the Ladder of the Intellect," they move from history and experience to natural history, to physic, to metaphysic, and finally come close to understanding God's summary law of nature ("Plan of the Work" and *De Augmentis*, in *Works*, 8:38, 507). When a person goes deep into the knowledge of philosophy, "then, according to the allegory of the poets, he will easily believe that the highest link of nature's chain must needs be tied to the foot of Jupiter's chair" (*Advancement of Learning*, in *Works*, 6:97). Although Bacon insists that human and divine knowledge should not be unwisely confounded — that people should not try to bring God down to their level — he firmly believes that natural philosophy is capable of drawing man up to God: "we ought not to attempt to draw down or submit the mysteries of God to our reason; but contrariwise to raise and advance our reason to the divine truth."[30] If philosophers will follow Bacon's humanitarian plans, humbly directing all their efforts to the glory of God, the pattern of degenerate, cyclical history that has been operative since the Fall can be reversed, and a new course of progression and ascent will begin, bringing mankind closer to nature and God.

Bacon's insistence on the necessity of directing all labors toward a proper goal reveals his dislike of endless activity. His preference for linear over circular movement is also a preference for that which is limited and has an end. "Circular motion is interminable, and for its own sake" (*De Principiis atque Originibus*, in *Works*, 10:368). It does not aim at an external goal in which it can rest. This self-centered motion is symbolic of man's pride, his absorption in his own fancies and glory. Bacon's description of the scholastic learning indicates the way in which the circle, endlessness, and pride all are interrelated. The schoolmen spun "laborious webs of learning" out of "no great quantity of matter, and infinite agitation of wit." Their books reveal only too well that if the mind works only "upon itself, as the spider worketh his web, then it is endless, and brings forth indeed cobwebs of learning, admirable for the fineness of thread and work, but of no substance or profit" (*Advancement of Learning*, in *Works*, 6:122). In contrast, linear motion is "to an end, and for the sake of something, and as it were to obtain rest" (*De Principiis atque Originibus*, in *Works*, 10:368). Bacon implies that all of God's works assume a linear pattern, for they "lead of a certainty to their end." His own divinely inspired plan for the reformation of knowledge, unlike the previous circular, endless philosophies, has a "true and lawful goal" (*Novum Organum*, in *Works*, 8:130, 113). With his inductive method, the mind will be properly limited to the study of nature and will thus be able to cease its restless wandering and "arrive at a knowledge of causes in which it can rest."[31]

This ideal of rest is central to Bacon's thought. His numerous references to the Sabbath reveal a profound longing for this peace. Although he clearly voices the newly emerging belief that change can be for the better, nevertheless his ultimate goal of rest suggests that Bacon could not entirely break away from the old ideal of perfection as stasis. It has been suggested that Bacon questioned the Ptolemaic/Aristotelian view of the world as having a fixed, stable center and believed that everything in the world is characterized by change and motion,[32] but he would not have agreed with Thomas Hobbes that cessation of motion is death, an end to be avoided. In Bacon's mind perpetual motion characterizes the false circles. He instead desires that path that will eventually lead science, and mankind, to rest in "sacred and inspired Divinity, the Sabaoth and port of all men's labours" (*Advancement of Learning,* in *Works,* 6:393), and it is with the consideration of divinity that *Advancement of Learning* appropriately concludes. When God finished the work of Creation, He rested ("Plan of the Work," in *Works,* 8:53). Human beings, too, should observe the Sabbath. Bacon criticizes the "incessant and sabbathless pursuit of a man's fortune" because it "leaveth not tribute which we owe to God of our time" (6:386). In the *New Atlantis* he significantly names the scientific institute the "House of Six Days Works," thus implying that our labors in natural philosophy, which were imposed on us by the Fall, are all directed toward the seventh day of rest.

Science and Salvation

Bacon's ultimate hope is that science will enable human beings to attain the most perfect Sabbath of all. In the beginning of *Great Instauration* he prays that "if we labour in thy works with the sweat of our brows thou wilt make us partakers of thy vision and thy sabbath" (8:54). The implication is that with God's blessing we might be able to effect our own redemption. Bacon's plan for the reformation of knowledge aims at the greatest instauration possible—the restoration of Adam's original knowledge that allowed him dominion over nature before the Fall. When we regain that perfect knowledge, we will attain the final Sabbath. The true end of learning is "a restitution and reinvesting (in great part) of man to the sovereignty and power (for whensoever he shall be able to call the creatures by their true names he shall again command them) which he had in his first state of creation. And to speak plainly and clearly, it is a discovery of all operations and possibilities of operations from immortality (if it were possible) to the meanest mechanical practice" (*Valerius Terminus*, in *Works*, 6:34). Although Bacon retains some doubts about man's ability to transcend his mortality through his own efforts, his faith that human beings can determine their own fortune is so strong that it leads him to suggest that mankind as a whole is capable of achieving its own salvation. God, of course, has preordained mankind's redemption, but Bacon implies that it might be possible to accelerate the process of time, to "abridge the circuits and long ways of experience." With his method, discoveries that would appear in the "revolution of many ages" now can be made "speedily and suddenly and simultaneously."[33]

Bacon suggests, however, that the forward advance of knowledge is paradoxically a return to the original state of wisdom before the Fall.[34] The linear path of progress that Bacon substitutes for the cycles of the past will actually complete the circle of history by leading us to the end of redemption that touches the prelapsarian state of bliss where the circle began. Mankind will have come full circle when philosophy reaches its goal of restoring perfect knowledge.[35]

There are major differences between this all-embracing cycle of universal history ordained by Providence and the corrupt cycles that Bacon condemns as having characterized man's erroneous philosophies and his past. Bacon's definition of circular motion indicates how the circle can symbolize perfection in God but sin in man: "the body . . . moves merely for the sake of moving and following itself and seeking its own embraces, and exciting and enjoying its own nature" (*Thema Coeli*, in *Works*, 10:469). Such a self-centered existence is the essence of pride. All human activities should be outwardly directed toward the benefit of mankind and the glory of God. Only God, who contains all within His circumference, can find perfection and completion in Himself.

The providential cycle of history differs from the corrupt cycles in yet another way. This one universal cycle returns to the same point at which it started—man's state of knowledge and bliss before the Fall—and thus completes what Bacon defines as "perfect circular motion" (*Thema Coeli*, in *Works*, 10:472). On the other hand, the cycles of the past exhibit "degenerate" circular motions (10:472), since each "revolution" of learning falls below the previous one. Most significant, however, the perfect circle of history, unlike the "endless" circles of error, has a goal in which it can rest—the salvation of mankind. Human history will not revolve interminably. When mankind's redemption is completed, historical time will cease, and "an eternal sabbath shall ensue" ("Confession of Faith," in *Works*, 14:50). The completion of this largest revolution of time will result, not in the perpetuation of further cycles, but in the Apocalypse.[36]

Only the advancement of knowledge is needed to bring about the end of the world. Bacon hopes for philosophers to "write an apocalypse or true vision of the footsteps of the Creator imprinted on his creatures" ("Plan of the Work," in *Works*, 8:53). When philosophers achieve this vision, they will have regained Adam's perfect knowledge and attained redemption. As in religion, so in science man's mind must first be "thoroughly freed and cleansed" of idols to attain this apocalyptic vision. Acquiring the perfect knowledge of nature becomes virtually the same for Bacon as attaining salvation in heaven: "the entrance into the kingdom of man, founded on the sciences, being not much other than the entrance into the kingdom of heaven, whereinto none may enter except as a little child" (*Novum Organum*, in *Works*, 8:99).

Bacon himself offers the means for redemption with his "new organon," his method for the reformation and advancement of knowledge. Only his method, he insists, can purify people's minds and make them capable and worthy of receiving an apocalyptic vision and entering the heavenly kingdom of knowledge. He claims in *Great Instauration* to "perform the office of a true priest of the sense (from which all knowledge in nature must be sought . . .) and a not unskilful interpreter of its oracles" ("Plan of the Work," in *Works*, 8:44). The evangelical fervor of his writings, the sense of urgency and importance, and his continual attempts to reach a large audience all result from his vision of himself as a Christ-like redeemer of mankind. Like Christ, his position is that of a mediator: his work ascends to God's glory and descends to the good of man (*Historia Naturalis et Experimentalis*, in *Works*, 9:373). In the preface to his *Great Instauration*, he prays that the Father, the Son, and the Holy Ghost "will vouchsafe through my hands to endow the human family with new mercies" (8:35). Bacon becomes the instrument of God's mercies, the true priest and prophet bringing news of salvation and the means for effecting it.

Bacon apparently had at least one disciple who believed in his redemptive role. Some forty years after Bacon's death, Abraham

Cowley's ode "To the *Royal Society*," which prefaced Thomas Sprat's *History*, proclaimed that Bacon "set [Philosophy] free" (st. 1).[37] Like Moses, the Old Testament type of Christ, Bacon showed us the way to the promised land, itself a type for the paradise that Christians hope to regain:

> *Bacon*, like *Moses*, led us forth at last,
>   The barren Wilderness he past,
>   Did on the very Border stand
>   Of the blest promis'd Land,
> And from the Mountains top of his Exalted Wit,
>   Saw it himself, and shew'd us it. (st. 5)

Though Bacon, like Moses, was not allowed to enter, Cowley prophecies that the Royal Society will actually "subdue" "These spacious Countries" (st. 6). The religious imagery and biblical parallels clearly suggest that Cowley not only recognized Bacon's sense of his redemptive role but also inherited Bacon's faith that the pursuit of science is essentially a religious one that can help bring about salvation.

Members of the Royal Society, which was founded to effect Bacon's plans for the advancement of science, continued to insist that their pursuits did not conflict with Christianity and were ultimately religious. Joseph Glanvill's *Plus Ultra* (1668) defended the society against charges that its members were atheists. And Robert Boyle argued that "by being addicted to *Experimental Philosophy*, a Man is rather Assisted, than Indisposed, to be a *Good Christian*."[38] Nevertheless, Bacon's words and ideas do have some important implications that undermine Christian assumptions. He believes that people can change the course of history, hasten the Apocalypse, build a new world for themselves, and work out their own salvation. Though God's blessings are needed, the process is human and natural, not divine. Moreover, the paradise that we will regain is not located in an afterlife, nor does it depend on God's creating a new heaven and earth. Rather, it is simply earthly existence, improved and refined by scientific discoveries and inventions. The secularization of Christian salvation appears perhaps most vividly in Bacon's *New Atlantis*. When the narrator enters the utopian island where natural philosophy is being perfected, it seems to him that "we had before us a picture of our salvation in heaven; for we . . . were now brought into a place where we found nothing but consolations. . . . we were come into a land of angels, which did appear to us daily and present us with comforts" (5:369). In comparing his visionary ideal of earthly life to life in heaven, Bacon does not really conflate the two. Earth is still a "picture" of heaven. But as human beings become capable of creating perfection in this world, the importance of God and the traditional Christian consolation of another world reserved for the saints must surely diminish. The next step is to conclude that salvation is of and in this world.

Bacon does not quite take this step, but he points the way. Although he usually adopts the traditional Christian position that this world is finite, at times he toys with the idea of its possible eternity. In *Thoughts on the Nature of Things,* he uses one biblical quotation to show that the universe is finite and mortal, but two to prove it eternal (10:315). His references to the Apocalypse omit the elements of destruction and devastation that typically constitute a large part of traditional Judaeo-Christian accounts. By ignoring the biblical idea that the creation of a new world must be preceded by the destruction of the old, he implies that the new heaven and earth will be simply a transformation of the existing ones. Even his conception of God reflects Bacon's passionate commitment to the natural world. God is the "Founder, Preserver, and Renewer of the universe" (*Historia Naturalis et Experimentalis,* in *Works,* 9:373). When such a beneficent God governs the universe, the future can hold no terror.

Notes

1. I have used *The Works of Francis Bacon,* ed. James Spedding, R. L. Ellis, and D. D. Heath, 15 vols. (Boston: Houghton Mifflin, 1861), and subsequent references will be included in the text where possible. For Bacon's discussion of history, see *Advancement of Learning,* in *Works,* 6:182–202; *De Augmentis Scientiarum,* in *Works,* 8:407–39.

2. Tuveson, *Millennium and Utopia,* pp. 66–67. On Bacon's belief in progress, see, e.g., Harry Levin, *The Myth of the Golden Age in the Renaissance* (Bloomington: Indiana University Press, 1969), pp. 149–54; Harris, *All Coherence Gone,* p. 132; and W. H. Greenleaf, *Order, Empiricism, and Politics: Two Traditions of English Political Thought, 1500–1700* (London: Oxford University Press, 1964), pp. 201-4. Other relevant discussions of Bacon's interest in history include Fussner, *Historical Revolution,* pp. 253–74; Leon-

ard F. Dean, "Sir Francis Bacon's Theory of Civil History-Writing," in *Essential Articles for the Study of Francis Bacon*, ed. Brian Vickers (Hamden, Conn.: Archon, 1968), pp. 211–35; and George H. Nadel, "History as Psychology in Francis Bacon's Theory of History," in ibid., pp. 236–50.

3. Nisbet, *History of the Idea of Progress*, pp. 113, 112–15.

4. Ibid., pp. 4–5.

5. Toward the end of Book I of *Advancement of Learning*, Bacon returns to the argument that there has been a concurrence of learning and the flourishing of empires—in moral virtue, in the felicity of the people, and in military prowess (*Works*, 6:146–65). Le Roy's thesis is stated in the long title of the English translation of his book: *Of the Interchangeable course, or variety of things in the whole world; and the concurrence of armes and Learning, thorough the first and famousest Nations: from the beginning of Civility, and Memory of man, to this Present.*

6. *Works*, 13:78–79. See also Bacon's comments about fables and ancient wisdom in the second book of *De Augmentis*, in *Works*, 8:443.

7. On *The Wisdom of the Ancients*, see, e.g., Paolo Rossi, *Francis Bacon: From Magic to Science*, trans. Sacha Rabinovitch (Chicago: University of Chicago Press, 1968), ch. 3; and James Stephens, *Francis Bacon and the Style of Science* (Chicago: University of Chicago Press, 1975), pp. 137–58.

8. F. H. Anderson, *The Philosophy of Francis Bacon* (Chicago: University of Chicago Press, 1948), p. 297, credits Bacon with the "complete emancipation of natural knowledge from the dominant conceptions of traditional theology." C. D. Broad, *The Philosophy of Francis Bacon* (Cambridge: Cambridge Univ. Press, 1926), pp. 18–19, remarks that "religion and morality have little to hope and nothing to fear from the advancement of natural philosophy. . . . It is evident that he was a sincere if unenthusiastic Christian." Although Moody E. Prior ("Bacon's Man of Science," in *Essential Articles*, ed. Vickers, pp. 140–63) recognizes a connection between Bacon's ideas about science and his fascination with the Fall, he tends to deprecate the depth and sincerity of Bacon's religious sentiments, which, he asserts, "sound like conventional embroidery" (p. 155). Harold Fisch, *Jerusalem and Albion: The Hebraic Factor in Seventeenth-Century Literature* (London: Routledge and Kegan Paul, 1964), pp. 72–92, has an interesting discussion of the mixture of religious and secular elements in Bacon's thought, but the note of disparagement once again emerges as he calls Bacon's Hebraism "perverted" and "distorted," and his ideas only "pseudo-religious."

9. Several scholars have begun to suggest that there is a serious religious dimension to Bacon's ideas. See Rossi, *Francis Bacon*, pp. 128–32, 162–64; Sidney Warhaft, "The Providential Order in Bacon's New Philosophy," *SLitI* 4 (1971), 49–64; Elizabeth McCutcheon, "Bacon and the Cherubim: An Iconographical Reading of the *New Atlantis*," *ELR* 2 (1972), 334–55; James S. Tillman, "Pygmalion's Idolatry and Hercules' Faith: Religious Themes in Bacon's Emblems," *South Atlantic Bulletin* 43 (1978), 67–74; and J. Samuel Preus, "Religion and Bacon's New Learning," in *Continuity and Discontinuity in Church History: Essays Presented to George*

Huntston Williams . . ., ed. F. Forrester Church and Timothy George (Leiden: Brill, 1979), pp. 267–84.

10. The four idols or "false notions" that are "in possession of the human understanding" are all manifestations of pride: each is a variation of the erroneous belief that human beings are the center and accurate measure of the universe. The Idols of the Tribe refer to the tendency of the race of man to distort "the nature of things, by mingling its own nature with it." The Idols of the Cave denote the predisposition of each individual to refract "the light of nature" according to his own "peculiar constitution." The Idols of the Market-place, created by the verbal intercourse of men, are those words that are imperfect names for things and that "overrule the understanding . . . and lead men away into numberless empty controversies and idle fancies." Human beings proudly become more concerned with their own language than with nature, God's creation. Finally, the Idols of the Theater refer to the false notions that men absorb from other philosophies that represent "worlds of their own creation after an unreal and scenic fashion." By worshipping these man-made notions, human beings engage in a form of self-worship. See *Novum Organum*, in *Works*, 8:72–78.

11. Bacon, *Cogitata et Visa*, trans. in Benjamin Farrington, *The Philosophy of Francis Bacon* (Liverpool: Liverpool University Press, 1964), p. 82.

12. Preface to *Great Instauration*, in *Works*, 8:29. See also *Valerius Terminus* and *Filium Labyrinthi*, in *Works*, 6:42, 426.

13. Preface to *Great Instauration*, in *Works*, 8:27. In the same passage Bacon insists that the history of mechanical arts, rather than following the same pattern as the intellectual sciences, exemplifies the idea of gradual perfection.

14. Because Bacon's optimistic prophecies about future advancements are often read as glorifications of present achievements, the misconception exists that he defended the actual superiority of the moderns over the ancients. R. F. Jones, "The Bacon of the Seventeenth Century," in *Essential Articles*, ed. Vickers, pp. 3–27, finds Bacon most enthusiastic about the future possibilities, but he still insists that Bacon "staunchly upholds the moderns in the controversy with antiquity" (p. 8).

15. *Works*, 6:199. This quotation from *Advancement of Learning* appears in a slightly different form in the later *De Augmentis Scientiarum*: "the learning of these our times not much giving place to the two former periods or returns of learning (the one of the Grecians, the other of the Romans), but in some respects far exceeding them" (8:435). This change seems to indicate Bacon's belief that between 1605 and 1623 the moderns had made significant progress and come closer to the level of the two previous cycles.

16. See Manuel, *Shapes of Philosophical History*, p. 65.

17. Bodin, *Method*, p. 300; Le Roy, *Of the Interchangeable course*, p. 107r.

18. Le Roy, *Of the Interchangeable course*, Bk. I, esp. p. 1r; Hakewill, *An Apologie*, sig. Clv and pp. 45–46.

19. Bacon's questioning of the traditional idea that fixed, unalterable

laws govern the universe is evident, for example, in his remark that "the human understanding is of its own nature prone to suppose the existence of more order and regularity in the world than it finds" (*Novum Organum,* in *Works,* 8:79), and in his belief that through science man will be able to control and alter nature in order to improve the condition of human life. James C. Morrison, "Philosophy and History in Bacon," *JHI* 38 (1977), 585–606, has suggested that Bacon's identification of knowledge and power means not just that knowledge gives man power to control nature but that "knowledge is *itself* an exercise of power over nature" (p. 592).

20. Virgil Whitaker, *Francis Bacon's Intellectual Milieu* (Los Angeles: William Andrews Clark Memorial Library, 1962), p. 22, notes Bacon's "evangelical fervor," but the importance of Bacon's apocalyptic thought has not been explored. Harold Fisch rightly acknowledges Bacon's "messianic call," "his sense of an approaching millennium of scientific advancement" (*Jerusalem and Albion,* p. 218), but then he accuses Bacon of lacking "the Hebraic vision . . . of a far-off divine event—other than simply human aggrandisement—to which the whole creation moves" (p. 113).

21. *Novum Organum,* in *Works,* 8:130. See also *De Augmentis* (*Works,* 8:435), *Valerius Terminus* (*Works,* 6:32), and *Advancement of Learning* (*Works,* 6:198).

22. See St. Augustine, *The City of God,* trans. Marcus Dods, 2 vols. (New York: Hafner, 1948), vol. 1, Bk. XII, chs. xiii, xvii, and xx.

23. Trans. in Farrington, *Philosophy of Francis Bacon,* p. 109.

24. Le Roy similarly describes the cyclical history of the arts and sciences as they flourished first in Egypt and Persia, then in Greece, Italy, and Sarasmania, and "finallie in this age." They "augment little by little" till they reach "their perfection"; then "they fall eftsoones, and finally perish. . . . when they haue bin a while let downe, they arise againe, and successiuelie recouer their former strength" (*Of the Interchangeable course,* p. 17r).

25. Charles W. Lemmi, *The Classic Deities in Bacon* (Baltimore: Johns Hopkins University Press, 1933), details Bacon's great debt to earlier mythographers but also indicates that Bacon usually added some original observations to these interpretations.

26. On Bacon's use of classical myth as a vehicle for his ideas about the reform of science, see Rossi, *Francis Bacon,* pp. 73–134, and Stephens, *Francis Bacon,* pp. 142–53.

27. Brian Vickers, *Francis Bacon and Renaissance Prose* (Cambridge: Cambridge University Press, 1968), pp. 179–86, presents an interesting discussion of Bacon's images of "journey" and "discovery."

28. Bacon, *Cogitata et Visa,* trans. in Farrington, *Philosophy of Francis Bacon,* p. 90.

29. Prior, "Bacon's Man of Science," p. 154, recognizes Bacon's distinction between pride and charity, but he underestimates the importance of Bacon's religious concern by denying that Christian grounds provide

the sanction for this insistence on charity: "The scientist must cultivate charity in consequence of being a scientist, not a Christian." Euguene Patrick McCreary's dissertation, "Charity and Related Principles in the Writings of Sir Francis Bacon and Sir Thomas Browne" (University of Illinois, 1969), places more emphasis on the religious element in Bacon's thought.

30. *Advancement of Learning*, in *Works*, 6:213.

31. Ibid., p. 122; "Plan of the Work," in *Works*, 8:52.

32. See Morrison, "Philosophy and History in Bacon," pp. 585–606, who argues for Bacon's modernism and sees him rejecting the old idea of the fixed, centered universe as well as the traditional distinction between nature *(phusia)* and art/artifice *(nomos)*.

33. *De Augmentis*, in *Works*, 8:507; and *Novum Organum*, in *Works*, 8:142. Bacon's interpretation of the myth of Atalanta also implies that it is ideally possible to speed up the natural course of time: "For Art, which is meant by Atalanta, is in itself, if nothing stand in the way, far swifter than Nature and, as one may say, the better runner, and comes sooner to the goal" (*Wisdom of the Ancients*, in *Works*, 13:143).

34. Rossi, *Francis Bacon*, pp. 127–30, is one of the few who have recognized that Bacon's plan for the advancement of learning is actually aimed at a "renewal of the past."

35. *Advancement of Learning* reveals Bacon's belief that a linear path could form a circle, for his orderly voyage or progress through the lands of learning completes the "Globe of the Intellectual World" (6:412). Although the Judaeo-Christian view of history is basically linear (see Patrides, *Grand Design of God*), it is also cyclical in this largest sense. Mircea Eliade, in *Cosmos and History*, trans. W. R. Trask (New York: Harper, 1959; originally published in Paris, 1949, under the title *Le Mythe de L'eternel retour*), pp. 102–47, also emphasizes the linear nature of this conception of history, but he indicates the important ways the cyclical idea of history was absorbed into Judaeo-Christian philosophy.

36. Eliade, *Cosmos and History*, pp. 111–12, observes that both Judaism and Christianity conceive of history as a single cycle from Creation and the Fall to Redemption and the final creation of a new world, whereas Hellenistic thought conceives of history as a series of repetitive cycles.

37. Abraham Cowley, "To the *Royal Society*," in *Works of Abraham Cowley*.

38. See the title page of Robert Boyle, *The Christian Virtuoso* (London, 1690).

CHAPTER III

John Donne: The Idea of Decay

Who would not bee affected, to see a cleere & sweet *River* in the *Morning*, grow a kennell of muddy land water by *noone*, and condemned to the saltnesse of *Sea* by *night*? And how lame a *Picture*, how faint a *representation*, is that, of the precipitation of man's body to *dissolution*? Now all the parts built up, and knit by a lovely *soule, now* but a *statue* of *clay*, and *now*, these limbs melted off, as if that *clay* were but *snow*; and now, the whole *house* is but a *handfull of sand*, so much *dust*, and but *a pecke of Rubbidge*, so much *bone*.

Devotions Upon Emergent Occasions, Meditation 18

W HEN SIR FRANCIS BACON LOOKED at the past, he concluded that history had been not only cyclical but also
degenerative. The natural course of time, which like a
river carries on whatever is "light" rather than "weighty" (*Works*,
8:29), seemed to provide evidence for the idea of decay. But Bacon
believed that the pattern of history could be changed. Indeed, the
very belief that decay is inevitable seemed to Bacon one of the
causes for the decline of the intellectual sciences, since it made
people despair of achieving any lasting progress.

The idea of universal, inevitable decay that Bacon attacked as
an obstacle to progress profoundly affected John Donne. Donne is
so admittedly various and complex a writer, and his skeptical mind
was so indisposed to accept unquestioningly any conventional idea,
that it might seem unlikely that there would be a single idea of
history that informs his work as a whole. There are, for example,
clear and important differences between the private poetry and the
more public prose, between secular and religious writings. Donne
himself encouraged others to see his own life, and thus his writings,
as exhibiting a discontinuity, since late in life he described himself
as having undergone a radical transformation—from Jack Donne,
rake and libertine, to Dr. Donne, devout dean of St. Paul's. This

69

sense of Donne's multiplicity has persisted to the present, despite arguments to the contrary, and even those readers who reject the notion that there was a clear-cut conversion recognize that Donne was by temperament changeable, as he himself was painfully aware. All his writings reveal a mind continually in motion—probing, questioning, changing. The *Songs and Sonnets* alone, with their varied personae and deliberate posturing, suggest his tendency to adopt, question, and revise a position, and then to start the process anew.

With our growing understanding of the complexity of Donne's mind and his works, it has become commonplace to stress the variety in Donne, the ways in which irony, paradox, and multiple meanings reflect a various, changeable intellect and temperament. There has thus been a tendency to suspect that an emphasis on the abiding, underlying patterns in his work may be reductive. I would insist, however, that there is in Donne—as in other seventeenth-century writers, indeed probably all good writers—a basic coherence and unity. As more than one recent critic has argued, "The distinctive structure of Donne's imagination was constant."[1] And an essential part of this structure of imagination was his sense of decay.

In Devotion 10 Donne remarked: "This is *Natures nest of Boxes;* The *Heavens* containe the *Earth,* the *Earth, Cities, Cities, Men.* And all these are *Concentrique;* the common *center* to them all, is *decay, ruine.*"[2] What Donne said about the universe, as he strove to understand his sickness in terms of a greater universal order, could well be said about his writings as a whole—the center of all is decay. Whether in the early *Elegies* and *Satyres* of the 1590s, the *Songs and Sonnets* (more difficult to date), the middle prose works such as *Biathanatos* (probably written in 1608) and *Ignatius his Conclave* (1611), or the later Sermons (1615–31) and *Devotions* (1623–24)—whether in his private or public voices, whether in prose or verse—there is a persistent preoccupation with what Sir Thomas Browne called time's "art" of making "dust of all things."[3] Donne's pervasive, abiding concern with time as a process of decay transcends the differences of form, genre, tone, and occasion that separate individual works, and it gives a distinctive voice to a complex, various, diverse body of writing.

The Process of Decay

For Donne, history has a clearly defined shape, with fixed, un-alterable limits. Bounded by Creation and Judgment, the history of the world is like a single day that progresses from dawn at morning to darkness at evening. "Truly, the *Creation* and the *last Judgment,* are the *Diluculum* and *Crepusculum,* the *Morning* and the *Evening* twi-lights of the long day of this world."[4] Like the sun, the world moves continuously toward its setting. Although for some writers this analogy indicated a cyclical pattern in which regener-ation follows decay, Donne avoids the suggestion of renewal. The life of the world constitutes a single cycle, a single finite day, and in these late times the sun's increasing proximity to the earth is a sign of the world's approaching end.[5]

With his belief in correspondence, Donne finds history's pattern repeated in the life of each person, indeed in the life of every created thing. As a microcosm, man recapitulates in his life the world's history: thus the sun's progress provides the pattern for the individual's life as well as the world's. When man is "in the best of his fortune, and in the strength of his understanding," he is at his "noone"; when he comes to die, his "Sun is ready to set."[6] Of course, for the virtuous Christian, death is not the final extin-guishing of light. As the *Second Anniversary* ("Of the Progres of the Soule") shows, what from the earthly perspective is a setting, from the divine is preparation for ascent. But, as we shall see, Donne insists that this resurrection is not part of the natural temporal order but contrary to it.

Occasionally his description of the temporal process implies that growth precedes decay. Such a pattern can be seen not only in the sun's arc but also in the biological cycle, which sometimes provides Donne with yet another analogy for the shape of history. The Jews had "their infancy" until the Flood, their adolescence until Moses, their "youth and strength" until Saul's reign, their "established vigor" under the kings, but finally "fell . . . into a wretched and miserable decay of old age, and decrepitnesse" (*Sermons,* 4:243).

Most frequently, however, Donne suggests that decline is contin-uous. From a perspective that stresses the teleological, the end to which things come, the growth to maturity or the ascent to the meridian becomes largely illusory, for the entire progress is a move-ment toward death. Even the sun's rising is but a movement toward setting. Thus Donne can suggest, as in the *First Anniversary,* that the world was at its meridian in its dawn, and that the apparent growth of the body from infancy to adulthood is actually a progressive decay. "We are *Borne* in a *Consumption,* and as *little* as we are then, we grow less from that time. . . . Before we can craule, we runne to meet death" (*Sermons,* 2:80). Donne images the body as mud-walls that begin to crumble not just at birth but perhaps even earlier: "from the first laying of these *mud-walls* in my *conception,* they have *moldred* away, and the whole course of *life* is but an *active death*" (*Devotions,* p. 96).[7] Donne both fears and is fascinated by such changes. The two *Anniversaries* detail the various ways in which all creatures have continuously declined from "the first houre" (*First Anniv.,* l. 201). In a universe where all decays, the only things that grow are disease and corruption. Every year produces "new species of wormes, and flies, and sicknesses, which argue more and more putrefaction of which they are engendred" (*Sermons,* 6:323).

Because decay is moral as well as physical, Donne finds that in this "Age of rusty iron" our corruption is much worse than in earlier, purer times.[8] Whereas Adam and Eve sold their souls "for (perchance) an Apple," ours "are now retailed every day for nothing." And this historical pattern of moral degeneration is recapitulated in the life of every individual: "Our youth is worse then our infancy, and our age worse then our youth" (*Sermons,* 1:159; 10:234).

Many of the same arguments for decay appear in Godfrey Goodman's *Fall of Man.* Observing that all creatures have declined "by degrees" since the original Creation, Goodman concludes that "corruption" is the law of nature.[9] Both Goodman and Donne attribute the cause of all this decay to the Fall of Adam, which precipitated the process of degeneration. Though the Fall may have occurred at one instant, in an important sense it has been continuous, extending throughout time, and affecting everything in time. In the *First Anniversary,* however, Donne suggests that the process of decay began even before Adam and Eve's Fall, indeed before Creation was finished: "before God had made up all the rest, / Corruption entred" when the angels rebelled (ll. 193–94). Donne has such an overwhelming sense of history as decay that he finds it difficult to believe that there ever was a time exempt from this process.

He typically emphasizes the downward movement of history. The first times were the highest, and the rest of history has been a continuous descent. The Fall provides the paradigm for the pattern of time. Both in the world at large and in human beings there is a force much like gravity that makes them tend downward. The sun has "falne" nearer the earth; the earth's color "sinke[s]"; the "body *falls* downe without pushing."[10] This natural tendency in things to fall or descend is evident even in childbirth, which is "orderly" only when children come head first "and fall upon / An ominous precipitation" (*First Anniv.*, ll. 96–98). A similar gravitational pull shapes the course of man's life as he becomes increasingly weighed down: though in youth we are relatively carefree, "in our declinations now, every accident is accompanied with heavy clouds of melancholy."[11] Not only do God's punishments depress us, but "man can adde weight to heavens heaviest curse" ("To Sir Edward Herbert, at Iulyers," l. 18). Donne's belief in this natural tendency toward descent lies behind his suggestion that human beings are more liable to decline into the sin of despair than to err in presumption. Though the first sin of the angels was pride, "the danger of man is more in sinking down, then in climbing up, in dejecting, then in raising himselfe."[12] As his remark that sin is "a sinking, a falling" suggests, the source of most "declinations" is sin. Sin is a weight that *"sinkes* a man, *declines* him, *crookens* him, makes him *stoop"*; it "bend[s] us downward from our natural posture, which is erect." Ultimately it "weigh[s]" man "t'wards hell."[13] And it is not just bodies that are affected by this gravitational pull. As Donne insists in the *Devotions,* "even *Angels,* even our *soules* . . . bend to the same *Center."* Were they not kept immortal by God's *"preservation,* their *Nature* could not keepe them from sinking to this *centre, Annihilation"* (p. 51). So ubiquitous is decay.

Both man and the world create the elements that will destroy them: "As the other *world* produces *Serpents,* and *Vipers,* malignant & venimous creatures, and *Wormes,* and *Caterpillars,* that endeavour to devoure that world which produces them, and *Monsters* . . . so this world, our selves, produces all these in us, in producing *diseases,* and *sicknesses* of all sorts."[14] And so Donne in the *Devotions* connects his self-engendered disease with those of the greater world: for both microcosm and macrocosm, such generation is perverse, characterized not by life but decay. We "kill our selves" with *"vapors"* that we ourselves *"breed"* (p. 63). Afflicted with diseases and sicknesses that are not invasions from without but evils that come from within, human beings work their own destruction. Their self-de-

structiveness is the counterpart of the irreversibly degenerative
nature of history. As perhaps the last step in the process whereby
man strives to bring himself back to "nothing," the dead body
actually breeds the worms that feed on it in the grave.[15] If people
are so active in bringing on their deaths, the difference between
natural death and suicide virtually disappears, for every man is "a
Murderer of himself" (*Sermons*, 1:257). It seems clear that Donne's
long tract on suicide, *Biathanatos*, explores a paradox that fascinated
him throughout his life.

The process of corruption and decay is a process of dissolution,
a loss of original wholeness or unity. When Donne speaks of man
before the Fall as existing in his "first integrity" (*Sermons*, 7:229),
he uses "integrity" in its root meaning of wholeness as well as in
the sense of purity or uprightness. With original sin man lost his
first integrity, or wholeness, and in the process of time the pieces
have become further separated. This process of fragmentation affected language when men tried to erect the Tower of Babel, and
one language was replaced by many. This condition in which every
person was divided from the others by his language foreshadowed
the divisive, individualistic state Donne laments in the *First Anniversary*:

> 'Tis all in pieces, all cohaerence gone;
> All just supply, and all Relation:
> Prince, Subject, Father, Sonne, are things forgot,
> For every man alone thinkes he hath got
> To be a Phoenix, and that there can bee
> None of that kinde, of which he is, but hee. (ll. 213–18)

In the course of time the force that binds the family and even
society has dissolved. This view of historical decay as a loss of
wholeness helps explain his praise of Elizabeth Drury as the one
"Magnetique force" that could have drawn "all parts to reunion"
(ll. 220–21). Despite the sense of pride in his own individualism
and separateness evident in the tone, postures, and subject of many
of the *Songs and Sonnets*, Donne here suggests that the growing
individualism characteristic of English society in the early seventeenth century is simply a further step in the loss of original integrity. This disintegration is evident, not only in society but also
in the life of each person. Dejection as well as calamity "scatters"

us "in the eyes of men" (*Sermons*, 8:112), and disease is quick in "dissolving this body" (*Devotions*, p. 13). Surely the plague as well as Donne's frequent illnesses and those of his family contributed to his sense that diseases repeatedly weaken and destroy our wholeness. All sicknesses culminate in death, which itself is a further dissolution, since the person "falls into a separation . . . of body and soul" (*Sermons*, 7:103). This concern with the progressive loss of integrity, the continual disintegration in time, lies behind Donne's seemingly obsessive detailing of the process of the body's decay in the grave. The scattering of dust is the final step in the process of dissolution that began with the Fall.

Fountains, Roots, Love, and Original Perfection

Donne's conception of the temporal process as one of decay involves a number of interrelated concerns and images in his writing that appear in both early and late works, in poetry as well as prose. Perhaps the most important assumption behind the idea of degeneration is the belief that the earliest state was the best. Like Goodman, who insists that all things were purest in "that first mould,"[16] Donne supposes that God created everything in the height of its perfection: "In the beginning of the world we presume all things to have been produced in their best state; all was perfect" (*Sermons*, 4:136). This notion of original perfection pervades Donne's thought and style. It makes him skeptical about discoveries and progress in knowledge, critical of innovations, and desirous of returning to the beginnings, the purest origins.

Donne believes that because God created everything at the first, there can be no true additions. All the stars, for example, "were created at once, with one Fiat" (*Sermons*, 3:369); no new stars can be born. Thus those that have been discovered by Galileo are not really new: existing since the beginning of time, they have merely become conspicuous, revealed by the sun, as "Loves Growth" suggests (11. 15–18).[17] Indeed, for all his interest in the new philosophy, Donne had little faith in the advancement of learning.[18] Like Fulke Greville, who insists that the founders of the arts "pierc'd" the furthest ("A Treatie of Humane Learning," st. 75), Donne believes that almost all knowledge is "rather conserved in the stature of the first age, then growne to be greater; and if there be any addition to knowledge, it is rather a new knowledge, then a greater knowledge; rather a singularity in a desire of proposing something that was not knowne at all before, then an emproving, an advancing, a multiplying of former inceptions" (*Sermons,* 6:260).

This view contrasts sharply with Bacon's faith that knowledge can grow through the cumulative efforts of men in successive generations. It is true that Bacon, like Donne, assumes that perfection existed at the beginning of time—his plan for science aims to restore Adam's perfect knowledge and control over nature—and that learning has degenerated over the course of history. But whereas Bacon thinks human beings can reverse this path of decline, Donne accepts the process of decay as inevitable and thus is skeptical about claims the new philosophy makes for advancing knowledge. He mocks scientists who have woven a "net" of "Meridians, and Parallels" to ensnare the heavens. The new science "calls all in doubt" rather than offering answers (*First Anniv.,* ll. 278–79, 205). Apparently it is but a further step in the disintegration of knowledge.

Because everything is best in its first state, any changes must be for the worse. Innovation is for Donne a term of disapprobation. As he flatly asserts in a sermon, "God loves not innovations" (*Sermons,* 2:305).[19] In *Ignatius His Conclave* innovations are relegated to the province of Lucifer, who in his rebellion against God was the first innovator, and the most "honourable" room in hell is reserved for the greatest innovators, those who "gave an affront to all Antiquitie, and induced doubts, and anxieties . . . at length established opinions, directly contrary to all established before."[20]

There is a curious disjunction between Donne's repeated attacks on innovation and his own role as an innovator in poetry. His own skeptical, questioning stance has much in common with the rejection of traditional authorities and opinions that he sees as characterizing the innovators he includes in *Ignatius His Conclave*—Copernicus, Paracelsus, Machiavelli, and Columbus. One thinks of the rebellious attitude toward conventional authority and received opinion in such poems as "The Canonization" and "The Sunne Rising." Donne's contemporaries recognized in his poetry his spirit of boldness, his inventiveness in poetic forms and diction, and his witty, often irreverent attitude toward poetic convention. In "An Elegie upon the death of the Deane of Pauls, Dr John Donne" Thomas Carew praised Donne precisely for being an original poet who had contributed something new to poetry.[21]

> The Muses garden with Pedantique weedes
> O'rspred, was purg'd by thee; The lazie seeds
> Of servile imitation throwne away;
> And fresh invention planted . . . .
> . . . . whatsoever wrong
> By ours was done the Greeke, or Latine tonque,
> Thou hast redeem'd, and open'd Us a Mine
> Of rich and pregnant phansie, drawne a line
> Of masculine expression . . . . (ll. 25–28, 35–39)

Despite the relapse that Carew foresees after Donne's death ("thy strict lawes will be / Too hard for Libertines in Poetrie," ll. 61–62), Carew credits Donne with innovations in poetry that bear comparison with Columbus's geographical discoveries that also made available new riches. Much as Bacon (who liked to compare himself with Columbus) consciously separated himself from what he saw as the corrupted derivative traditions of his predecessors in natural philosophy, so Donne is presented here as similarly distinguishing himself, reforming the decayed "Muses garden," banishing the "old Idolls" (l. 69), and rejecting "servile imitation" in favor of his own "fresh invention." Perhaps Donne thought that in his bold poetic experiments, and his revitalization of lyric poetry, he was working against the forces of degeneration evident even in the history of poetry. Nevertheless, there is a basic, unresolved tension between Donne's own literary stance as an innovator and the dislike of innovations that is very much a part of his obsession with universal decay.

The connection between Donne's characteristically negative attitude to innovation and his view of history as degenerative is particularly evident in his interpretation of church history. As St. Ignatius's role in the *Conclave* suggests, Donne sees the Jesuits in particular and the Roman Catholic church more generally as guilty of innovations in religion.[22] Just as all the stars were created at once and created perfect, so "the *Christian doctrine necessary* to salvation, was delivered at once, that is intirely, in one spheare" (*Sermons*, 3:369). Christianity being purest in its early form, later "traditions and Postscripts" are "unwholesome and putrifying." Defending the English Protestant Reformation against the charge that it was simply another innovation, Donne follows the traditional view from John Foxe in the sixteenth century to Bishop Gilbert

Burnet at the end of the seventeenth and insists that the Reformation was rather a restoration of the original purity of the Catholic church, an orderly cure of the diseases the church had contracted (*Pseudo-Martyr*, pp. xvii, 15).

In explicating a difficult passage of Scripture, Donne prefers the "Interpretation of the Fathers" to that of the schoolmen (*Pseudo-Martyr*, p. 225), for we get farther from original purity as we descend in time, as he implies when he prefaces his discussion of scholastic interpretation of a text with the comment, "To come lower, and to a lower rank of witnesses, from the Fathers to the Schoole" (*Sermons*, 7:200). As "the eldest," the church fathers are those to whom "most reverence will belong."[23] Similarly, he opposes new terms in divinity, insisting that people use the language "pure antiquity" spoke: "Old doctrines, old disciplines, old words and formes of speech in his service, God loves best" (*Sermons*, 1:255; 2:305). Indeed, he favors the earliest words in divinity—the language and phrase of the Bible—and envisions himself in his sermons "restoring" to their true sense scriptural passages that the Roman church "detorted" (*Sermons*, 2:171–72, 325).

As a consequence of his belief in original perfection, Donne thinks that the farther one goes back, the closer one gets to truth and purity. "Though truth and falshood bee / Neare twins, yet truth a little elder is" ("Satyre III," ll. 72–73), and thus in this third satire he recommends that the seeker of the true religion "aske thy father which is shee, / Let him aske his" (ll. 71–72). But given the declining course of history, to go back farther into the past is also to ascend to "higher" times. Throughout his sermons, when Donne announces that his discourse will concern earlier times or biblical figures, he characteristically sees himself making an ascent. For example, in discussing the trouble men have had because of women, he mentions St. Jerome, then Solomon, then Samson, and finally goes "as high as is possible, to *Adam* himself" (*Sermons*, 1:202–3; cf. 3:365; 6:216). In one sense Donne may mean that in the process of meditating on these things he is spiritually ascending, but he also suggests that one needs to rise higher to see into the past since we have fallen lower with time. All this explains why in "Satyre III" Donne follows the suggestion that man go farther back into the past to find truth, with the image of truth standing on "a huge hill" (l. 79). In order to reach her, the seeker "about must, and about must goe; / And what th'hills suddennes resists, winne so" (ll. 81–82). Donne has not changed his mind within these few lines about how one gets to truth. Rather the two images of going deeper into the past and ascending the hill are quite complementary, once we recognize that truth exists in a past that is also the highest point in time. Moreover, if truth is only to be found at the original source, then a skeptical, even irreverent approach to later, subsequent authorities (religious, political, or literary) would be in order.

As we might expect from his view of historical decay, Donne is frequently concerned with tracing things to their sources or origins, for that is the way people come closest to truth. For Donne, priority is a temporal as well as a metaphysical principle. In *Pseudo-Martyr* he traces almost all schisms in the church to Pope Gregory VII, whose letter about the pope's supreme authority was the source of later attempts to deny the sovereignty of magistrates: "here seemes the first fire to have been giuen, and the first drop of poyson to have been instil'd of all those virulencies and combustions, with which the later Authors in that Church, are inflam'd and swollen vp, in this point of auiling [*sic*] Princes" (pp. 28, 76–77). And in order to defend the authority of the king, he pursues the origin of "Magistracie" all the way back to God: "Magistracie and Superioritie is so naturall and so immediate from God, that Adam was created a Magistrate, and he deriv'd Magistrate by generation vpon the eldest Children" (p. 83). Here as elsewhere Donne uses "derive" in the sense of drawing something from a source (OED, 6) as well as handing it down (OED, 4b).

An interesting image that reflects his concern with sources and origins is that of the fountain, spring, or head and the rivers and streams that descend from it.[24] Just as the rivers of paradise "flow'd from one head," so "the sentences of the Scripture flow all from one head, from the Holy Ghost" (*Sermons*, 2:325). As an emblem of the word of God, the sun is the "Fountaine" of light (*Biathanatos*, p. 154). The most pessimistic conclusion that Donne can reach is that the fountain or spring has been poisoned, for then nothing that descends from it can possibly be pure. Since original sin has "poisoned the fountaines, our hearts," none of our actions can be "perfit" (*Pseudo-Martyr*, p. 98). Our first mother, Eve, "poison'd the well-head, / The daughters here corrupt us, Rivulets" (*Metempsychosis*, ll. 93–94).

Ultimately God is the pure "fountaine" (*Sermons*, 3:354) from

whom all streams flow. This image becomes central in the third
satire as Donne examines the extent to which human beings are
bound to obey earthly powers.

> As streames are, Power is; those blest flowers that dwell
> At the rough streames calme head, thrive and prove well,
> But having left their roots, and themselves given
> To the streames tyrannous rage, alas, are driven
> Through mills, and rockes, and woods, 'and at last, almost
> Consum'd in going, in the sea are lost:
> So perish Soules, which more chuse mens unjust
> Power from God claym'd, then God himselfe to trust.
>
> (ll. 103–10)

God is clearly the source of all power, the head from which the
"streames" or earthly powers, such as kings, priests, and popes,
derive. Because streams may become corrupted ("unjust") and
violent as they descend from the source,[25] those who wish to "thrive"
must like the flowers "dwell" at the "calme head." If they leave
their "roots" in God, they will be carried downstream by the "tyr-
annous" current of the stream only to "perish" in the sea. In order
to thrive, man must remain at the source or head.

But what if he is already downstream? Is it possible to return to
the head? "Satyre V" implies that in the world of politics man may
not be able to go upstream. Once in the current, he risks drowning.
Just as earthly powers were compared to streams in the third satire,
so here the courts are a stream that can "sucke thee in" (l. 47).
Deploring the corruption of the legal system, Donne despairs of
any appeal. When a person goes "upwards" "Against the stream"
(l. 50), those he complains against enlarge into "great seas" over
which he must "make golden bridges" by giving bribes, but "all
thy gold was drown'd in them before" (ll. 53–55). In the sermons
Donne is more confident in suggesting that man's proper motion
is to go upstream against the current, for there he seeks, not an
earthly magistrate, but the true head, God. "He that seeks upwards
to a River, is sure to finde the head" (*Sermons*, 4:229).

Donne's fundamental impulse to go against the flow of time, to
return to the source, is the counterpart of his view of history as a
process of continual decay, and it underlies not only the fountain
imagery but also the image of the root, which he is particularly

fond of.[26] He uses the word *root* in the sense of the source or origin of all that grows out of it, as is evident in his comment that at Creation God stocked the earth and sea with those creatures "which were to be the seminary, and foundation, and roote of all that should ever be propagated" (*Sermons*, 2:335). Whatever grows comes from the root and is nourished by it. Thus Donne implies that the root actually *contains* all in essence. God "show[s] that in the bough which was hid in the root" (*Sermons*, 3:71). The root includes all that becomes visible later. Thus it becomes an image of containment and wholeness, as indicated by Donne's remark that God's "name of *Iehovah*" is the "root" that "includes all his other names" (*Sermons*, 5:324).

Donne is fascinated with the way in which the entire plant is originally hidden within the root and emerges in time. He loves to describe Jehovah as the "roote" and Christ as "the bud and blossome, the fruit and off-spring of Jehovah."[27] This plant image provides a particularly apt description of the Father and Son because it implies that both were coeternal (they were always together in the root) and that Christ actually appeared only later, just as the bud, blossom, and fruit are subsequent emanations. God thus becomes the entire plant—root, branch, flower, and fruit. "This one God is such a tree, as hath divers boughs to shadow and refresh thee, divers branches to shed fruit upon thee" (*Sermons*, 3:258).

The Fall marks our separation from the root—God, the source of all life. In *Metempsychosis* what happens to the apple suggests an analogue for man's fate, which was soon to follow. When the "serpents gripe" plucked the apple, he "broke the slight veines, and tender conduit-pipe" that connected the fruit to the root. Once the connection was severed, the fruit could no longer "draw / Life, and growth" from "the trees root" (ll. 121–25). Like a plant that cannot thrive once it has been cut off from the root, man began to "wither" (*Sermons*, 7:272) and decay when he divorced himself from God.

Such ideas help to explain Donne's concern with fruitfulness. Criticizing those who choose a barren retirement, he insists that people must *act* in this world, must produce works which are their "fruit" (*Sermons*, 1:207; 5:102). Bacon, too, values fruitful activity. He rebukes philosophers who withdraw into arid contemplation, and he defines his scientific ideal largely in terms of its ability to yield works that will nourish mankind. For Bacon this fruitfulness can result only when scientists return to the source of empirical truth—nature. Donne sends people directly to God.

If people are cut off from God, they cannot bear fruit. In the letters written at Mitcham (1607–9?), Donne anguishes over his sense that he must *do* something but is unable. As he complains to his friend Sir Henry Goodyer, "Every tuesday I make account that I turn a great hour-glass, and consider that a weeks life is run out since I writ. But if I aske my selfe which I have done in the last watch, or would do in the next, I can say, nothing" (*Letters*, p. 48). Such statements reveal a gnawing fear that his barrenness is the consequence of having somehow been cut off from God. His bitterness surfaces poignantly in another letter (dated 17 April [1615?], probably written several months after his ordination), where he paradoxically describes his procreative fertility as spiritual barrenness: "I see that I stand like a tree, which once a year beares, though no fruit, yet this Mast of children" (p. 272). A *mast* is a weight, but it also refers to fruit from forest trees that was used as food for swine (*OED*). His children are not only a burden to him (he often complains of the sorrow that their number, illnesses, and deaths cause him), but unwholesome fruit that withers. One by one they die. The many periods of his own illness that his letters record seem to him only further evidence of his sterility. Behind so much of his depression in these years is his belief that to be resurrected one "must be rooted in faith, and then bring forth fruit, and fruit in season" (*Sermons*, 6:278).

Donne's religious prose reveals some interesting versions of this concern with roots. Sometimes he thinks of a particular verse as the root of a larger section of the Bible. In *Essays in Divinity* he analyzes the first verse of Exodus because "radically and virtually it comprehends all the book." God's mercy, power, justice, and judgment are "radically and contractedly in that first *verse*, but diffused and expansively through the whole book" (pp. 41, 62). Donne, in fact, has an especially organic view of the Bible. Pained by expositors who "excerpt and tear insignificant rags of a word or two," who "stub up these severall roots, and mangle them into chips," he desires to preserve the wholeness of this marvelous plant, insisting that the words not be "broken, but taken intirely" (*Essays in Divinity*, pp. 39, 41). Because the Bible is so close to God that "it is *he*" (p. 39), those who mutilate it virtually crucify God. Moreover, since the Bible *is* God, the closer a person gets to it the nearer he approaches God. As all branches lead to the root and all streams to the head, so "all the Scriptures lead us to Christ" (*Sermons,* 4:124). This is why Donne insists on remaining close to the language of the text, why he tries to understand as completely as possible the full meaning of the words. Donne's attitude toward the Scriptures thus reflects an overriding concern to regain both the original wholeness and the connection with the source that have been lost in the degenerative course of history.[28]

Even Donne's etymological analysis of the specific words of his biblical text reveals his preoccupation with going back to the source. His interest in derivations is similar to the ancient Greek and Latin writers' concern with etymologies.[29] As W. S. Allen has shown, this early Greek and Latin concern with etymology seems to have assumed that the process of linguistic or phonetic change was a process of deterioration.[30] In Plato's *Cratylus,* Socrates presents numerous etymologies of words—some fanciful and ironic, mocking the excesses and absurdities of many etymologists, others apparently serious and insightful—and he suggests that in the course of time, words have altered so that the original names have been buried, disguised, or twisted.[31] The implication is that if we can trace a word back to its earliest form we will arrive at (or come closest to) the name that was originally intended to express the nature of the thing named. Donne's conception of degenerative history leads him to share these assumptions. In tracing etymologies he considers the "roote and Originall signification" of the Hebrew words in the text, as if that is the way to approach its true meaning (*Sermons,* 9:262).[32] He also examines the Latin and Greek roots of English words. But his analyses of the roots of English, Latin, or Hebrew words share a common assumption that because the original root meanings are earliest, they are purest and thus closest to "truth": "To know the nature of the thing, look we to the derivation, the extraction, the Origination of the word" (*Sermons,* 3:171). Donne seems to accept the idea that there is originally a natural connection between the words and the things they signify,[33] since he suggests that to learn the "origination" of the word is to "know the nature of the thing." Although he avoids complete identification of word and thing,[34] he does imply that the close connection, which existed earlier, has been weakened with the passage of time. And so he examines the origin of the word *scandall,* for example, in order to reveal scandal's true nature: "The word from which scandall is derived (*Scazein*) signifies *claudicare*, to halt; and thence, a scandall is any trap, or Engin, any occasion of stumbling, and laming, hid in the way that I must goe, by another person."[35]

His belief that the first state of things is purest informs his use of language, for he characteristically tries to restore the earlier linguistic purity. He uses many words in the earlier significations, often emphasizing the Latin roots from which the English words descend.[36] We have already seen this in his use of *derive* and *integrity*. But there are many other examples. To *depart* usually means to go away from truth, to go into error; *aversion* is a turning away; *reconciliation* is a bringing together again of that which was originally united but has become separated (*Sermons*, 3:176; 5:80; 9:399; 10:120). As one might expect, Donne's concern with maintaining a living connection with these roots is most prominent in the sermons.

Donne's conception of the root as something that contains in original form all that may be visibly extended is very similar to his idea of the epitome. The human body is an epitome or microcosm, since it recapitulates all God had done in the six days of Creation (*Sermons*, 7:272). But the microcosm is not the only form of epitome that interests Donne. His sermons often dwell on a single person, word, or verse, which contains in small a much larger mass. The word *Iudgement*, for example, "embraces and comprehends all" (*Sermons*, 2:312). Some biblical figures, particularly David, Adam, and Christ, contain all men. David's "example is so comprehensive" that his history "embrace[s] all"; and consequently Donne in his sermons on the Psalms repeatedly says that *"Davids* case is our case, and all these arrowes stick in all us" (*Sermons*, 5:299; 2:69). All mankind "was collected" in both Adam and Christ (*Sermons*, 2:75). Moreover, when Donne says that every man was in Adam's "loines" (*Sermons*, 2:69), we can see the way in which the epitome may also be the root, for Adam contained all *originally* and thus was the source of all later men. The possible identification between root and epitome is even more evident in Donne's remark in *Essays in Divinity* that the first verse of Exodus "radically... comprehends all the book; which being a history of Gods miraculous Mercy to his, is best intimated or Epitomized in that first part" (p. 41). Often the figure of the circle emerges in Donne's descriptions of the epitome as something that contains all that is "dilated" in the larger context. In the first chapter of John "is contracted all that which is extensively spred, and dilated through the whole Booke" (*Sermons*, 3:348). Yet another sermon finds that the "spirit and soule" of the Psalms are "contracted" into one psalm, and the soul of this psalm is further "contracted" into a single verse (*Sermons*, 7:52). As something small that contracts the larger sphere encompassing it, this epitome is like the epitomes that abound in the *Songs and Sonnets.*

When man and woman are united in true love, they become epitomes of the larger world, thus approaching the state of wholeness, the compacted perfection that has been lost in the degenerative course of history and that is Donne's ideal throughout all his works. In "A Valediction: of the Booke," the lovers' letters contain all knowledge. The lovers in "The Canonization" "extract" the "whole worlds soule," and their mirrorlike eyes "epitomize" "Countries, Townes, and Courts" (ll. 40, 43–44). In "The Goodmorrow," each of the lovers is a "world" or microcosm, and as two "hemispheares" together they form a more perfect world than the larger one where "sea-discoverers" and "others" look for multiple "worlds," thus moving farther from the original, ideal state of unity the lovers hope to embody (ll. 14, 17, 12–13). The epitome is far more valuable than the things epitomized because it contains all in unity. It is this sense that leads the lovers in "The Sunne Rising" to feel that "nothing else is" (l. 22) once they have "contracted" (l. 26) the world. As an epitome, the lovers in reuniting what has been scattered are working to restore the "integrity" that existed at the beginning of time; and thus the sun need only "Shine here" (l. 29) to them.

As the spherical wholeness that the lovers embody suggests, love to some extent counters the fragmenting, degenerative course of history. Donne does not have Bacon's faith that people can alter the pattern of history, but neither does he share Goodman's complacent acceptance of universal decay as part of God's providence. Repeatedly he seeks to find some antidote for the destructive effect of time, which brings all things to dissolution. Some of his finest poems, such as "The Good-morrow," "The Sunne Rising," and "A Valediction: Forbidding Mourning," offer the hope that intensely mutual love may be able to transcend decay.

> If our two loves be one, or, thou and I
> Love so alike, that none doe slacken, none can die.
> "The Good-morrow," ll. 20–21

He often betrays a desire to arrest the movement of time, as in "A Lecture upon the Shadow," where he longs for a love that can maintain the "brave clearnesse" (l. 8) of noon.[37] In an important way Donne's celebration of the immortality of love is a response to the pattern of time that he sees, for in love people seek to find a refuge from the temporal process of decay. "The Anniversarie," with its claim that these lovers' love miraculously resists the seemingly universal, gravitational movement toward ruin, gives most explicit voice to the hope that underlies so many of Donne's love poems:

> All other things, to their destruction draw,
>   Only our love hath no decay;
> This, no tomorrow hath, nor yesterday,
> Running it never runs from us away.
> But truly keepes his first, last, everlasting day. (ll. 6–10)

And in "A Lecture upon the Shadow," the speaker insists that perfect love, as "a growing, or full constant light" (l. 25), defies the natural movement of the sun toward setting. It embodies either a stasis that is impervious to change or a pattern of continuous growth that contrasts with the natural process of decay.

But love is not always an entirely reliable remedy for Donne. If some of the *Songs and Sonnets* praise the transcendent immortality of love, others suggest quite different attitudes as Donne through his various personae repeatedly explores, redefines, and questions the nature and value of love. Poems such as "The Indifferent" and "Communitie" question the assumption that constancy is either possible or desirable in love. "Loves Alchymie" scoffs at lovers (like the one in "The Sunne Rising"?) who think to find a "centrique happinesse" (l. 2) in love. And having lost his faith in love, the speaker in "Farewell to Love" insists that he will no longer "dote and runne / To pursue things which had, indammage me" (ll. 33–34). Even the lover in "The Canonization" has paid richly for his love, with his "ruin'd fortune" (l. 3) and his gout, though he insists that such penalties are unimportant, indeed even signs of his special prestige. He may imitate Christ's death and resurrection when he dies and rises "the same" (l. 26), but he also recapitulates Adam's example in sacrificing all for a woman. From the cynical perspective of poems like "Loves Alchymie," this saint in the religion of love is in one sense just another man who has lost his "ease," "thrift," "honor," and "day" for love. As the collection of *Songs and Sonnets* as a whole suggests, there is a fundamental tension in Donne between the desire to find in love the ability to transcend or reverse the degenerative effect of time, on the one hand, and the suspicion that man's love for woman participates in, or even accelerates, decay, on the other.

The skeptical, disparaging view of human love becomes more insistent in the sermons. As they make clear, this negative view is at least in part a consequence of the Judaeo-Christian tradition that sees the seductive Eve as the instrument of Adam's fall away from God. In one sermon Donne's praise of marriage as the highest human love is soon followed by the observation that though women have souls and sometimes have acted for "the advancement of Gods glory," they have been associated more with man's "ruine" than with his salvation. "The Virgin *Mary* had not the same interest in our salvation, as Eve had in our destruction." Throughout this sermon, as in poems such as "Farewell to Love," "Loves Alchymie," or "The Blossome," runs the refrain that women are dangerous to men. "What good Mariner would anchor under a Rock? . . . What Fish would chuse his food upon a Hook? What Mouse at a Trap?" (*Sermons*, 1:200, 202). Though love has the potential to "raise us to the contemplation of the Creator" (*Sermons*, 1:243), all too often it fails to reverse the downward, degenerative direction of time.

When Donne discusses the expression "to fall in love," he reminds his congregation of the connection between the Fall and man's love of woman. "Man was borne to love; he was made in the love of God; but then man falls in love; when he growes in love with the creature, he falls in love. . . . to grow in love with [God's creatures] is a fall" (*Sermons*, 6:69–70). "Even the love of the husband to the wife, is a burthen, a submitting, a descent" (*Sermons*, 5:115). The sermon that Donne preached for the marriage of the earl of Bridgewater's daughter again insists that love of a woman is a descent. Taking as his text Matthew 22:30 ("For, in the Resurrection, they neither mary nor are given in mariage, but are as the angels of God in Heaven"), he sternly remarks that the angels whom God sent down to protect men "fell in love with *Women*, and maried them"; they "never returned to God againe, but fell, with the first fallen, under everlasting Condemnation." For all his exaltation of married love elsewhere, Donne here flatly asserts that in heaven the angels of God "doe not mary" (*Sermons*, 8:107). It must have been a sobering sermon for the couple marrying.

Clearly Donne's position in these sermons is more rigid, more unequivocal than in the love poetry. In part, it may be a matter of age. Moreover, in the sermons Donne is speaking in an authoritative, public voice, and his position as spiritual guide would encourage a harsher view of human love and the pleasures of the body. Nevertheless, even in the secular poetry one senses Donne's recurring suspicion, evident as early as the *Elegies*, that love is an inadequate remedy for time. Though he was strongly attracted by the possibility that love might be able to counter the decay that resulted from the Fall, Donne was also disturbed by the fear that man's love for woman might be yet another example of the self-destructive tendency of man and indeed the entire created universe.

Memory as Remedy

There is, however, another remedy for the degenerative course of time—one less fraught with problems than love. Whereas Donne's desire to find in love an antidote to time appears most frequently in the *Songs and Sonnets*, from the *Anniversaries* on we see him turning instead to memory.[38] Given his view of history as a decline from an ideal perfection at the beginning of time, it is not surprising that he should attribute special prominence to the faculty of the mind that is concerned with the past.

According to Augustinian tradition, memory is one of the three parts of the rational soul that God imprinted on man at Creation. As a trinity the three faculties (memory, understanding, and will) constitute the image of God in man.[39] Donne, however, gives an unusual weight to memory, for, rather than seeing the three faculties of the soul as equal, he finds memory the most reliable for leading man to God.

Memory is the faculty that has been least impaired by the Fall. Understanding is an uncertain faculty, which is not easily "settled," and will is even less reliable, since it is the "blindest and boldest faculty," "untractable, and untameable" (*Sermons*, 2:236, 235). But memory is "so familiar, and so present, and so ready a faculty, as will always answer, if we will but speak to it, and ask it, *what God hath done for us, or for others*" (*Sermons*, 2:73). Whereas people through their understanding may interpret God's words in separate, conflicting ways, all people find a bond or harmony through their memory. Thus memory becomes a unifying force where understanding and will foster disagreement and dissension. "Present the history of God's protection of his children . . . to the memory, and howsoever the understanding be beclouded, or the will perverted, yet both Jew and Christian, Papist and Protestant, Puritan and Protestant, are affected with a thankfull acknowledgment of his former mercies and benefits, this issue of that faculty of their memory is alike in them all" (*Sermons*, 2:237). As a unifying force, memory works against the division, fragmentation, and dissolution that Donne believes have occurred during the course of time.

The importance Donne attributes to memory finds a precedent in St. Augustine. Although *De Trinitate* insists on the interdependence of the three parts of the soul, implying their equality, St. Augustine singles out memory for his most eloquent praise: God has elected to dwell in the memory. Because all that a person learns is stored in the memory, God, too, must be there, once He has been learned. Therefore the way to find God is through memory.[40] When we lose something, that is, when we forget, it is in the memory that we must search till we find it (*Confessions*, X, xix). In a similar way, when we seek God (whom we have learned or found before), we must look for Him in the memory. Thus St. Augustine concludes that he has found God and all things concerning Him "in memory" rather than outside it, and he finds God only "when I call Thee to remembrance" (X, xxiv).

We see here an interesting precedent for Donne's selection of memory as the single faculty that leads us to the divine, but the importance he attributes to memory is particularly a consequence of his view of history. If the course of time has led us farther from goodness, truth, and perfection, it is necessary to exercise the faculty that enables us to return, at least mentally, to the purer, earlier, higher times. As Donne decisively remarks, "The wiseman places all goodnesse in this faculty, the memory" (*Sermons*, 9:84–85). The emphasis that Donne places on memory separates him radically from Bacon, who believes that men's hopes of regaining the perfection that existed before the Fall lie in their willingness to apply themselves to experiment and the close observation of nature. Bacon relies on sense and understanding, supported and guided by induction. But Donne turns to memory, advising us to turn inward—precisely the solution that Bacon attacked. Moreover, whereas Bacon calls for the cooperative effort of men to increase knowledge and deliver it to their successors to be further augmented, the exercise of memory must of necessity be an individual matter. Though all believers are united in the body of Christ, each person must himself seek God through memory. He cannot learn from or build on the wisdom others have gained.

We find a radical concern with memory throughout Donne's religious writings. His sermons propose to stimulate the memory of his congregation.[41] Since Donne can assume that his Anglican congregation has already learned God and the principles of Christianity, his teaching will simply be "a remembring, a refreshing of those things, which Christ . . . had taught before" (*Sermons*, 8:253).[42] He repeatedly counsels his listeners to "remembrances" and reminds them of their connection with men in the past. "*Davids* case," for example, becomes "our case" (*Sermons*, 2:69), and our remembrance creates a bond between past and present. Similarly in the *Devotions* Donne tries to understand his sickness by recalling biblical history, by discerning parallels between himself and those whom, despite their suffering, God blessed. He consoles himself for his solitude by recalling that only when Jacob was alone did God come to him. Frequently he is reminded of Christ's suffering and crucifixion, which were necessary before He could be glorified. Like Christ, Donne is pained by the "*brambles, & thornes* of a sharpe sicknesse" (p. 14); he is "nayled" to his bed (p. 16); his "sick bed" becomes God's "*Altar*," and he becomes the "*Sacrifice*" (p. 68).

As one might expect, memory also plays a crucial role in Donne's poetic devotions, the *Holy Sonnets*. He calls to remembrance his former sins, defining his own sinfulness in terms of biblical history. Donne becomes Adam, and the pattern of his life recapitulates the history of mankind from Creation through the Fall to Redemption.[43] Memory becomes not simply something private and individual, but rather a kind of typological memory, linking Donne with biblical history and mankind as a whole. In the sonnet "I am a little world made cunningly," he recognizes that he must personally reenact biblical history in order to expiate his sin. Just as in Noah's time the sinful world had to be punished with the Flood, so now Donne longs to "Drowne my world with my weeping earnestly" (l. 8). But the postdeluvian world continued to sin, and Donne, too, will need a more devastating punishment. He prays for an apocalyptic fire that will at once destroy and recreate him anew, much as God will do to the world at the end of time:

> . . . burne me o Lord, with a fiery zeale
> Of thee 'and thy house, which doth in eating heale. (ll. 13–14)

The importance of memory is nowhere clearer than in the two *Anniversaries* written on the death of Elizabeth Drury. With Elizabeth's death, the world has "lost [its] sense and memory" (*First Anniv.*, l. 28), which Donne seeks to awaken. Significantly, the loss of memory is here explicitly associated with the world's decay — in this most degenerate time of the world "Prince, Subject, Father, Sonne, are things forgot" (l. 215) — and Donne's purpose in this poem is as much to remind us of the original perfection as to anatomize the dead world. Thus his eulogy of Elizabeth as the embodiment of perfection serves not just to teach that even the best are mortal because of the Fall, but also to stimulate us to remember the perfection that existed only at the beginning of the world. There is, in fact, some suggestion that memory may have regenerative powers. In this "last long night" (l. 69) of the world, the "twi-light of [Elizabeth's] memory" (l. 74) remains in the world. Her memory is "a glimmering light, / A faint weake love of vertue," which "Reflects from her" on those who recognized her worth (ll. 70–72). Although the dead world "can never be renew'd" (l. 58) this light of her memory can create "a new world" (l. 76): "the matter and the stuffe of this, / Her vertue, and the forme our practice is" (ll. 77–78). Donne suggests that if we keep alive the memory of Elizabeth, that is, the memory of the lost perfection, embodying it in our practice of virtue, a new world can be born. At the end of the *First Anniversary*, he returns to this explicit emphasis on memory: not only will his verse "enroule" Elizabeth's "fame" while heaven "keepes" her soul and the grave her body (ll. 473–74), but he compares his poem to the song God had Moses deliver to the Israelites to preserve God in their memory (Deuteronomy 31:16–21). Like Jehovah, Donne chooses verse because of its special hold on memory. Just as Jehovah knew the song would "not be forgotten out of the mouths of [the Israelites'] seed" (Deut. 31:21), so Donne has faith that poetry will last in the memory when "the Law, the Prophets, and the History" (l. 465) are forgotten.[44]

In the *Second Anniversary* Donne despairs because there are so few remaining who have even a faint recollection of Elizabeth and perfection. All have lost their memory, "drown'd" in a flood of "Lethe"; "All have forgot all good" (*Second Anniv.*, ll. 27–28). In this general flood of forgetfulness, Donne now seeks to save himself rather than others. Since there are no receptive people left, this *Second Anniversary* addresses not the world at large but his own soul, counseling it to "remember" (e.g., ll. 122, 220). Donne offers a picture "Of the Progres of the Soule," which contrasts with and is a response to the temporal decay that infects the world and the flesh. While on earth, he must "Forget this rotten world" and "Looke upward" toward heaven in order to prepare for the soul's "long-short Progresse" after death when, freed from its "shell," it will ascend to heaven (ll. 49, 65, 219, 184). This preparation for the final ascent is accomplished through meditation. In the process of meditating, memory enables Donne to rise, as his soul tries to "worke up againe" to its "first pitch" (l. 435). Though Donne appears to descend in his contemplation of death and the corruption of the body, actually he rises as he "remembers" what will be in heaven.[45] Repeatedly spurring his soul "up" (ll. 339, 345, 347, 351, 353, 356), he feels his soul ascend in an "extasie" that is not really a mystical experience but a vision achieved through exercising the memory in meditation.[46] Similarly, in his sermons, he carries his meditation progressively "higher," attempting to "raise" the devotion of his congregation, to lift their spirits through his appeals to memory (*Sermons*, 7:217; 3:133, 362; 7:68–69), and typically the sermons end with an ascent. Such an exercise of memory elevates the preacher as well as the congregation: as Donne writes, "The Pulpit . . . [is] my exaltation" (*Letters*, p. 314). Countering the degenerative process of time, the ascent through memory paradoxically leads us forward to salvation.

For Donne, memory's supreme value lies in its ability to reestablish the link between human beings and God. Ever since the Fall, we have become progressively estranged from health, goodness, and truth, as we have moved farther away from the beginning of time and the source of all perfection, God. But by turning within to our memory, we can find God again. Donne says that memory is "the neerest way" to God (*Sermons*, 2:235). Memory contains numerous pictures of God's mercies toward us in the past, each picture capable of leading us back to God Himself, as if through studying the image one can reach back to the thing it represents:

"every man hath a pocket picture about him, a manuall, a bosome book, and if he will turn over but one leaf, and remember what God hath done for him even since yesterday, he shall find even by that little branch a navigable river, to sail into that great and endless Sea of Gods mercies towards him, from the beginning of his being" (*Sermons*, 2:238). Though the understanding may be a light, since it is "beclouded" we cannot easily follow its beam to the source. The will is even more benighted. But memory contains rivers that are "navigable"—and surely lead to the sea. Whereas sin and the course of time separate us from God, memory leads us back. In the sermon on Ecclesiastes 12:1 ("Remember now thy Creator in the Dayes of thy Youth"), Donne insists that through the exercise of memory we can and should go back to the Creator at the beginning of time which was the Creation. In this regressive act, we pass over all the creatures that threaten to distract us and to separate us from God. "*Remember the Creator then . . .* that thou maist stick upon nothing on this side of him." Though the "best" of the creatures can be a "way to the Creator," we must be careful not to "stop upon the creature."[47] There is always danger of shipwreck; "there is no safe footing" until we come to the Creator Himself.

The Holy Sonnet "If poysonous mincralls" is one of the most striking examples of the way in which Donne's holy meditations are affected by his sense that it is memory rather than understanding or will that best leads a person to God. The poem begins as the speaker asks a series of questions whose argumentative nature suggests his rebelliousness:

> If poysonous mineralls, and if that tree,
> Whose fruit threw death on else immortall us,
> If lecherous goats, if serpents envious
> Cannot be damn'd; Alas; why should I bee?
> Why should intent or reason, borne in mee,
> Make sinnes, else equall, in mee, more heinous?
> And mercy being easie, 'and glorious
> To God, in his sterne wrath, why threatens hee?

These questions, products of man's skeptical reason, suggest the speaker's separation from God—his lack of proper understanding, his reluctance to accept God's judgments or his responsibility for his sins. But the poem (and the speaker's spiritual state) turns abruptly at line 9 as he remembers his unworthiness; significantly, this act of memory marks the speaker's direct address to God for the first time in the poem. "But who am I, that dare dispute with thee?" This question, unlike the previous ones, is an admission of humility, not a proud assertion of self. Once Donne remembers his unworthiness, he can pray for a "heavenly Lethean flood," made of his tears and Christ's blood, which will "drowne" the "blacke memorie" of his sin (ll. 11–12). His remembrance of his sin leads him to long for the restoration of his original harmony with God, which can only take place if God blots out or forgets Donne's sinfulness. And so the poem concludes paradoxically:

> That thou remember them, some claime as debt,
> I think it mercy, if thou wilt forget.

But it is not just memory of his sinfulness that helps restore the connection between man and God. Memory of God's many mercies work a similar effect. The recollection that God originally created him as a "temple of thy Spirit divine" and redeemed him "when I was decay'd" compels Donne to "resigne" himself to God (Holy Sonnet, "As due by many titles"). Once a person remembers that God made "his Temple" in man's breast, chose him to be "Coheire to'his glory," and "was slaine" in order to redeem him, that person will come to "love God, as he thee" (Holy Sonnet, "Wilt thou love God"). All memory's paths ultimately lead to God.

Since memory connects human beings with God, it is a necessary step in the process of salvation. As Donne describes the "Gallery of the soul" filled with pictures of God's mercies, he explains how remembering God can lead to the rectification of the other faculties of man's rational soul: "as a well made, and well plac'd picture, looks alwayes upon him that looks upon it; so shall thy God look upon thee, whose memory is thus contemplating him, and shine upon thine understanding, and rectifie thy will too" (*Sermons*, 2:237). Behind this passage lies the Augustinian notion that God resides in memory. If a person looks toward the image of God in his memory, God Himself will illumine the rest of his rational soul. There is almost a sense that this process of illumination is inevitable, once man rightly uses his memory. The intimate, almost mirrorlike relationship between memory and God, which is evident in Donne's description of this gallery, appears also in the poem "Goodfriday,

1613. Riding Westward," written some six years earlier than this sermon. As Donne rides westward, going forward in time, his soul in its meditation "bends toward the East" (l. 10) and moves into the past, thus countering the westward movement toward death. Although the events of the Crucifixion are absent "from mine eye, / They'are present yet unto my memory" (ll. 33–34). Not only does memory transcend time, make the past present, but it also establishes that special intersection of God's vision and man's. His memory "looks towards" the Crucifixion, and "thou look'st towards mee, / O Saviour, as thou hang'st upon the tree" (ll. 35–36). At this point, when the eye of memory meets God, Donne can ask God to "Restore" the divine "Image" in him so he can look on God face to face. While man goes forward in time, memory can move backward to repair in part the bond with God that was severed, thus enabling him with God's grace to complete the circle and regain paradise.[48]

But there is still one further sense in which memory brings us closer to our first perfection. As Donne often observes, remembering is "recollection," a bringing together of things that were previously united but since have become separated,[49] and in this sense it is an attempt to restore original wholeness or, as Donne says, "integrity." Not only must human beings "recollect" God's mercies in the past, thus finding God through their thankfulness, but they must also recollect their sins. This recollection of sin is purgative; once a person "gathers" his sins "in his memory," he must "poure them out in a true *Confession*" and empty them into the saving sea of Christ's blood (*Sermons*, 6:199).[50] Only then will he be able to regain his original purity. Thus both recollections are necessary to unite man with God. Perhaps most important, however, the recollection of memory is an image, an anticipation, of the resurrection we will have at the Apocalypse when God shall "re-collect" all the "scattered" grains of dust, "re-compact" the body, and finally "re-unite" body and soul (*Sermons*, 7:103). Since memory can effect a resurrection that prepares us for God's, Donne can confidently conclude that the proper exercise of memory is "the art of *salvation*" (*Sermons*, 2:73) and will lead to man's final glorious resurrection by God: "He that rises to this Judgment of recollecting, and of judging himselfe, shall rise with a chearfulnesse, and stand with a confidence, when Christ Jesus will come in the second" (*Sermons*, 7:117).

God as Remedy

As Donne's reference to the Resurrection suggests, it is ultimately God who has the supreme power to work against the naturally degenerative course of time. Though human beings can rise through the proper exercise of memory, their ascent will be neither continuous nor steady, for, as Donne repeatedly suggests in both poetry and prose, inconstancy is the condition of life.[51] Since there is no stability in this world, "as long as we are, we are subject to be worse then we are. . . . I am still in a slippery state, and in evident danger of being the greatest sinner" (*Sermons*, 1:318). One can fall or decline at any moment, thus succumbing to the gravitational pull of time. Indeed, even rising itself may be a way to fall, as Donne concludes in *Devotions* when he meditates upon the spiritual significance of his physical dizziness: "I am readier to fall to the Earth, now I am up, than I was when I *lay* in bed: O *perverse way, irregular motion* of *Man;* even *rising* it selfe is the way to *Ruine*" (p. 110). Donne sees change as so much a condition of man's life that he finds that even before the Fall man was "subject to *alteration*," and "every *alteration* is in a degree . . . a *suffering*" (*Sermons*, 2:79).

In this life of unevenness, human efforts to combat the downward pull of nature are insufficient. Despite Donne's emphasis on the efficacy of memory, some of the Holy Sonnets imply that memory's ability to reunite man and God is limited. In the Holy Sonnet "What if this present were the worlds last night," Donne's remembrance of the Crucifixion fails to assure him completely that he will be saved. Though his vivid recollection of Christ's suffering, His tears, and His forgiving nature prompts Donne's pity and makes him feel that Christ will not "adjudge" him "unto hell" (l. 7), this assurance is punctured by Donne's fear, evident throughout this disturbing sonnet, that he can indeed be damned. In the sestet memory gives way to understanding, as Donne anxiously tries to persuade both himself and Christ that he will be saved:

> . . . as in my idolatrie
> I said to all my profane mistresses,
> Beauty, of pitty, foulnesse onely is
> A signe of rigour: so I say to thee,
> To wicked spirits are horrid shapes assign'd;
> This beauteous form assures a pitious minde. (ll. 9–14)

Donne often reveals a deep sense of man's essential helplessness. Especially in the *Holy Sonnets,* man seems a very passive creature, incapable of avoiding on his own the tendency to fall into sin and to sink to hell. As a "usurpt towne," he seems a victim, hardly responsible for being "betroth'd" to Satan, and rescue depends on God's actions rather than his own—"Divorce mee, 'untie, or breake that knot againe, / Take mee to you, imprison mee" ("Batter my heart," ll. 11–12). He is a temple of God's spirit, which the devil has taken over. Although in the Holy Sonnet "As due by many titles" memory instills in Donne a sense of his sinfulness and of God's love and mercy and thus leads him to resign himself to God, the "devill" continues to "usurpe" on him (l. 9). Unable to resist the attack, he can only ask God to "rise and for thine owne worke fight" (l. 11). More than human effort is needed to counter the effects of decay. As Donne laments in the *Devotions,* though "*Heaven is the center of my Soule,*" the soul does not return there of its own unaided efforts: "My *body* falls downe without pushing, my *Soule* does not go up without pulling" (p. 11). Since natural motion is downward, it takes a higher force to pull the soul back up to its home. Ultimately, it is only God's "*preservation*" that prevents even the angels "from sinking to this *centre, Annihilation*" (p. 51).

Donne's conception of God's opposition to the natural, degenerative pattern of time is evident in the way he uses traditional sun imagery in talking about God.[52] Although the analogy between God and the sun is conventional, Donne's use of it reflects his view of time. In contrast to the natural sun, whose cycle Donne characteristically identifies with the pattern of decline, the divine sun of God never sets. Whereas the world's sun inexorably declines toward the west, God is the full "noon" that the speaker in "A Lecture upon the Shadow" sought to find in human love (*Sermons,* 6:172; 9:50). Though human love may strive to be a full growing or constant light, only God's love can be that, for He is the only sun that never sets ("Goodfriday," ll. 11–12).

The progress of God's revelation to mankind throughout history contrasts with the degenerative course of time, for not only did "the Sun" of revelation continuously ascend to full light, but ever since it reached its meridian it has maintained its height without decline. After the Fall God's revelation was in "the *winter Tropick,* short and cold, dark and cloudy dayes"; during the time of the Jewish law, it "advanced higher" to Libra, "as much day as night";

but finally with Christianity "the Sun is in a *perpetuall Summer Solstice*," "a perpetuall *Meridian*, and *Noon*. . . . in that height in the Christian Church" (*Sermons*, 7:349–50). Whereas in the course of time man falls farther from God, God works to counter this natural movement, coming closer to man in time, bringing salvation "nearer" to us than it was to the Jews (*Sermons*, 2:268; 5:151; *Essays in Divinity*, p. 92). Although traditionally Christianity does not see God and nature in opposition but rather finds God working through nature, Donne's language often suggests that God is at odds with the course of nature: "Ruine" is the pattern of nature; as he remarks in the *First Anniversary*, even in the Garden of Eden it "labour'd to frustrate . . . Gods purpose" (ll. 100–101).

It is true that Donne sometimes shows God working through the process of time as He effects mankind's salvation. In these instances God's hand is visible behind the process of decline: He casts man down finally to raise him up ("Hymne to God my God, in my sicknesse"). Christ sanctified this pattern when he descended so that He (and mankind) might rise. Nevertheless, Donne frequently implies that the natural, temporal pattern of decline conflicts with God's force, though there is never any doubt that God's power is infinitely the stronger. It is this opposition between God and time that distinguishes Donne's view of history from the traditional Judaeo-Christian one, which assumes that God's providence directs the course of time.

God provides an antidote against the natural pattern of decay and decline by giving us the "supernaturall food, Religion," which may be able to keep our spiritual growth from becoming "withered" (*Second Anniv.*, ll. 188–89). The Eucharist itself is a cordial that works against decay, offering Donne hope of "quickning in this world" as well as immortality in the next (*Devotions*, p. 39). If we follow the "motion" of His church, we may "stand firme" ("Upon the Annunciation and Passion," l. 30). Because the preacher is assisted by God's grace, he perhaps can "save [people] from falling into future sinnes" by preaching God's word and administering his sacraments (*Sermons*, 3:302). Indeed, "in every word" of the Bible "the soule findes a rise, and help for her devotion" (*Sermons*, 5:171). That only God's magnetic force can fully counter the gravitational pull of sin and time is evident in Donne's remark that Christ "rose; others are but raised" (*Sermons*, 4:359). Weighed down by sin and tempted by the devil, we cannot "sustaine" ourselves "one houre," but need God "like Adamant" to "draw [our] iron heart" (Holy Sonnet, "Thou hast made me," l. 14). Donne's descriptions of God's power to raise man are sometimes so vivid that the images assume a startlingly physical, tactile quality, as in his comment that, when "thy soule comes to set in thy deathbed, the Son of Grace shall suck it up into glory" (*Sermons*, 10:52). The instantaneousness of being sucked up contrasts with both the slow sinking and the precipitous falls that characterize earthly life.

In addition to raising man, God also reunites him. Though memory makes a beginning, it is only God who fully restores our wholeness and our connection with Him. In instituting the sacrament of the Eucharist, He offered a way for human beings to join with Him, partaking of His Body and Blood. But the Bible also makes possible a similar union: through hearing (or reading) the word of God, we incorporate and assimilate divinity much as we do in receiving the eucharist. "As the end of all bodily eating, is Assimilation, that . . . that meat may be made *Idem corpus*, the same body that I am; so the end of all spiritual eating, is Assimilation too, That after all Hearing, and all Receiving, I may be made . . . the same spirit, that my God is" (*Sermons*, 6:223).

The most complete reunion of man and God, however, will only occur at the Resurrection, when our wholeness will be perfectly and finally recreated. Though baptism restores us to "the integrity which *Adam* had before the fall" (*Sermons*, 7:231), God will bring us "to a better condition, than we were in, at first," making us "partakers of the divine nature" (*Sermons*, 1:163–64). Whereas time works to dissolve and scatter man, God will gather all the grains of dust, reform the atoms of dust, and unite the body and soul (Sermons, 7:103), thus completing the process memory began. Only at the Resurrection, at the end of time, will we find a permanent remedy for the destructive, dissolving effects of time. In heaven we will find continual growth of joy without decay. There "every thing, is every minute, in the highest exaltation, as good as it can be, and yet super-exalted, and infinitely multiplied, by every minutes addition" (*Sermons*, 7:82).[53]

Notes

1. The remark is John Carey's, in *John Donne: Life, Mind, Art* (Oxford: Oxford University Press, 1981), p. 10. Terry G. Sherwood, *Fulfilling the Circle: A Study of John Donne's Thought* (Toronto: University of Toronto

Press, 1984), has also argued for the consistency of Donne's thought, though the consistency he sees is quite different from Carey's.

2. John Donne, *Devotions Upon Emergent Occasions,* ed. Anthony Raspa (Montreal: McGill-Queen's University Press, 1975), p. 51.

3. Browne, *Works,* 1:164. Earl Miner has observed that "most of Donne's writing supports the view of historical decay" (*Metaphysical Mode,* p. 51). See also Harris, *All Coherence Gone.* On Donne's obsession with change— his interest in the fluidity and inconstancy of the created world—see Carey's discussion in *John Donne,* ch. 6.

On the dating of Donne's works, see esp. R. C. Bald, *John Donne: A Life* (Oxford: Oxford University Press, 1970), and Helen Gardner's introductions to her editions of *"The Elegies" and the "Songs and Sonnets"* (Oxford: Clarendon Press, 1965) and *The Divine Poems,* 2d ed. (Oxford: Clarendon Press, 1978).

4. John Donne, *Essays in Divinity,* ed. Evelyn M. Simpson (Oxford: Clarendon Press, 1952), p. 19. Subsequent references to the *Essays* are to this edition.

5. See "To the Countesse of Huntingdon," ll. 17–18, in *John Donne: The Satires, Epigrams, and Verse Letters,* ed. W. Milgate (Oxford: Clarendon Press, 1967); cf. *First Anniv.,* ll. 273–74. On the connection between the Renaissance idea of the decay of nature and the preoccupation with the Apocalypse, see Tuveson, *Millennium and Utopia,* ch. 2.

I have used Gardner's editions of *"The Elegies" and "The Songs and Sonnets"* and *The Divine Poems,* and W. Milgate's edition of *The Epithalamions, Anniversaries, and Epicedes* (Oxford: Clarendon Press, 1978).

6. *The Sermons of John Donne,* ed. George R. Potter and Evelyn M. Simpson, 10 vols. (Berkeley: University of California Press, 1953–62), 4:321. Subsequent references for the sermons are to this edition and will be cited in the text by volume and page number. Sir Thomas Browne similarly describes old age as the "Evening" that "conclude[s] the Day" (*Works,* 1:263).

7. Cf. *Sermons,* 2:83; 1:273.

8. See "Satyre V," l. 35; *First Anniv.,* l. 426; and *Sermons,* 1:159.

9. Godfrey Goodman, *The Fall of Man, or the Corruption of Nature* (London, 1616), pp. 84–85, 15.

10. *First Anniv.,* ll. 274, 373; *Devotions,* p. 11.

11. John Donne, *Letters to Severall Persons of Honour* (London, 1651), p. 135.

12. *Sermons,* 9:377–78; Cf. *Biathanatos* (London, 1644), p. 28.

13. *Sermons,* 6:69; 2:132, 97; and Holy Sonnet, "Thou hast made me," 1.8.

14. *Devotions,* p. 20. Cf. Goodman, *Fall of Man,* p. 24: "euery thing containeth in it selfe the inbred seedes of corruption." Donald Ramsay Roberts, in "The Death Wish of John Donne," *PMLA* 62 (1947), 958–76, discusses Donne's "conception of *the existence within life of a contrary destructive principle, an anti-life or death principle*" (p. 964).

15. *First Anniv.,* l. 157; *Second Anniv.,* ll. 117–18; *Sermons,* 4:333.

16. Goodman, *Fall of Man*, pp. 84–85. Cf. Browne, in *Works*, 1:255: "we are fallen . . . from a primitive and pure Creation."

17. In "To the Countesse of Huntingdon," the speaker, referring to the stars in "the firmament" (l. 7), says, "There no new things are" (l. 8).

18. For Donne's interest in the new philosophy, see Charles Monroe Coffin, *John Donne and the New Philosophy* (1937; rpt. New York: Humanities Press, 1958). Murray Roston, *The Soul of Wit: A Study of John Donne* (Oxford: Clarendon Press, 1974), convincingly argues that Donne's poetry reveals his rejection of empiricism and the new science (pp. 18, 74–83, 109, and passim).

19. Cf. Goodman's attack on Ramus for his "barbarous innouation" (*Fall of Man*, p. 268); like Donne, Goodman laments that "nouelty and strangenesse moues the minde of man" (ibid., p. 307).

20. John Donne, *Ignatius His Conclave*, ed. T. S. Healy (Oxford: Clarendon Press, 1969), p. 9. See also *Sermons*, 1:223.

21. *The Poems of Thomas Carew*, ed. Rhodes Dunlap (Oxford: Clarendon Press, 1949), pp. 71–74.

22. This was a standard Anglican view of the Roman Catholic church. See, e.g., Hall, *Olde Religion*, and Ussher, *An Answer to a Challenge made by a Jesuite in Ireland*.

23. *Pseudo-Martyr* (London, 1610), p. 225. Goodman similarly reveres "the first Fathers which did neerer approch to the times of the Apostles" and thus "had a greater measure of knowledge" (*Fall of Man*, p. 363).

24. William R. Mueller, in *John Donne: Preacher* (Princeton: Princeton University Press, 1962), p. 139, mentions Donne's frequent use of water as a symbol, and Potter and Simpson in their discussion of Donne's sources briefly note that the symbol of the river (which appears in Genesis and the Revelation of St. John) is "always in the background of Donne's mind" (*Sermons*, 10:306).

25. In describing man's increasing "imperfection" the farther he is from "the first mould," Goodman's fountain imagery recalls Donne's— "so [man] incurres the more imperfection and weaknesse; as the streames of a fountaine, the further they runne through vncleane passages, the more they contract the corruption" (*Fall of Man*, p. 349).

26. Potter and Simpson have noted Donne's fondness for the Tree of Life as a symbol (*Sermons*, 10:306), but as far as I know no one has discussed Donne's use of the root image.

27. Ibid., 3:327, 250; 8:131. Donne's imagery here recalls representations of the Tree of Jesse. The conception of the Tree of Jesse is based on Isaiah 11:1: "And there shall come forth a rod out of the stem of Jesse, and a branch shall grow out of his roots." In the representations the tree rises from Jesse's body, and the ultimate flower it produces is Jesus. See Arthur Watson, *The Early Iconography of the Tree of Jesse* (London: Oxford University Press, 1934). As Watson shows, Jesse himself is the root, but Donne emphasizes that God is the root as well as the flower.

28. Winfried Schleiner, *The Imagery of John Donne's Sermons* (Providence,

R.I.: Brown University Press, 1970), pp. 165–66, observes that "in the exposition Donne usually managed somehow to follow the word order of his text. . . . Thus the text was not only left intact but was pointed to at the various steps of the exegesis." Joan Webber suggests, in *Contrary Music: The Prose Style of John Donne* (Madison: University of Wisconsin Press, 1963), that "with his sacramental view of the Word, he sees the sermon as a point of connection between God and man" (p. 125).

29. For a discussion of the older Greek and Latin concern with etymologies, see Otto Jespersen, *Language* (1921; rpt. New York: Norton, 1964), p. 19; Alfons Nehring, "Plato and the Theory of Language," *Traditio* 3 (1945), 13–48; W. S. Allen, "Ancient Ideas on the Origin and Development of Language," *Transactions of the Philological Society* (1948), pp. 35–60.

30. Allen, "Ancient Ideas," p. 58.

31. See Plato's *Cratylus*, in *The Dialogues of Plato*, trans. B. Jowett, 3d ed. rev., 5 vols. (Oxford: Clarendon Press, 1892), 1:358, 362–63, 366.

32. Some scholars have suggested that Donne's knowledge of Hebrew was limited (see, e.g., D. C. Allen, "Dean Donne Sets His Text," *ELH* 10 [1943], 208–29; and Potter and Simpson in *Sermons*, 10:307–8), but the issue has not been resolved or fully explored.

33. On theories of language, see Plato's *Cratylus;* Frederick Sontag, "The Platonist's Concept of Language," *Journal of Philosophy* 51 (1954), 823–30; Nehring, "Plato," pp. 13–48; and Allen, "Ancient Ideas," pp. 35–60.

34. Nehring argues that Plato's ultimate position is that "language is not a source from which truth can be learned" ("Plato," p. 33). Socrates says that "the knowledge of things is not be derived from names. No; they must be studied and investigated in themselves" (Plato, *Cratylus*, p. 387). Similarly, St. Augustine in *De Magistro* insists that man cannot learn the thing through the name: "words possess only sufficient efficacy to remind us in order that we may seek things, but not to exhibit the things so that we may know them" (in *Concerning the Teacher and On the Immortality of the Soul*, trans. George G. Leckie [New York: Appleton-Century, 1938], p. 46; see chs. x–xiv).

35. *Sermons*, 3:171–72; cf. 7:302; 5:308. Although St. Augustine insists that we cannot actually learn truth through words, sometimes he discusses the origin of a word as if it were a means of getting closer to truth: "if we also trace back the origin of the word 'discovery' [*inventio*], what else does it mean, than that to discover is to come into that which is sought?" (*The Trinity*, trans. Stephen McKenna, The Fathers of the Church, vol. 45 [Washington, D.C.: Catholic University of America Press, 1963], p. 304, Bk. X, ch. vii; subsequent references to *The Trinity* will be to book and chapter number).

36. Webber has observed that "sometimes he dwells upon a single word, staying very close to its original meaning, but pulling that meaning out into expanded versions or more vivid renderings" (*Contrary Music*, p. 44);

and Roston (*Soul of Wit*, p. 95) suggests that Donne's wordplay is often concerned with the earlier meaning of the word.

37. On Donne's concern with love's ability to defeat mutability and death, see esp. Anne Ferry, *All in War with Time: Love Poetry of Shakespeare, Donne, Jonson, Marvell* (Cambridge, Mass.: Harvard University Press, 1975), ch. 2. Carey, *John Donne*, has remarked on Donne's "wish to stop time" (p. 181) and concludes that "his desire for something stable is born of and struggles with his sense of instability" (p. 190).

38. G. F. Waller, "John Donne's Changing Attitudes to Time," *SEL* 14 (1974), 79–89, argues that in the *Anniversaries* and the later sermons and essays Donne flees "the deepest source of inspiration in the early poems, the trust in the value of his own restless aspiration to find eternity through the intensity of human experience. Love is now seen as deceptive" (p. 84).

39. See St. Augustine, *The Trinity*, X, xi; St. Bernard (attrib.), *Saint Bernard His Meditations . . . vpon our Sauiours Passion* (London, 1614), pt. 2, p. 6; and St. Bonaventure, *The Mind's Road to God*, trans. George Boas (Indianapolis: Bobbs-Merrill, 1953), pp. 22ff. See also Donne's *Sermons*, 2:72–73.

40. St. Augustine, *Confessions*, trans. E. B. Pusey (New York: Dutton, 1907), Bk. X, ch. xxiv, p. 226. Subsequent references will be to book and chapter number.

41. See Webber's brief but excellent discussion of Donne's concern with memory in *Contrary Music*, p. 22, n27. Other valuable discussions include Dennis Quinn, "Donne's Christian Eloquence," *ELH* 27 (1960), 276–97; Robert L. Hickey, "Donne's Art of Memory," *Tennessee Studies in Literature*, 3 (1958), 29–36; and Donald M. Friedman, "Memory and the Art of Salvation in Donne's Good Friday Poem," *ELR* 3 (1973), 418–42. Recently Terry G. Sherwood, in *Fulfilling the Circle*, has argued against this emphasis on the importance of memory (see esp. pp. 21–62). While he valuably insists that "the importance of reason is considerably greater" in Donne (p. 35) than usually recognized, his deprecation of the importance of memory is a distortion of Donne, who grants powers to memory that Sherwood would restrict to reason.

42. Cf. St. Augustine, *Concerning the Teacher*, ch. 11. St. Augustine's idea that the teacher simply reminds us of what we already know is similar to Plato's idea of learning as remembering (*Phaedo* 73–76, in *Dialogues of Plato*, 2:213–19). Frances A. Yates, in *The Art of Memory* (Chicago: University of Chicago Press, 1966), describes St. Augustine as "a Christian Platonist, believing that knowledge of the divine is innate in memory" (p. 48). But Etienne Gilson, in *The Christian Philosophy of Saint Augustine*, trans. L. E. M. Lynch (New York: Random House, 1960), suggests that though St. Augustine in his early years may have accepted the Platonic doctrine that ideas of things are present in the soul from birth (pp. 71–72), he restricted the meaning of Platonic language later on, insisting that "we discover truth not in memories deposited previously in the soul, but in the divine light which is constantly present there" (p. 82); "truth is

always within our grasp" because we always have the "inner master," Christ, within us (p. 75).

43. See Barbara Kiefer Lewalski's discussion of the Protestant view that biblical history is recapitulated in the life of the individual (*Protestant Poetics*, pp. 131–44, 254–65).

44. Several times Donne refers to this biblical passage as indicative of God's special preference for song. See *Essays in Divinity*, p. 204; *Sermons* 2:171; 4:179.

45. Neither Donne nor St. Augustine restricts memory to the past. See St. Augustine, *The Trinity*, XIV, xi; *Confessions*, X, viii; Donne's *Sermons*, 2:74; 9:84–85.

46. Louis L. Martz, *The Poetry of Meditation* (1954; rev. ed. New Haven: Yale University Press, 1962), p. 248, points out that this "ecstasy is metaphorical only. 'Meditation' is always discursive . . . it is only the preparation for ascent to the truly mystical state."

47. *Sermons*, 2:246. Cf. St. Augustine, *The Trinity*, IX, viii.

48. Cf. the final remarkable pages of Donne's last sermon, "Deaths Duell," where his meditation on the Crucifixion bridges the gap between past and present, between Christ, on the one hand, and Donne and his congregation on the other (*Sermons*, 10:245–48).

49. Perhaps Donne also had in mind the state of "Recollection," which Evelyn Underhill defines as the first part of mystical introversion: "All the scattered interests of the self have here to be collected; there must be . . . a deliberate expelling of all discordant images from the consciousness" (*Mysticism* [New York: Dutton, 1911], p. 374). Donne, of course, was not a mystic. Whereas he, like St. Augustine, identifies recollection with remembering, for the mystics, Underhill insists, recollection is *not* "remembrance" since all the faculties have their part in "the wilfull production of this state of consciousness" (pp. 375–76).

50. Cf. Donne's comparison of the recollection of sins in confession to physic in the tenth Expostulation of the *Devotions*: "As *Phisicke* works so, it drawes the *peccant humour* to it selfe, that when it is gathered together, the weight of it selfe may carry that humour away, so thy *Spirit* returns to my *Memory* my former sinnes, that being so recollected, they may powre out themselves by *Confession*" (p. 54).

51. See *First Anniv.*, ll. 387–400, and Holy Sonnet "Oh, to vex me, contraryes meet in one."

52. Potter and Simpson note (*Sermons*, 10:302–3) that Donne in the early part of his ministry made relatively little use of the sun as a symbol of God, but later it became more important.

53. As he says in the *Second Anniv.*, we shall find in heaven that our joy "doth every day admit / Degrees of growth, but none of loosing it" (ll. 495–96).

CHAPTER IV

Ben Jonson: Stoic Constancy and Cyclical Vicissitude

Tis onely [virtue] that can time and chance defeat.

"Epistle to Katherine, Lady Aubigny"

BEN JONSON'S INTEREST IN HISTORY and in history-writing is easy to document. His plays *Sejanus* and *Catiline* reveal a fascination with Roman history and an immersion in classical historians such as Sallust, Dio Cassius, and Tacitus. Apparently some time after writing these two historical tragedies, Jonson attempted a prose history of Henry V, which was lost in the fire that destroyed his library.[1] Throughout his poetry there is also evidence of Jonson's familiarity with the work of contemporary English historians as well as with contemporary translators of ancient historians. In addition to his poem on William Camden, his teacher at Westminster and the learned author of *Britannia* (*Epigrammes*, XIV), Jonson wrote poems to John Selden on the occasion of his *Titles of Honor* (*Under-wood* 16), Clement Edmonds for his translation of Julius Caesar's *Commentaries* (*Epigrammes*, CX, CXI), Sir Henry Savile for his translation of Tacitus (*Epigrammes*, XCV), and Thomas May for his translation of Lucan (*Uncollected Poetry*, 47). His poem "The Mind of the Frontispice to a Booke" (*Under-wood* 26), which was printed facing the frontispiece of Sir Walter Raleigh's *History of the World*, repeats many of the commonplaces about the nature and value of history as it explicates the symbolism of the engraving. Late in his life (1628) Jonson was appointed historiographer of London.[2] As one might expect, Jonson had a clearly formulated idea of the pattern of history; and it is not surprising, given his interest in classical historians, that his view of history was essentially cyclical.

Behind Jonson's works and the Stoic ethic that informs them is a cyclical view of history, which shapes all of his writing, from the early works such as *Cynthia's Revels* (1600) to late plays like *Staple of News* (1626), and links the plays, the masques, and the nondramatic poetry. Like Sir Francis Bacon, Jonson is disturbed by the direction history has taken, but he does not share Bacon's faith that it can be changed. Whereas Bacon believed that mankind could replace the cycles with progress, Jonson retreats into Stoicism, finding in it an antidote to the temporal cycles that the individual seems powerless to alter. As he places his hopes in the virtuous person's ability to become superior to cyclical vicissitude, Jonson typically moves away from the temporal world to that which is not subject to change, and thus he reveals an antihistorical impulse that, I suggest, is characteristic of Stoicism in general. His overriding desire for what is permanent prevents him from giving too much value to history per se, since by its nature history concerns the changing, the transient. For him as for many others in the Renaissance, history is primarily important for teaching transcendent moral lessons,[3] and the lesson that it teaches him is the necessity of rising above the times. Of course, Jonson was not an unworldly recluse. He was keenly interested both in his contemporary world (apparent in his role as satirist and in the substantial body of occasional poetry addressed to his contemporaries) and in Roman history (as we know from *Catiline* and *Sejanus*). But Jonson is a paradoxical writer, for while he is indeed interested in the past and in his own times,[4] he insists on the necessity of transcending the realm of history.

The Cycles of History

There is a close relationship between Stoic ethics and the cyclical view of history. In the Roman empire the cyclical idea had been commonly identified with Stoicism, and in the Renaissance a renewed interest in Stoicism accompanied the revival of the classical view that history moves in cycles.[5] Jonson reveals particularly well how Stoicism is based upon, and indeed is a response to, a cyclical view of history. But before defining this relationship more fully, it is necessary to examine Jonson's sense of the shape of history.

As might be expected, Jonson's clearest definition of the pattern of history occurs in his two Roman plays, which portray a nation in the process of decline. *Sejanus* presents the cyclical view of history to account for Rome's corruption. Arruntius, Cordus, Lepidus, and

Silius all expose the decay from the past, as they bitterly lament
that Rome no longer has a Cato, a Brutus, or a Cassius (I.87–104).
But it is Silius who points out that this decay results from Rome's
giving reign to her "affections" rather than reason. As John Milton
was also to observe, it is but a short step from this servitude within
man to tyranny on the political scale:

> We, that (within these fourescore yeeres) were borne
> Free, equall lords of the triumphed world,
> And knew no masters, but affections,
> To which betraying first our liberties,
> We since became the slaues to one mans lusts:
> And now to many. (I.59–64)

The nation ruled by her appetites may enjoy prosperity for a while
(Rome was master of the world even though subject to "affections"),
but eventually she will decline.

In *Catiline* the historical context of Rome's decline receives even
more attention. At the end of the first act, the Chorus offers as
an explanation of Catiline's villainy the cyclical interpretation of
history:

> Can nothing great, and at the height
> Remaine so long? but it's owne weight
> Will ruine it? Or, is't blinde chance,
> That still desires new states t'aduance,
> And quit the old? Else, why must *Rome*,
> Be by it selfe, now, ouercome? (I.531–36)

Jean Bodin had similarly observed that the "Flourishing estate" of
a commonwealth "cannot be of any long continuance, by reason
of the chaunges of worldly things, which are so mutable and vncer-
taine, as that the greatest Commonweales oftentimes fall euen all
at once with the weight of themselves."[6] Like Bodin, Jonson here
raises the possibility that cyclical decline is inevitable.

Although at times mistaken and uncertain in its knowledge, the
Chorus does recognize that Rome is involved in the process of
decay, as history was eventually to confirm. Despite its initial impulse
to absolve Rome from responsibility by blaming fortune, or even
merely chance, the Chorus revises its understanding of cyclical
history to include the idea of human responsibility. States are subject

to such cyclical decay because of inner weaknesses—greed, lust, the desire for material riches and power. Rome "builds in gold" (I.551): "Her women weare / The spoiles of nations" (I.555–56); her men are effeminate and "prostitute" (I.563).

> Hence comes that wild, and vast expence,
> That hath enforc'd *Romes* vertue, thence,
> Which simple pouerty first made:
> And, now, ambition doth invade
> Her state, with eating auarice,
> Riot, and euery other vice. (I.573–78)

As in *Sejanus,* Jonson suggests that the cyclical decline of a nation results when the people become ruled by appetites rather than reason. Moreover, by suggesting that Rome's earlier virtue was the result of poverty, the Chorus implies that Rome's virtue was dependent on external circumstance. Since Jonson believes that true virtue is unaffected by such material conditions, it would seem that Rome never really was virtuous. Her vices simply did not at first have the opportunity to reveal themselves.

Jonson's cyclical view of history leads him to find parallels between Rome and England, and between himself and the classical poets. His strong identification with Horace, for example, is based on more than just his admiration for his predecessor's moral and poetic virtues. In satires and odes Horace had attacked "perverted greed" as the basic cause of Rome's corruption (see *Satires*, I.i; *Odes*, III.xvi; and especially *Odes*, III.xxiv.48–49). Jonson's satires similarly focus on avarice; the plays as well as the poems relentlessly expose the extent to which gold has become the basis for all relations in his society. Behind Jonson's criticism of his age's corruption lies his awareness of its similarity to ancient Rome's.

As is apparent from *Catiline,* Jonson shared the view of Latin writers such as Horace and Sallust that avarice was one of the main causes of Rome's decline, and Jonson's conception of the cyclical pattern of history would have suggested to him the parallels between Rome's history and England's. *Sejanus* and *Catiline* constitute an implicit warning to England that she too may be involved in the process of decay.[7] Indeed, his lifelong attack on avarice and moral corruption in England indicates that he believed England was repeating the pattern of Rome and that her ultimate decline was probably imminent. Like Bodin, Jonson assumed that his country would undergo the same cycle as others had in the past. In these days

> Our Delicacies are growne capitall,
> And even our sports, are dangers! what we call
> Friendship is now mask'd Hatred! Justice fled,
> And shamefastnesse together! all lawes dead
> That kept man living! Pleasures only sought!
> Honour and honestie, as poore things thought
> As they are made. (*Under-wood* 17, ll. 37–43)

Already this cyclical decline was evident in letters. "*Sir Thomas Moore*, the elder *Wiat; Henry*, Earle of *Surrey* . . . began Eloquence with us." Sir Philip Sidney and Richard Hooker developed it even further, but it is Bacon "who hath fill'd up all numbers; and perform'd that in our tongue, which may be compar'd, or preferr'd, either to insolent *Greece*, or haughty *Rome*." In Bacon's time the greatest perfection was reached, but now England has embarked on the downward swing of the cycle: "Now things daily fall: wits grow downeward, and *Eloquence* grows backward" (*Timber*, ll. 902–22). Since language and style reflect the public state (*Timber*, ll. 954–58), this degeneration of eloquence points to the larger political decline of the nation.

Jonson's cyclical view of history receives its most explicit statements in *Sejanus*, *Catiline*, and *Timber*. But it also affects what he believed was the heart of his work: the discrimination between virtue and vice. He characteristically defines virtue and vice in terms of their radically different relationships to the cycles of time.

Vice and Vicissitude

The vicious person is intimately involved with time and "the times." Peni-boy Senior, the evil usurer in *Staple of News*, places supreme importance on being "on time," and Sir Petronell Flash wants a "*Time-fitted* Conscience" (*Eastward Ho* II.ii.308). Like the virtuous Crites in *Cynthia's Revels*, Jonson repeatedly criticizes the corrupt courtier who "serues the time" (III.iv.44). Significantly, it is Jonson's fools and villains who usually voice the *carpe diem* motif, which has been considered central to Cavalier poetry. Moria advises her ladies to "make much of time, and place, and occasion, and opportunitie," and Amorphus wants to "take our time by the forehead" (*Cynthia's Revels* IV.i.124–25; IV.v.101). And one of the most beautiful lyric expressions of the *carpe diem* theme, "Come, my *Celia*, let us proue, / While we can, the sports of loue," is, we must remember, sung by Volpone (III.vii.166–83). Apparently Jonson was less convinced of the importance of seizing the moment than were his poetic successors.

Those who concern themselves with what comes through time foolishly seek to find security in things that are themselves affected by temporal vicissitude. Mammon believes that gold will confer on him "a perpetuitie / Of life, and lust" (*The Alchemist* IV.i.165–66). Some place their happiness in clothing, which is even more obviously transitory. Like Asotus and Amorphus, who exchange clothes as a token of friendship (*Cynthia's Revels* I.iv), many characters in the plays value their tailor more than their virtue. Sir Diaphanous Silkeworme well exemplifies the folly of such ambitions, for he hopes by diet, baths, and clothes "to immortalize / Mortality it selfe" (*Magnetic Lady* I.vi.7–8).

Another manifestation of this foolish love of the transitory is the interest in novelty and "news," which Jonson so frequently satirizes. John Donne, as we have seen, also rejects innovation. But whereas Donne prefers the old because he believes that the best and truest things existed earliest, Jonson's dislike of novelty and news is based on his assumption that the permanent alone should be valued. He criticizes the audience of his plays for desiring novelty and indicts those who are curious to hear news rather than truth.[8] Moria, who ironically desires to "be a wisewoman," wants to know all the low gossip concerning "court, citie, and countrie. I would know what were done behind the arras, what upon the staires, what i' the garden, what i' the *Nymphs* chamber, what by barge, & what by coach. I would tel you which courtier were scabbed, and which not; which ladie her owne face to lie with her a-nights, and which not; who put off their teeth with their clothes in court, who their haire, who their complexion; and in which boxe they put it" (*Cynthia's Revels* IV.i.140–49). Not only is all this news concerned merely with the physical, which is subject to time's corruption, but also news by its nature implies transience. Something that is new soon will become old. It lacks true value, not only because it is so tied to the moment, but also because it is subject to the cyclical process of time and decay.

The vicious or foolish person shares the inconstancy and instability of time. Seeking things dependent on time and chance, he himself partakes of the everchanging fluctuation of time and the times to which he is tied. Like the revolutions of time, the courtiers of *Cynthia's Revels* are "Still turning giddie, till they reele like drunkards" (I.v.30). Corvino's insatiable desire for gold effects a remarkable alteration in him as the jealous husband suddenly becomes a pimp who insists that his wife must satisfy Volpone's lust. In *Sejanus* Natta and Satrius continually change their behavior to secure the favor of their patron (I.i.33–41). Often the inconstancy of the vicious characters takes the form of a desire for variety. Mammon wants an exquisite variety in his food, and Volpone thinks that his lust will be satisfied only if he and Celia reenact all the classical myths and the "more moderne formes" as well (*Volpone* III.vii.221–33).

One of the most fascinating versions of inconstancy is the tendency of vicious people to metamorphose themselves, to change shape repeatedly and to assume disguises. Crites describes the "subtle PROTEUS" he meets, a figure who reappears under different names in Jonson's plays: he is "one [who] / Can change, and varie with all formes he sees" (*Cynthia's Revels* III.iv.42–43). In *Staple of News,* lawyer Picklock boasts he is a

> . . . *Vertumnus,*
> On euery change, or chance, vpon occasion,
> A true *Chamælion,* I can colour for't. (III.i.34–36)

Mosca, as a parasite, can "Present to any humour, all occasion; / And change a visor, swifter, then a thought!" (*Valpone,* III.i.28–29). But Face is the most protean character. His very name indicates his superficial, everchanging nature. Like Shift in *Every Man out of His Humour,* whose many names signify his "varied" self which changes as the wind (II.vi.189–99), Face is known by many names— Face, Ullen, Lungs, Captain, and finally Jeremy.[9] We are, in fact, never sure of his true identity, for even at the end Jeremy may be only "a new Face" (*Alchemist,* V.iii.21).[10]

Jonson's belief that masks, disguises, and varying roles reflect the inconstancy of vice and folly recalls a particularly interesting passage in Seneca. Since this passage helps explain the symbolic import of the masks, the shifting identities that appear so often in Jonson's characterization of vice, it is worth quoting in full:

Everyone changes his plans and prayers day by day. Now he would have a wife, and now a mistress; now he would be king, and again he strives to conduct himself so that no slave is more cringing; now he puffs himself up until he becomes unpopular; again, he shrinks and contracts into greater humility than those who are really unassuming; at one time he scatters money, at another he steals it. That is how a foolish mind is most clearly demonstrated: it shows first in this shape and then in that, and is never like itself—which is, in my opinion, the most shameful of qualities. Believe me, it is a great role—to play the role of one man. But nobody can be one person except the wise man; the rest of us often shift our masks. At times you will think us thrifty and serious, at other times wasteful and idle. We continually change our characters and play a part contrary to that which we have discarded. (Epistle CXX.21–22)[11]

Like Jonson, Seneca defines the foolish person in terms of his multiplicity, his lack of a stable, single identity. Interestingly, Seneca describes the inconstant person's proclivity for changing shapes in terms of drama: like an actor playing several parts, he is continually changing roles.[12] Such fluctuation is the counterpart of the vicissitudes of time.

Slaves to their inconstant passions, vicious and foolish people are inevitably ruled by fortune. In many of Jonson's plays we witness the wheel of fortune turn. Fortune's cycle underlies the structure of *Every Man out of His Humour,* in which all the foolish characters appear in the "height of their humours" and then suddenly are "laid flat" (IV.viii.168). This pattern is only too clear in *Staple of News,* where we see the young heir, Peni-boy Junior, followed by a beggar "at his first entry into fortune" (II.iv.211). The cyclical pattern of time's vicissitudes is explicitly defined by Peni-boy Senior, who realizes that other wealthy men have witnessed the revolution of fortune's wheel but blindly believes that his prosperity will last. He teases Fitton, Shunfield, and Madrigal about their loss of fortune:

> . . . I remember too,
> When you had lands, and credit, worship, friends,
> I, and could giue security: now, you haue none,
> Or will haue none right shortly. This can time,

And the vicissitude of things. I have
All these, and money too, and doe possesse 'hem. (II.iv.183–88)

But the rest of the play shows that he is as subject to the vicissitudes as the others were.

The Alchemist provides a more complex examination of the relationship between vice and fortune. The play is full of references to fortune, both as money or wealth, and as the shaping principle in the lives of the vicious and foolish characters.[13] Indeed, for Jonson these two meanings are closely related, since fortune is both a personification of cyclical vicissitude and the term for worldly goods which are subject to this vicissitude.

All the characters are fortuneseekers. Dapper wants a "familiar" so he will be lucky at games. Drugger wants to know how he can build his shop so he will have "good fortune" (II.vi.49). Dame Pliant "do's strangely long to know her fortune" (II.vi.39), both in the sense of what the future holds for her and also what wealth she will gain through marriage. The cheaters, too, are concerned with their fortunes. At the end of the play, Face still wants to "make the best of [his] fortune" (V.iii.82), despite the fact that his master has discovered his villainy. Subtle considers his "Fortune" "better than my birthright" (IV.iii.14). Not content with the goods he gets from his victims, he wants to marry the rich widow Pliant, whom he calls his "fortune" (IV.iii.13). Although Surly seems more of an honest man than the others, he too pursues the widow, not because he loves her virtue, but because he could use her money. It would make him "a man" (IV.vi.13). And the less than exemplary Lovewit is willing to forgive his servant if he gets both the money that has been taken from the fools *and* the rich widow Face offers as a bribe.

As this connection between love and money would suggest, there is a great deal of concern in this play with prostitution, which Jonson sees as symbolic of man's worship of fortune.[14] Lovewit's house has become a "bawdy-house" (II.iii.226) with Face as the "pimpe" (III.iv.44) and Dol the whore. And Subtle appropriately counsels Dame Pliant, who is at first reluctant to accept the wealthy Spanish Don, to "fit her loue, now, to her fortune" (IV.iv.27). All the characters similarly prostitute themselves, selling their virtue for gold. Fortune herself is a whore, and men are willing to sacrifice all their riches to enjoy her,[15] as Jonson implies in the scene where Dol, as Queen of Faery, presents her "petticote of FORTUNE"

(III.v.7) to Dapper in return for "all [his] worldly pelfe" (l. 17). Since she is supposedly the source of his hoped-for fortune, Dapper must pay to gain her favors. This scene nicely suggests that in seeking fortune men are courting a whore. They are foolish to expect constancy from either. And the degradation involved in the pursuit of fortune is tellingly illustrated by Dapper's imprisonment in *"Fortunes* priuy lodgings" (III.v.79)—the outhouse.

Machiavelli counsels that the man who pursues fortune should treat her roughly like a mistress in order to control her (*The Prince,* ch. xxv), and Bacon similarly believes people can "mould" their own fortune (*Works,* 12:215). But Jonson insists that the vicious, ambitious man is not able to master fortune, since by desiring her gifts he has placed himself under her power. Subtle's victims are clearly passive characters, obeying his commands to bring him their riches. The cheaters think they have more control over the pattern of events. But chance occurrences such as Lovewit's early return or the victim's unexpected visits continually disturb their plans. Subtle, Dol, and Face begin to lose control of the situation as Mammon inconveniently appears when Dol is engaged with Dapper. Soon after, the Spanish Don arrives. Too many gulls are coming to the house at once, and Face realizes that his seemingly perfectly ordered scheme threatens to collapse.

Indeed, the careers of both fools and villains in *The Alchemist* follow the cycle of fortune's wheel. The fools give away their worldly goods in the hopes of gaining their fortune, and thus they bring about their own downfall. As Subtle ironically tells Mammon when the furnace explodes, these are "the curst fruits of vice" (IV.v.77). But blinded by his own greed, Subtle fails to realize that what he has told Mammon predicts his own end: he will lose all the wealth that he thought he had gained. In the opening scene where Dol predicts that Face and Subtle will "ore-throw all" (I.i.92), Jonson suggests the inevitability of this cycle. The precarious order they try to establish collapses at the end. Their apparent rise is in fact a fall.

If vice brings about its own ruin, it would seem that justice operates in the cyclical process. In *The Alchemist,* as in *Volpone, Staple of News,* and *Case is Altered,* the cheaters are cheated, and the process of justice is apparent as fortune's wheel turns. It was, indeed, common to assert that Providence controls the cyclical pattern of crime and retribution. Raleigh in *History of the World* sees God's judgments in the fall of kingdoms and princes who through blood-shed and cruelty have tried "to make them-selves . . . maisters of the world." Sir Thomas Browne similarly insists that the "hand of God" moves the "wheele . . . whereby all States arise to their Zenith and verticall points, according to their predestinated periods."[16] But Jonson refrains from ascribing control of these cycles to Divine Providence. Whereas Raleigh confidently proclaims that "ill doing hath alwaies beene attended with ill successe,"[17] Jonson's view that these cycles sometimes effect justice is complicated by the fact that fortune's cycles fail to reward the good and that vice is not always punished.

The Alchemist ends cynically with the triumph of vice, as Face, absolved by Lovewit, turns to his audience for more victims. Jonson implies that there are always people who seek the gifts of fortune and thus are quite willing to be cheated. On the other hand, Face is not secure in his position—his fortune, which came partly through accident, can be lost in the same way. The cycles continue.

Fortune is to the individual what the cycles of history are to the state or nation, as *Sejanus* most clearly reveals. Set within the larger context of Rome's history, Sejanus's career parallels the history of Rome. Like Jonson's other vicious characters, Sejanus's life follows the pattern of the wheel of fortune as he rises to power only to be thrown down.[18] Though he believes that he can control fortune (I.362–65), his worship of her as "Queene of human state, / Rectresse of action, Arbitresse of fate" (V.178–79) suggests he has surrendered "all power" (l. 180) to her. Ruled by vicious appetites and a passion for power, Sejanus, like other foolish people, has deified fortune, as Lepidus insists (V.733–35). By placing his felicity in things which come through time, he has immersed himself in the realm of cyclical vicissitude and made himself vulnerable to the Machiavellian machinations of Tiberius.

Throughout the play Jonson emphasizes the parallel between Sejanus and the society that has produced him. Like Sejanus, the Romans are slaves to their passions, as we see in the violent end that Sejanus and his family meet at the hands of the mob. The analogy between Sejanus and Rome suggests that just as a country ruled by vicious appetites brings about its own decline, so the individual's passions make him subject to fortune's vicissitudes. The wheel of fortune is a microcosm of the cycles of history.

Virtue, Constancy, and the Poet

Whereas the vicious, always concerned with time, are ruled by its cyclical vicissitudes, the virtuous people define themselves by their opposition to these cycles. Jonson's good man is essentially the Stoic wise man who seeks things unaffected by time.[19] With its cyclical process of growth and decay, time is an enemy of happiness. As Cicero explains, "No one can be happy except when good is secure and certain and lasting. . . . For nothing of all that goes to make a happy life should shrivel up, nothing be blotted, nothing fall to the ground" (*Tusculan Disputations*, V.xiv.40).[20] The assumption is that true happiness depends on transcending time, since human beings cannot control its destructive powers.

Through reason and philosophy the wise person can become impervious to the temporal vicissitudes that, like Jonson, the Stoic writers identify with fortune.[21] In Horace and Seneca as in Jonson these vicissitudes are imaged by "stormy waters" whose waves are suggestive of cyclical flux. But philosophy enables a person to be "always armed against the assaults of fortune" (*Tusculan Disputations*, V.vii.19). Jonson praises the ability of virtue (which he equates with reason) to raise people above the injuries of fortune. Hence the noble count in *Case is Altered* claims that though he "be wrack't on Fortunes wheel," he will "prepare with steeled patience / To tread on torment" (IX.ii.17–19). The vicissitudes simply do not affect his inner virtue, which is, as Seneca would say, "so steeled against the blows of chance that she cannot be bent, much less broken" (*De Constantia*, v.4).

The good person stands in opposition to fortune and seeks to create in himself the stability that counters the inconstancy of life.[22] Since numerous calamities are incident to man in this life, the best solution, as Cicero says, is to maintain "an unruffled temper, an unchanging mien, and the same cast of countenance in every condition of life" (*Offices*, I.xxvi.90).[23] Thus Jonson counsels a friend to remain unchanged despite the changes of fortune. No matter what "face thy fate puts on," he must not "shrinke or start . . . but be alwayes one" (*Under-wood* 17, ll. 185–86). In contrast to the protean, everchanging nature of the vicious person, the good person is always the same.[24] The virtuous Crites is unperturbed by Hedon's and Anaides's insults; as Hedon remarks, "How confidently he went by vs, and carelesly! neuer moou'd! not stirr'd at any thing!" (*Cynthia's Revels* III.ii.13–14). Jonson himself boasts that "though forsooke / Of *Fortune*," he has "not alter'd yet my looke, / Or so my selfe abandon'd" (*Forest* XIII, ll. 15–17).

A "calme" mind and "an even gate" (*Under-wood* 86, 9, ll. 163, 165) protect the virtuous person from being pulled into the dangerous flux. Jonson counsels Lady Aubigny that though the "turning world" (l. 64) is "Giddie with change" (l. 67), she must

> . . . keepe an even, and unalter'd gaite;
> Not looking by, or back (like those that waite
> Times, and occasions, to start forth, and seeme).
>
> *Forest* XIII, ll. 61–63

Whereas the vicious person is a time-server, the virtuous individual usually stands in opposition to the times, which Jonson associates with corruption and multiplicity. Throughout Jonson's poetry runs the fear of being sucked into the world of change and death, imaged so frequently by the stormy sea. In order to preserve his life, the Stoic person must remain poised, "keeping a just course" (*Forest* XIII, l. 91) and trying to insulate himself "'Gainst stormes, or pyrats, that might charge your peace" (l. 93).

Jonson's concern with being "one," with constancy as a device for protecting oneself in a world of change, affects his poetic style. Behind his preference for the so-called plain style is his conviction that the wise man is always one and consequently his voice is, too. As Seneca advises, "You should therefore force yourself to maintain to the very end of life's drama the character which you assumed at the beginning. See to it that men be able to praise you; if not, let them at least identify you" (Epistle CXX.22).[25] While Face's name continually changes throughout *The Alchemist*, Jonson has only to "name" Pembroke to praise him (*Epigrammes*, CII) because his name is as constant as his virtue.[26] Jonson's own constancy is confirmed by the fact that he usually speaks in his own voice in his nondramatic verse, unlike Donne, whose personae reflect his Montaignian sense that the self is multiple and everchanging. Jonson's style is the counterpart of his Stoic belief that the wise person is stable and thus should "play the role of one man" (Seneca, Epistle CXX.22).[27]

Jonson's writings reveal his resistance to the world of change in yet another way. In opposition to the cyclical flux of time and history, he presents the Horatian ideal of the virtuous person as a centered circle—self-sufficient, constant because of his center of virtue. The stability of the centered circle contrasts with the continual fluctuation of the cyclical vicissitudes. In *Cynthia's Revels*, Crites exemplifies this ideal figure: he "(like a circle bounded in it selfe) / Contaynes as much, as man in fulnesse may" (V.viii.19–20). Similarly, King James "in his own true circle still doth run, / And holds his course as certain as the sun" (*Oberon*, 11. 269–70). Such a man is impervious to the flux of fortune, as Jonson asserts in his praise of Sir Thomas Roe's "gather'd selfe" (*Epigrammes*, XCVIII, l. 9):

> He that is round within himselfe, and streight,
>   Need seeke no other strength, no other height;
> Fortune upon him breakes her selfe, if ill,
>   And what would hurt his vertue makes it still. (ll. 3–6)

Jonson himself will "dwell as in my Center" (*Under-wood* 49, l. 60), keeping "mine owne fraile Pitcher" (l. 56) from injury by the storms and "waves" (l. 57) that surround him, the dangerous vicissitudes of the corrupt, injurious times. Not that Jonson thinks of virtue as inert. For all his insistence on fixedness and stability, Jonson presents virtue's constancy as itself a strong, forceful act.[28]

Able to repel the assaults of fortune, the virtuous individual at the same time can draw all that is good from the external world to his center of virtue. This center has a magnetic force that orders the world around it. Jonson emphasizes this magnetic quality not only in the movement of the masques, where the king is the ordering center, but also in "To Penshurst" (*Forest* II), where the virtuous lord who "dwells" (l. 102) at home similarly provides the moral and physical center to which all else moves in the poem: "Fat, aged carps . . . runne into thy net" (l. 33); "The earely cherry, with the later plum, / Fig, grape, and quince, each in his time doth come" (ll. 41–42). "All come in, the farmer, and the clowne" (l. 48), even King James and Prince Henry (ll. 76–81). Jonson's conception of true imitation reflects this centripetal movement as the poet draws out the best from other authors, assimilates it, and transforms it into something of his own (*Timber*, ll. 2466–79).

The virtuous, "gather'd" person orders time as well as space, figuratively giving history a pattern that contrasts with the cyclical one Jonson associates with fortune. All the virtuous people of the past are drawn to the good person, as once again he provides the center to which the external world moves. In *Masque of Queens* Jonson brings together eleven queens from the past who were famous for their virtue. All these through their virtue transcended the limitations of time and history and now "live eternised in the House of Fame" (l. 389). But because England's queen contains "all virtues, for which one by one / They were so famed" (ll. 393–94), they have all come to her, "wanting then a head / To form that sweet and gracious pyramid / Wherein they sit" (ll. 394–96). As the pyramid figure suggests, all the best of the past meets in the virtuous person. Jonson often praises his virtuous contemporaries as epitomizing the good people of the past. Allen, the English actor, "contract[s]" all the graces of past actors "in thy selfe" (*Epigrammes*, LXXXIX, ll. 9, 11), and Jonson tells Mary Lady Wroth that if all history and fables had been lost, they could be created again from her (*Epigrammes*, CV). Similarly, King James "cherish[es] every great example / Contracted in yourself" (*Masque of Queens*, ll. 412–13). By contracting the best of the past, the virtuous person becomes greater than each of those who lived before him, and thus Jonson implies a kind of individual moral progress, which contrasts with the cyclical pattern of history. Similarly, as a good poet truly imitating Horace, Martial, and other great classical writers, Jonson incorporates the best of the past into his present work, thus joining the transcendent community of great poets and at the same time hoping to surpass his predecessors' achievements. In a sense, this ideal recalls Bacon's idea of cumulative progress in which a person takes the best of the past and adds to it, but Jonson restricts such progress to the realm of poetry and (possibly) the supremely virtuous person. The centered circle of the good individual, the contracted society composed of good people from all ages, and the virtuous person's ability to epitomize and perhaps even surpass the best of the past provide alternatives to the temporal cycles.

Finally, although virtuous people are themselves superior to fortune, Jonson believes that the poet has the power to raise them even further above the times. Behind Jonson's conviction that the poet's remarkable talent lies in his ability to apotheosize his subjects is his fundamentally antihistorical attitude, his desire to transcend the vicissitudes of time and history.[29] "Envy would hold downe" virtue's fame "in shade / Of Death, and Darknesse" (*Under-wood* 86, 1, ll. 3–5), but the true poet "keepes Vertue up" by immortalizing it in poetry (*Under-wood* 77, l. 152). By praising men and women in his panegyrics, he hopes to keep their virtue constant, unaltered by shifting times and fortune's vicissitudes. Moreover, Jonson typically sets the virtuous person within the context of the corrupt times only to separate him and to raise him well above them. His version of the classical idea of the poet's ability to immortalize his subjects significantly places a greater emphasis on elevation as he promises almost literally to raise them above history:

> It is the *Muse*, alone, can raise to heaven,
>   And, at her strong armes end, hold up, and even,
> The soules, she loves.
>
> *Forest* XII, ll. 41–43; cf. Horace, *Odes*, IV. viii

Apotheosizing his virtuous subjects in his panegyrics and masques, Jonson places them more securely above time, fortune, and death than virtue alone can.

Stoicism as Reaction to History

As has long been recognized, Stoicism forms the basis of Jonson's ethical discrimination between virtue and vice. But what is of special interest is that Stoicism is fundamentally a response to history and, in a sense, a rejection of history, as its exponents in different ages reveal. Emerging from a vision of history as characterized by cyclical flux, vicissitude, calamities, and the prevalence of vice, Stoicism attempts to provide a solution to the cycles for the individual. Zeno, the founder, attempting to liberate himself from what he saw was a "morally debased" age, stressed the importance of being independent from external things—neither desiring them nor being affected by them.[30] Seneca, a later exponent of Stoicism, experienced great fluctuations of fortune in his own life. After a successful career in the Senate, he was banished in Claudius's reign to Corsica for eight years. When he was finally recalled, he again grew in wealth, power, and honor only to be forced to commit suicide when he was charged with involvement in the conspiracy of Piso. Given his own history, Seneca's insistence on the importance of being impervious to the cyclical vicissitudes of fortune gains an added significance. Apparently for him Stoicism was a way of dealing with historical changes over which the individual otherwise had little control. That Stoic ethics is essentially a response to history becomes particularly clear as Seneca presents Cato, "standing erect amid the ruins of the commonwealth," as an example of the true wise man (*De Providentia,* ii.9). Though "all the world has fallen under one man's [Caesar's] sway . . . Cato has a way of escape"; through the final act of suicide he is able to "deliver" himself from "human affairs" (*De Providentia,* i. 10). Suicide exemplifies the ultimate withdrawal from history.[31]

Even Christians for whom suicide was a sin found in Stoic ethics a solution to history. For Lipsius, too, Stoicism provides the proper way of dealing with political upheaval. His *Discourse of Constancy* (1584; translated into English, 1595) is set within the context of the civil war in which his country was engaged. Lipsius desires to flee his country, but his friend Languis advises him to forsake his passions rather than his country, so he may enjoy "*Rest* among *Troubles,* and *Peace* in the midst of *Warre.*"[32] The civil war is simply part of the cyclical pattern of history,[33] and since there is nothing one can do to change this pattern, the only solution is to adopt the Stoic alernative of inner rather than physical withdrawal—to rise above history simply by becoming unconcerned with it. Since cyclical change characterizes everything, the constancy of a person's virtue is the only possible alternative. If he cannot determine his fate, he can at least control the way he faces it. Common to Stoicism in various ages is a sense that the forces of history are beyond human control. And this assumption radically contrasts with Bacon's belief that man can not only mold his fortune but also shape the course of history.

Jonson's Stoicism also seems to be a response to history. He frequently voices his disapproval of the changes he saw in his times: the new money, the decay of hospitality and the old order, and what he believed was the moral corruption of his age.[34] His political conservatism is part of his deeper opposition to change, and he seeks to counter the alterations he sees in his society by maintaining an inner constancy that allows him to rise above all vicissitudes. In spite of his interest in history and his preoccupation with his own times, Jonson often seems indifferent to history and the particularities of contemporary politics.[35] In "An Epistle Answering to One That Asked to be Sealed of the Tribe of Ben" (*Under-wood*

49), which begins with the Stoic idea that "Men that are safe, and sure, in all they doe, / Care not what trials they are put unto" (ll. 1–2), Jonson expresses this indifference:

> What is't to me whether the French Designe
>   Be, or be not, to get the *Val-telline?*
> Or the States Ships sent forth belike to meet
>   Some hopes of *Spaine* in their West-Indian Fleet?
> Whether the Dispensation yet be sent,
>   Or that the Match from *Spaine* was ever meant? (ll. 31–36)

This passage recalls Lipsius's similar queries in his *Discourse:* "Do you think it troubles Me, what *French,* or *Spaniards* are plotting? who *keepes,* or who *loses* the Scepter of *Belgia?* That the Tyrant of *Asia* threatenes us by *Land,* or by *Sea?*" (p. 81). The virtuous person cannot become too involved with such things.

Jonson shares with these Stoic writers the belief in the necessity of rising above, sometimes even withdrawing from, history and the times. He often feels that involvement with the world means contagion by its corruption. In the dramatic monologue "To the World: A Farewell for a Gentlewoman, Vertuous and Noble" (unusual for Jonson in its use of a persona), the speaker rejects the "False world," "resolv'd to tread / Upon thy throate, and live exempt / From all the nets that thou canst spread" (*Forest* IV, ll. 1, 6–8). Although this speaker's *contemptus mundi* attitude may be extreme, it is not very different from the one Jonson expresses in his own voice in the epistle "To Katherine, Lady Aubigny" (*Forest* XIII) when he advises her to "tread" the path of virtue:

> . . . what if alone?
>   Without companions? 'Tis safe to have none.
> In single paths, dangers with ease are watch'd:
>   Contagion in the prease is soonest catch'd. (ll. 55–58)

Such a rejection of the world has a basis in that part of Christianity that emphasizes that people can be saved only by avoiding the lures of the world. This religious view of man's relationship with the temporal world can seem to offer a sanction for Stoic ethics, and thus we find that Jonson's Stoicism characteristically assumes certain Christian values.

The ideal of withdrawing from the corrupt world also underlies the ode "To the Immortall Memorie, and Friendship of that Noble Paire, Sir Lucius Cary, and Sir H. Morison" (*Under-wood* 72). The poem begins with one of the most bizarre examples of the virtuous person's retreat from the calamitous vicissitudes of history. The "Brave Infant of *Saguntum*" (l. 1), "coming forth in that great yeare" (l. 2) when Hannibal razed the town of Saguntum, withdrew into the womb when he saw the horrors of the life he was about to enter. The child's decision to flee from the world was in Jonson's opinion "wise." He left man "a circle . . . Of deepest lore" (ll. 9–10), an example of the proper action of the virtuous man in the corrupt world: "could they but lifes miseries fore-see, / No doubt all Infants would returne like thee" (ll. 19–20). It would at first seem that this example of a literally escapist response is out of place in a poem praising Morison as a soldier and insisting that life should be "measur'd" "by the act" (ll. 21–22). Jonson suggests, however, that such withdrawal from the world is a proper action. In fact, his description of Morison's death implies that it was just as willful a flight from the awful world as the exemplary infant's:

> Hee leap'd the present age,
> Possest with holy rage,
> To see that bright eternall Day. (ll. 79–81)

Stoic ethics blends with the Christian's holy desire to reach heaven. Even a man of action like Morison seems, in Jonson's mind, to be motivated by a desire for permanence, an impulse to transcend the flux of history and its corruption.

Clearly in Jonson there is a strong impulse to retreat from or transcend the cyclical vicissitudes of history. Like the Stoics (and ultimately the Greeks), he radically separates time from eternity and suggests that only the permanent and eternal are to be valued. This antihistorical attitude can find some support in the strain of Christianity that believes the temporal world is a temptation to be resisted, but it has little in common with the orthodox Christian perspective that asserts that history has religious value and that, because of the Incarnation, believes that the eternal intersects and includes the temporal.[36]

Sejanus, too, presents the Stoic ideal of remaining detached from and therefore superior to the vicissitudes of history. The good, virtuous person in this play can only try to remain constant like

Cordus, who is "not moou'd with passion" (III.463), or like Silius, who stands firmly, unshaken by the misfortunes that befall him, and shows his scorn for them by committing suicide. Or the virtuous person can during his lifetime withdraw even further than Cordus and Silius from the political world. Lepidus seems to be Jonson's most exemplary figure in this play, and the "artes" that have "preseru'd" him (IV.290–91) are

> None, but the plaine, and passiue fortitude,
> To suffer, and be silent; never stretch
> These armes, against the torrent; liue at home,
> With my owne thoughts, and innocence about me,
> Not tempting the wolves iawes: these are my artes. (IV.294–98)

In this way he hopes to become invulnerable — not that he will escape being attacked or even killed, but he will not really be harmed since such injuries cannot touch his inner, immortal virtue.

Stoic detachment, however, can seem an inadequate response to corruption. It reflects a defeatist spirit, a sense that the individual is powerless to control the world he lives in. In *Sejanus* withdrawal at times seems a less than satisfactory way of confronting cyclical decline, since it has no reforming effect on the world. But the fate of the virtuous Germanicus family demonstrates that heroic action is no more effective. It, too, does not arrest decline. In seeking to gain power, Nero and Drusus Junior become caught in the cyclical pattern and fall victim to Sejanus's machinations. Jonson presents a dilemma.[37]

In *Catiline* the situation is rather different. Here the virtuous man acts to save his country. It is interesting that Senecan Stoicism dominates *Sejanus*, whereas in the later *Catiline* the emphasis is on Cicero as an active force of virtue. Far from withdrawing from the political corruption, Cicero attempts to stop it. In his own writings Cicero had been rather vehement about the necessity of public action; private withdrawal seemed to him a distinctly inferior reaction.[38] Though he absorbed many Stoic doctrines, he was, in fact, quite critical of Stoic apathy. But Jonson's position in *Catiline* is not clear-cut: he is not simply stating that Stoic apathy is ineffectual and that one must actively combat vice, even if it means resorting to Machiavellian deception, as Cicero indeed does to trap the conspirators. Jonson's admiration of Cicero seems qualified, for the play indicates that Cicero, for all his good intentions, remains blind to Caesar's corruption and involvement in the conspiracy.[39] Cicero refuses to believe that Caesar is part of the corruption that plagues the state, and so, though Catiline is checked, Caesar remains free at the end of the play. Vice is not eradicated, and Jonson relies on our awareness of history to realize that this play represents merely a segment of Roman history—what follows is the continuation of the process of the empire's decline. For all his virtue, Cicero lacks a complete enough vision of the corruption that permeates his age. Perhaps his involvement in the times blinds him somewhat as the pursuit of fortune blinds others, since this involvement makes it impossible for him to attain the comprehensive vision a more detached person who was above the times would have. Any any rate, Jonson's play emphasizes that Cicero is clearly not able to stop the process of cyclical decline.[40]

The Problem of Action: Detachment versus Involvement

Sejanus and *Catiline* thus suggest what is for Jonson a recurrent problem: what kind of action the virtuous person should take in a world given over to vice. Should he withdraw from history and attempt to transcend it? Or should he become involved with the times in trying to reform the vice that characterizes them?[41] This dilemma points to the essential ambivalence of Jonson's attitude toward history. As we have seen, Jonson's poetry repeatedly insists that the wise man must remain stable, untouched by vicissitude, unmoved by the corruption of the world. In *Sejanus* Lepidus's speech, in which he advises that it is best to live at home, not tempting the "wolves iawes," finds its echo in Jonson's own declaration in "An Ode. To Himselfe" (*Under-wood* 25) that he too will retire to remain safe. But despite such emphasis on withdrawal, Jonson at times reveals an underlying discomfort with the transcendence he poses as an ideal. Although like Seneca he asserts the importance of viewing history unconcerned as a *"Spectator"* of the *"Play of Fortune"* (*Timber,* ll. 1106–9; cf. Seneca's *De Constantia,* vi.3 and xiii.5), he also often finds involvement not only necessary but desirable.[42] Jonson's work reveals, I believe, a deep-seated tension between Senecan withdrawal or unconcern and the Ciceronian emphasis on the active public life. In the *Offices* Cicero praises the life of action over that of contemplation, suggesting that even a contemplative man, "absorbed in the investigation and study of creation," should "drop all those problems and cast them aside, if the word were suddenly brought to him of some critical peril to his country, which he could relieve or repel" (I.xliii.154). Political involvement is necessary. Cicero believes that a public life, involved with affairs of state, is superior to the "life of retirement" (I.xxi). Jonson, too, insists on the importance of action, though he usually describes action in moral rather than political terms. Convinced that "all great life" is "exercis'd" in the battle between "vice, and vertue" (*Epigrammes*, CII), he himself is actively engaged in this war as he continually "fewd[s] / With sinne and vice" (*Forest* XIII, ll. 9–10).

The extent of Jonson's involvement in this battle is apparent from the large amount of his work that forms a satirical attack on the corruption in contemporary England. Just as Horace attacked Roman degeneracy in his poetry, so Jonson attacks the prevalence of vice in his own times. But if England is already in the process of cyclical decline, the question arises: can this cycle be stopped and reform effected?

Although his works reveal a strong desire for the restoration of the golden age in which virtue and reason ruled, they do not suggest a great deal of optimism about the possibility of this restoration. Often the golden age seems revived only in select individuals such as Benjamin Rudyerd (*Epigrammes*, CXXII) or Sir Thomas Egerton (*Epigrammes*, LXXIV). His masques are more optimistic, since by incorporating the antimasque into the masque, Jonson can symbolically demonstrate the effective reformation of vice, as imperfection is either destroyed and replaced or transformed into constant virtue (see, for example, *Masque of Queens*). As the very title of *Golden Age Restored* indicates, it is in the masques that the golden age is revived. In *Hymenae* reason controls the four humors and affections: all fall into the figure of the circle whose center is reason (ll. 361–88). In *Love Restored* Plutus, god of money, who is masquerading as the god of love (Cupid), is exposed as an imposter and the true Cupid restored. Jonson's hope is that the moral lessons of the masques will extend beyond the evening's entertainment — that the courtiers and nobles, even the king and queen, will become more virtuous. But although the masques bespeak Jonson's hope for reform in the world, success is still clearly limited to the confines of the fictional world.[43] The masques present an ideal rather than his actual expectations. Since history itself shows that Cicero and Horace were unable to alter the historical pattern of cyclical decline, it appears unlikely that Jonson would be able to arrest it.[44]

If it is not possible to stop the process of decay and effect a reformation, then there is a certain futility in continuing to write satires; and, moreover, the satirist runs the danger of being sullied by the corruption he attacks. In his attacks on vice, Jonson often emphasizes that he is standing far above it, trying to assure us that he retains his purity like the hawk, which provides an example for the good satirist:

> She doth instruct men by her gallant flight,
>   That they to knowledge should toure upright,
> And never stoupe, but to strike ignorance.
>
> *Epigrammes*, LXXXV, ll. 5–7

Nevertheless, in attacking vice the satirist may become so involved with the times that he loses his stable control.[45] In fact, this is what occasionally happens to Jonson in his virulent attacks on Inigo Jones. By criticizing Jones so personally and passionately, he reveals that, unlike the exemplary Crites in *Cynthia's Revels*, he has been moved by the insults of his censurers.[46]

A few late poems, written when Jonson was in poor health and in need of money, reflect a sense that in spite of his Stoic ethics the virtuous poet is indeed dependent upon external, material circumstances. Thanking Charles I for sending him £100 after the poet had been paralyzed by a stroke, Jonson praises the king for trying "To cure the *"Poëts Evill*, Povertie" (*Under-wood* 64, 1.6). His "To the Right Honourable, the Lord High Treasurer of England. An Epistle Mendicant" admits that because of *"Disease"* and *"Want"* his "Muse peepes out" only one day out of a hundred (*Under-wood* 73, ll. 4, 5, 9).[47] In these poems Jonson recognizes, as John Dryden will more fully at the end of the century, that poetry requires a favorable climate to thrive.

Complete withdrawal is not possible for Jonson, but he realizes the limitations and dangers of involvement, as his portrayal of Cicero's partial blindness in *Catiline* suggests. His uneasiness with his involvement in the times becomes particularly apparent in the two odes to himself in which he announces that he will turn away from the stage. In "An Ode. To Himselfe" (*Under-wood* 25), Jonson refuses to be "a Page" any longer "to that strumpet the Stage" (ll. 33–34). He suggests that in writing for the stage he has been seeking popular applause, with which the Stoic should not be concerned. As Cicero had remarked, the wise man who has a proper "exaltation of soul" should "be independent of popular approval" rather than "trying to win applause" (*Tusculan Disputations*, II.xxvi.64). Jonson recognizes he "Should not on fortune pause," since "'Tis crowne enough to vertue still, her owne applause" (ll. 17–18). Not only does drama as an "Image of the times" (*Every Man in His Humour*, "Prologue," l. 23) necessitate involvement with the corrupt times that the wise man should be superior to, but also Jonson seems to realize that, as a dramatist, he has had to depend on the applause of the ignorant mob in a way that a nondramatic poet need not. In order for one's plays to continue to be performed, they must meet with the approval of the audience. For this reason, drama is a rather imperfect instrument for satire. Jonson finds himself in the dilemma of seeking approval from an audience who shares the vices that are being attacked in the plays, and thus who is implicitly being criticized in them. And in depending on popular applause, Jonson is risking the self-sufficiency that he posits as the essential characteristic of the virtuous person. He becomes like those he criticizes for seeking the rewards of fortune: he foolishly depends on what comes through chance and time.[48]

Both "An Ode. To Himselfe" (*Under-wood* 25) and "Ode to Himselfe" (*Uncollected Poetry*, 53) conclude with Jonson moving away from the stage and the corrupt times to a higher kind of poetry concerned with transcendence, the poetry of praise. In his work Jonson typically moves between involvement and transcendence, between satire, which criticizes the times, and panegyric, which is concerned with immortal virtue and exalts the virtuous men and women above the vicissitudes of time and fortune. Perhaps Jonson comes closest to a resolution of this tension between involvement and transcendence in his conception of apotheosis.

In the ode "To the Memory of My Beloved, The Author Mr. William Shakespeare" (*Uncollected Poetry*, 42), he transforms Shakespeare into a star that, significantly, is not only superior to the time's vicissitudes but also can "influence" the times (l. 8). Transformed into a star by the poet, the virtuous man embodies Jonson's ideal, for he is in a fixed, unalterable position—he can never be pulled down into the corruption of the age—yet, at the same time, as a star he can exert an influence upon the times. He can possibly effect a reformation without endangering his constancy, self-sufficiency, or superiority. Moreover, the image of the star suggests the spherical quality that Jonson attributes to the virtuous person who is a centered circle. In "To the Immortall Memorie, and Friendship of . . . Sir Lucius Cary, and Sir H. Morison" (*Under-wood* 72), Jonson similarly stellifies these two virtuous men, but, more important, in this ode he also refers to the poem itself as a constellation, a "bright *Asterisme*" (l. 89). He implies that his own poem is above the vicissitudes of time yet able to affect the times. This stellar position is apparently the one Jonson himself wished to attain as a poet: superior to fortune and history's vicissitudes yet capable of reforming the world.

Notes

1. Jonson mentions the history of Henry V in "An Execration Upon Vulcan" (*Under-wood* 45). For the poems I have used *The Complete Poetry of Ben Jonson*, ed. William B. Hunter, Jr. (New York: Doubleday, 1963); for the plays and prose I have used *Ben Jonson*, ed. C. H. Herford and Percy and Evelyn Simpson, 11 vols. (Oxford: Clarendon Press, 1925–52); and for the masques, my quotations refer to *Ben Jonson: The Complete Masques*, ed. Stephen Orgel (New Haven: Yale University Press, 1969).

2. See Herford and Simpson's "Life of Ben Jonson," in *Ben Jonson*, 1:93.

3. Felix Gilbert, "The Renaissance Interest in History," in *Art, Science, and History in the Renaissance*, ed. Charles Singleton (Baltimore: Johns Hopkins University Press, 1967), pp. 373–87, argues that in the Renaissance history was primarily important as it provided examples for teaching moral philosophy.

4. Studies of Jonson have repeatedly emphasized his interest in history. Edward Partridge, "Jonson's *Epigrammes*: The Named and the Nameless," *SLitI* 6 (1973), 153–98, remarks that Jonson "had an historian's sense of the holiness of fact" (p. 194), and those who have written on *Sejanus* and *Catiline* similarly stress Jonson's respect for history. Perhaps Joseph Allen Bryant, Jr., "*Catiline* and the Nature of Jonson's Tragic Fable," *PMLA* 69 (1954), 265–77, most forcefully describes Jonson's concern with history: "For Jonson, history was an end in itself; it was man's best source of truth outside the realm of supernatural revelation" (p. 275).

5. Manuel, *Shapes of Philosophical History*, p. 9, notes the connection between Roman Stoicism and the cyclical theory of history. On the revival of the cyclical view in the Renaissance, see ibid., pp. 48–69, and Peter

Burke, *The Renaissance Sense of the Past* (London: Edward Arnold, 1969), pp. 87–89.

6. Bodin, *Six Bookes*, p. 406.

7. B. N. De Luna, *Jonson's Romish Plot: A Study of "Catiline" in Its Historical Context* (Oxford: Clarendon Press, 1967), has argued that Jonson saw parallels between Roman and English history, specifically between Catiline's plot and the Gunpowder plot. Angela G. Dorenkamp, "Jonson's *Catiline*: History as the Trying Faculty," *SP* 67 (1970), 210–20, also notes that Jonson shared the "Renaissance faith in historical parallels" (p. 211), but she does not define the "larger issues" that the historical event adumbrates. Neither De Luna nor Dorenkamp has noted that the parallels may have suggested to Jonson that England was also, like Rome, involved in the process of cyclical decline. On Jonson's concern with historical parallels between Rome and England in his two Roman tragedies, see also Annabel Patterson, "'Roman-cast Similitude': Ben Jonson and the English Use of Roman History," in *Rome in the Renaissance: The City and the Myth*, ed. Paul A. Ramsey (Binghamton: Center for Medieval and Early Renaissance Studies, 1982), pp. 381–94.

8. See Jonson's *News from the New World Discovered in the Moon* and *Staple of News*, especially Jonson's address "To the Readers," which precedes Act III, for an attack on his age's concern with news. He felt that much seventeenth-century news was really fiction masquerading as fact.

9. Edward B. Partridge, *The Broken Compass: A Study of the Major Comedies of Ben Jonson* (New York: Columbia University Press, 1958), p. 118, observes that Face is "nothing in himself, but living only in the disguises or 'faces' which he assumes."

10. While masks and disguises are almost always in Jonson's plays associated with vice, the world is so corrupt that sometimes virtue must work disguised in order to be effective. But most often even those who use disguise to expose vice are not truly virtuous. In *Bartholomew Fair* Justice Overdoo is better than most of the other characters in the play, but he is still far from perfect, as is apparent not only in his name but also in his treatment of Grace Welborn as a mere commodity (III.v). In *The Alchemist* Surly, though he uses his Spanish disguise to uncover villainy, is hardly exemplary. Just like the other greedy characters, he desires a fortune; it is simply that he does not believe that Subtle will give it to him. Lovewit, wearing a Spanish cloak, deceives the rather foolish Dame Pliant into thinking she is marrying the Spanish don. Like Surly, Subtle, and Face, he is attracted by her wealth and superficial beauty rather than her virtue. The one place in Jonson's works where supposedly virtuous people wear disguise is in the masques, but here, as Stephen Orgel notes, these masks do not suggest deceit or inconstancy, but rather reflect the person's true identity (*The Jonsonian Masque* [Cambridge, Mass.: Harvard University Press, 1965], p. 117).

11. Seneca, *Epistulae Morales*, trans. Richard M. Gummere, 3 vols. (Cambridge, Mass.: Harvard University Press, 1934), vol. 3. Subsequent quotations of the *Epistles* are from this edition and volume.

12. Arthur F. Marotti, "The Self-Reflexive Art of Ben Jonson's *Sejanus*," *TSLL* 12 (1970), 197–220, has noted that in *Sejanus* role-playing is associated with the villains and is distasteful to the more virtuous characters in the play. Jonas A. Barish, "Jonson and the Loathed Stage," in *A Celebration of Ben Jonson*, ed. William Blissett et al. (Toronto: University of Toronto Press, 1973), pp. 27–53, discusses the foolish characters' addiction to change, mimicry, and metamorphosis as evidence of Jonson's antitheatricality. Alexander Leggatt similarly links the "shape-shifting" of the vicious characters with Jonson's interest in the false worlds created by artist figures in the masques and plays (*Ben Jonson: His Vision and His Art* [London: Methuen, 1981], pp. 13–18).

13. Horace in *Epistles*, I.i.65–69, seems to use "fortune" in a similarly double sense:

> isne tibi melius suadet, qui "rem facias, rem
> si possis, recte, so non, quocumque modo, rem,"
> ut propius spectes lacrimosa poemata Pupi,
> an qui Fortunae te responsare superbae
> liberum et erectum praesens hortator et aptat?

(Does he advise you better, who bids you "make money, money by fair means if you can, if not, by any means money," and all that you may have a nearer view of the doleful plays of Pupius; or he who, an ever present help, urges and fits you to stand free and erect, and defy scornful Fortune?) Horace, *Satires, Epistles, Ars Poetica*, trans. H. Rushton Fairclough, Loeb Classical Library (Cambridge, Mass.: Harvard University Press, 1961). Burke, in *Renaissance Sense of the Past*, remarks that in the sixteenth century "Fortune . . . becomes less and less anthropomorphised, less and less the goddess one must grasp by the forelock, and more of a name for the impersonal forces in history" (p. 77).

14. This symbolism also operates in the epistle "To Elizabeth Countesse of Rutland" (*Forest* XII), where Jonson complains that "all vertue now is sold" for "almightie gold" (ll. 1–2), and throughout *Staple of News*, where Pecunia is described as "the *Venus* of the time" (II.v.34).

15. The image of fortune as a whore appears frequently in Jonson. See *Every Man out of His Humour* I.iii.ll; *A Tale of a Tub* II.v.38–39; and *Staple of News* IV.iii.82.

16. Raleigh, *History of the World*, sig. A2v–A3r; Browne, *Works*, 1:27. Baker, *Race of Time*, pp. 60–66, discusses the way the cyclical view of history was accommodated within a Christian providential scheme: God's providence was seen behind cyclical alteration.

17. Raleigh, *History of the World*, sig. A3r.

18. Robert E. Knoll, *Ben Jonson's Plays: An Introduction* (Lincoln: University of Nebraska Press, 1964), pp. 71–74, places *Sejanus* in the medieval and Renaissance tradition of the rise and fall of great men. The fullest treatments of fortune in this play, however, are Gary D. Hamilton's "Irony and Fortune in *Sejanus*," *SEL* 11 (1971), 265–81, and especially Frederick

Kiefer, *Fortune and Elizabethan Tragedy* (San Marino: Huntington Library, 1983), pp. 271–79.

19. On Jonson's Stoic ethics, see Clarence Beverly Hilberry, *Ben Jonson's Ethics in Relation to Stoic and Humanistic Ethical Thought* (Chicago: University of Chicago Press, 1933), and Isabel Rivers, *The Poetry of Conservatism, 1600–1745: A Study of Poets and Public Affairs from Jonson to Pope* (Cambridge: Rivers Press, 1973), pp. 28–33.

20. Cicero, *Tusculan Disputations*, trans. J. E. King, Loeb Classical Library (Cambridge, Mass.: Harvard University Press, 1966). Subsequent quotations are from this edition.

21. See, e.g., Seneca, *De Constantia* v.4, in *Moral Essays*, trans. John W. Basore, Loeb Classical Library, 3 vols. (Cambridge, Mass.: Harvard University Press, 1958), vol. 1. Subsequent quotations are from this edition and volume.

22. See Seneca, *De Providentia* ii.2–4 and iv.2–3, in *Moral Essays*, vol. 1. Miner, *Cavalier Mode*, pp. 43–99, discusses the ideals of constancy, self-sufficiency, and the *integer vitae* in Cavalier poetry.

23. Cicero, *De Officiis*, trans. Walter Miller, Loeb Classical Library (Cambridge, Mass.: Harvard University Press, 1947).

24. Arthur F. Marotti, "All About Jonson's Poetry," *ELH* 39 (1972), 208–9, suggests that Jonson, despite his pronouncements, actually reveals an attraction to such protean variety and is himself often involved in what Marotti labels "role-playing."

25. Cf. Cicero's remark, "If there is any such thing as propriety at all, it can be nothing more than uniform consistency in the course of our life as a whole and all its individual actions" (*De Officiis*, I.xxxi.111).

26. See Partridge, "Jonson's *Epigrammes*," pp. 190–98, for a discussion of the importance of "naming" in Jonson's poetry. See also Martin Elsky, "Words, Things, and Names: Jonson's Poetry and Philosophical Grammar," in *Classic and Cavalier: Essays on Jonson and the Sons of Ben*, ed. Claude J. Summers and Ted-Larry Pebworth (Pittsburgh: University of Pittsburgh Press, 1982), 91–104. Anne Barton, *Ben Jonson, Dramatist* (Cambridge: Cambridge University Press, 1984), ch. 8, discusses Jonson's handling of characters' names in the comedies.

27. Jonson's insistence in his poems on his single identity contrasts with the masks and disguises that characterize the fools and villains in the plays. As Barish has observed, Jonson's antitheatricality, his hostility to role-playing, is closely linked to his ideal of stasis, his sense that value resides only in the immutable ("Jonson and the Loathed Stage," pp. 27–53).

28. For a discussion of the centered circle in Jonson, see Thomas M. Greene, "Ben Jonson and the Centered Self," *SEL* 10 (1970), 325–48, but the connection between Jonson's concern with the centered circle and his view of history has not been recognized. Richard S. Peterson, *Imitation and Praise in the Poems of Ben Jonson* (New Haven: Yale University Press, 1981), pp. 25–29, argues against what he sees as Greene's over-emphasis on stasis as a supreme value in Jonson. Peterson insists that

Jonson's ideal actually includes both "fixity" and "motion": "Jonson's sympathies were equally divided between the center and the circumference [;] . . . the 'turning,' with its inclusiveness, its rich fullness, its animation, and its hints of transforming power . . . is as important as the 'standing,' the ability to hold fast to one's center" (p. 29). Leggatt, too, has emphasized that Jonson presents virtue as far from inert: it is typically surrounded by adversity against which it must strive (*Ben Jonson*, ch. 4). See also William E. Cain, "Self and Others in Two Poems by Ben Jonson," *SP* 80 (1983), 163–82.

29. Miner, *Cavalier Mode*, pp. 137–46, discusses apotheosis as a "remedy of time." Peterson has argued that Jonson's belief in the poet's ability to raise his subjects "strikingly resembles the figure of History," engraved on the title page of Raleigh's *History of the World*, as she stands, "arms extended upward, raising the world to fame" (p. 50). I would suggest that when Raleigh praises history for its ability to triumph over time, to provide a kind of immortality for man (sig. A2r–A2v), he reveals a desire for transcendence, an antihistorical attitude akin to Jonson's.

30. Eduard Zeller, *The Stoics, Epicureans, and Sceptics*, trans. Oswald J. Reichel (1879; rev. ed. New York: Russell and Russell, 1962), p. 400.

31. For another example of Stoicism as a response to history's vicissitudes, see Seneca's description of Stilbo's constancy when his estate had been plundered, his daughters raped, and his city captured (*De Constantia* v.6–7).

32. Justus Lipsius, *A Discourse of Constancy*, trans. R. G. (London, 1654), p. 3.

33. Ibid., pp. 42–51. The cyclical pattern is "the Eternall Law, from the beginning pass'd upon, and denounc'd to the World, to be *Born*, and *Die; to Rise and Set*" (p. 46). Commonwealths and kingdoms "*begin:* they *Encrease*, they *Stand*, they *Flourish;* and all this, onely that they may fall" (p. 48).

34. See L. C. Knights, *Drama and Society in the Age of Jonson* (1937; rpt. New York: Norton, 1968), especially ch. 7.

35. Miner, *Cavalier Mode*, p. 175, has observed that in his poems Jonson "paid little attention to specific events in their historical aspect. . . . Jonson's view of the times was essentially moral."

36. On how the Christian view of time differs from that of the ancient Greeks, see C. A. Patrides's introduction, in *Aspects of Time*, ed. C. A. Patrides (Toronto: University of Toronto Press, 1976), p. 4; Catherine Rau, "Theories of Time in Ancient Philosophy," in ibid., pp. 21–29; and Baker, *Race of Time*, pp. 54–55. Collingwood, *Idea of History*, pp. 20–21, discusses the antihistorical tendency of Greek thought, which held that only "the permanent" could be "an object of genuine knowledge." But he argues that "the Greek pursuit of the eternal was as eager as it was precisely because the Greeks themselves had an unusually vivid sense of the temporal" (p. 22). Much the same could be said of Jonson.

37. Marvin L. Vawter, "The Seeds of Virtue: Political Imperatives in Jonson's *Sejanus*," *SLitI* 6 (1973), 41–60, argues that Jonson is criticizing

Stoic apathy. It seems, however, that although there are some implicit suggestions of the inadequacy of Stoic apathy, Jonson in large part adopts the moral perspective of his source, Tacitus, who, as Collingwood suggests (*Idea of History*, pp. 39–40), shares with Stoic philosophy "the assumption that the good man cannot conquer or control a wicked world" but can only learn "how to preserve himself unspotted from its wickedness."

38. See *De Officiis* I.xxi; II.i.

39. Although C. G. Thayer, *Ben Jonson: Studies in the Plays* (Norman: University of Oklahoma Press, 1963), sees Cicero as "designed to be a genuinely sympathetic character and a model statesman as well" (p. 118), other critics have noted that Jonson's praise for Cicero is qualified. See Bryant, "*Catiline* and the Nature of Jonson's Tragic Fable"; Michael J. C. Echeruo, "The Conscience of Politics and Jonson's *Catiline*," *SEL* 6 (1966), 341–56; and Dorenkamp, "Jonson's *Catiline*."

40. George K. Hunter, in "A Roman Thought: Renaissance Attitudes to History Exemplified in Shakespeare and Jonson," in *An English Miscellany, Presented to W. S. Mackie*, ed. Brian S. Lee (London: Oxford University Press, 1977), pp. 93–115, concludes that *Sejanus* and *Catiline*, in contrast to Shakespeare, show that the large forces of history defeat the individual.

41. Robert C. Jones, "The Satirist's Retirement in Jonson's 'Apologetical Dialogue'," *ELH* 34 (1967), 447–67, detects in Jonson "the ambivalence of an author who wants to claim, on the one hand, that his art is too lofty to affect that bawd the world, and, on the other, that he can transform the world with his art" (p. 465). Gabriele Bernhard Jackson, *Vision and Judgement in Ben Jonson's Drama* (New Haven: Yale University Press, 1968), notes a tension between Jonson's belief that his poetry should "suit the times" to communicate and his sense that his moral insight might be compromised in the process (pp. 51–52). Leggatt has observed that "while [Jonson] is sometimes attracted by the idea of retreat from the world, he also has a powerful impulse to go on fighting" (*Ben Jonson*, pp. 142–43). Such tensions as Jones, Jackson, and Leggatt describe reflect Jonson's ambivalent attitude toward history.

42. Jonson criticism usually emphasizes Jonson's belief in the poet's important responsibility to society. E.g., Paul M. Cubeta, "A Jonsonian Ideal: 'To Penshurst,'" *PQ* 42 (1963), 14–24, comments, "The fact that most of Ben Jonson's non-dramatic poetry is social verse reveals how seriously he took the responsibility of the artist toward his community" (p. 14).

43. The limit of Jonson's hope is recognized by Orgel (*Jonsonian Masque*), who concludes his discussion of "Pleasure Reconciled to Virtue" with the observation that "Jonson the masque writer retains the sensibility of a satirist. . . . Before our eyes now, the scene 'closeth, and is a Mountaine againe, as before.' All the masque can do, Jonson seems to say, is to offer a moment in which a vision of an ideal becomes a poetic and dramatic experience—becomes, in other words, a reality" (p. 185).

44. Jackson, *Vision and Judgement*, p. 163, and Alvin B. Kernan, "Al-

chemy and Acting: The Major Plays of Ben Jonson," *SLitI* 6 (1973), 1–22, have noted Jonson's general pessimism about change. This pessimism perhaps accounts for the rather static quality Knoll (*Ben Jonson's Plays*) finds characteristic of the plays, for all their apparent bustle: especially in the early and middle plays "the major characters do not learn from their experience" (p. 8); and in most of the plays "there is no development of character, situation, or philosophy. There is, rather, the exposition of a settled philosophic system" (p. 9).

45. J. A. Bryant, Jr., *The Compassionate Satirist: Ben Jonson and His Imperfect World* (Athens: University of Georgia Press, 1972), especially pp. 30–37, argues that the satirist in the plays typically runs the risk of succumbing to pride in his attacks on the vice of others.

46. Jonas A. Barish, *Ben Jonson and the Language of Prose Comedy* (Cambridge, Mass.: Harvard University Press, 1960), pp. 87–88, has observed a "buried" tension in Jonson, who "cannot, like the Stoic he longs to be, remain indifferent to the vicissitudes of fortune. He cannot despise the acclaim or the scorn of others; he exults in approval and smarts painfully under criticism."

47. John Lemly, "Masks and Self-Portaits in Jonson's Late Poetry," *ELH* 44 (1977), 248–66, recognizes that in these poems Jonson no longer maintains the tone of detachment that characterizes his earlier works.

48. L. A. Beaurline, *Jonson and Elizabethan Comedy* (San Marino: Huntington Library, 1978) ch. 1, has argued that although Jonson ultimately loathed the stage, "he came to see the need to accommodate his audience" (p. 34). Such accommodations, though necessary, lessen the distance between the poet and the imperfect world that is the object of satire, and thus they threaten to contaminate the poet and his moral visions.

CHAPTER V

Robert Herrick: "Repullulation" and the Cyclical Order

What though my Harp, and Violl be
Both hung upon the Willow-tree?
What though my bed be now my grave,
And for my house I darknesse have?
What though my healthfull dayes are fled,
And I lie numbred with the dead?
Yet I have hope, by Thy great power,
To spring; though now a wither'd flower.

"To God, on his sicknesse," N-84

THROUGHOUT SO MUCH OF *Hesperides* (1648) the spirit of play and fancy reigns that it might seem overly serious to talk about Robert Herrick's view of history. The very brevity and self-conscious lightness of many of his lyrics; his fanciful, mythological explanations of such things as "How Roses Came Red"; his seemingly voyeuristic descriptions of his mistresses' legs, breasts, clothes; the tendency of Herrick's persona at times to present his poems as a delightful respite from the unpleasant and crude realities of life—all these qualities might lead us to think that Herrick would not be very interested in the larger, weighty problems of history. But as some recent criticism has begun to suggest, Herrick's poetry is more importantly and subtly concerned with (and indeed a reaction to) the pressures of contemporary history than has been previously believed. Some poems directly address the political situation.[1] In others, Herrick's celebration of art, imagination, and anacreontic pleasures often constitutes an implicit response to the patterns and problems of time and history that he perceives. Much of the special quality of Herrick's poetry comes from the interplay between the seemingly light or even frivolous tone or pose of many poems and Herrick's quite serious concern with the pattern of time—a concern that is pervasive and especially striking when his entire collection of poems is viewed as a whole.

As a "son of Ben," Herrick shares Jonson's belief that the pattern of time and history is cyclical, but his attitude toward the cycles is quite unlike his mentor's. Jonson associates the cycles with the recurrence of vice and with the political/moral degeneration that is the consequence of people's allowing themselves to be swayed by passions rather than reason. But Herrick typically sees in the cycles order rather than disorder. His sense of the pattern of time reflects his feeling for the progress of the seasons—the movement from spring through summer to autumn and winter and the renewal of the process with the return of spring. In its recurrent cycles history exemplifies the seasonal pattern, and the individual's life, too, follows the natural order, progressing from the spring of youth to winter and death. The seasonal cycles link nature, history, and man.

But despite his participation in this cycle, man lacks the inherent capacity to renew, which nature and even history manifest. Whereas Jonson tends to regard the cycles of time with either disdain or hostility, Herrick finds that in a sense the cyclical order embodies an ideal, since it is an assurance of regeneration. Seeking the renewal that nature denies to the individual, Herrick turns to art and religion, which alone offer people the chance for a second spring.

History and the Cycles of Nature

Herrick reflects the Renaissance inclination to assume a correspondence between the realms of history and nature, to see history, in a sense, as part of the natural world. For John Donne, the decay of nature finds its parallel in the process of degeneration that he believes history records. But Herrick sees a different pattern uniting nature and history. Because his view of history is so intertwined with his view of nature, we must examine both in order to understand more fully his attitude toward time.

Hesperides reveals an especially close relationship between human beings and nature.[2] Cherries grow on Julia's lips (H-53) and roses in her cheeks (H-45 and H-295).[3] Adolescent boys and girls bud like plants (H-178), and Herrick's dainty mistresses are flowers—

"a *Tulip*," "a lovely *July-flower*," "a sparkling *Rose* i'th'bud" (H-216). These maidens share not only the beauty but also the fragility of these flowers. In much the same way as Herrick's men and women embody certain attributes of plants, especially flowers, so nature typically assumes human characteristics in his poetry. Violets are poor, neglected "Girles," "Maids of Honour" who wait upon the spring (H-205). Like people, roses need funeral rites (H-686). Herrick frequently finds a sympathy between man and nature. If Sappho becomes sick and "droop[s]" like a flower, "Lillies will languish; Violets look ill; / Sickly the Prim-rose: Pale the Daffadill" (H-118). When Julia recovers from her illness, roses, violets, and primroses are similarly resurrected (H-9). The strength of Herrick's identification with this natural world is clear in his instruction to his namesake, *"Robin Red-brest,"* to write his epitaph: *"Here, here the Tomb of Robin Herrick is"* (H-50).

What links human beings to the plants and flowers is the natural, cyclical order that governs all life. Each human life parallels the seasons of the year, and soon "Growes old with the yeere, / That dyes with the next *December*" (H-534). As Herrick warns a proud lady who despises him for his gray hairs, in old age the "Rose-bud" no longer will bloom in her cheek; she too will "weare / Such frost and snow upon her haire" (H-164A). Such descriptions are not unusual in Cavalier *carpe diem* poetry, which typically assumes that human life follows the same cycle as the seasons. Thomas Carew's "To A. L. Persuasions to Love" reminds a reluctant mistress that when her "Summer's done" (l. 48), her hair will grow "white and cold as Winter's snow" (l. 40); "in the cheek, chin, nose, / No lily shall be found nor rose" (ll. 43–44).[4] We briefly flourish in our spring only "to languish and decay" like "these Garden-glories" that are our "Flowrie-sweet resemblances" (H-522). Because of this "resemblance" or correspondence, Herrick frequently reads in the "leaves" of nature's book lessons about man.[5] The blossoms that fall from the tree are

> . . . lovely Leaves, where we
> May read how soon things have
> Their end, though ne'r so brave.
>
> *"To Blossoms,"* H-467

The lessons he discovers are characteristically those of transience and death. "We have as short a Spring" as the "Daffadills"—"As

quick a growth to meet Decay" (H-316). Herrick tells young virgins
to learn of their frailty by looking at "Bright Tulips" whose "Fading-
time do's show, / That Ye must quickly wither" (H-493). He is like
a tree, and the loss of one of his fingers ("One of the five straight
branches of my hand") reminds him of his approaching death:
"First dyes the Leafe, the Bough next, next the Tree" (H-565).
All are subject to the same inexorable process of time.

Part of the classical view of time's cyclical pattern that Herrick,
like Jonson, adopts is the notion that the temporal process is characterized by vicissitude and the succession of opposites.[6] As he says
to Corinna, such change is the essence of life:

> You have changes in your life,
> Sometimes peace, and sometimes strife:
> You have ebbes of face and flowes,
> As your health or comes, or goes;
> You have hopes, and doubts, and feares
> Numberlesse, as are your haires.
> You have Pulses that doe beat
> High, and passions lesse of heat.
> You are young, but must be old.
>
> *"The Changes to* Corinna," H-232

The seasonal change from youth to age, from spring to autumn,
is part of the general pattern of vicissitude, of cyclical "ebbes" and
"flowes." As the harvest succeeds planting, so labor is followed by
pleasure that makes "paine" "spring againe" (H-250). Herrick's
attitude toward change and vicissitude distinguishes him sharply
from Jonson, for whom vicissitude constitutes a threat to the virtuous person whose stability and constancy are clearly set in opposition to such changes. But in Herrick's view, vicissitude is neither
chaotic nor evidence of mere chance. Quite the contrary, it is
orderly and gives a certain stability to the temporal processes and
to human life. As Louis Le Roy observed, everything in the world
is "conserued" by "contraries" whose alteration provides a healthy
balance and sometimes even a kind of pleasure: "The sweetnesse
of the Springtime is more esteemed by the sharpenesse of Winter;
the happinesse of peace, by the calamities of warre; and faire weather
after long rayne."[7]

All things are subject to cyclical change: the person who is "most
fortunate" in the morning will be "in poore estate" in the evening

(H-583). Unlike Jonson, Herrick recognizes that the rotation of the temporal wheel of fortune may itself be a source for qualified optimism:

> Times bad
> And sad
> Are a turning:
> And he
> Whom we
> See dejected;
> Next day
> Wee may
> See erected.
> *"Anacreontike,"* H-993

As fair weather follows foul in the natural order of things, good events succeed bad. In *An Apologie of the Power and Providence of God,* George Hakewill had found that the cyclical pattern of time could provide consolation to those whose fortunes had fallen: men should not "cast away all hope, and fall to despaire," since "private families" as well as nations "haue their seasons and appointed times of returning againe."[8] For Herrick, too, vicissitude gives cause for hope that just as "Clouds will not ever powre down raine," so unfortunate times will not last forever (H-725). Thus he consoles the bishop of Lincoln that his present miseries are part of the cycle, like the night that alternates with day:

> Never did Moone so ebbe, or seas so wane,
> But they left Hope-seed to fill up againe.
> So you, my Lord, though you have now your stay,
> Your Night, your Prison, and your Ebbe; you may
> Spring up afresh; when all these mists are spent,
> And Star-like, once more, guild our Firmament.
> *"Upon the Bishop of* Lincolne's *Imprisonment,"* H-146A

Symbolized by the ebb and flow of the moon and seas, this succession or alternation of opposites insures that in people's lives, too, there is always hope that their ill fortune will improve, and they will "Spring up afresh" after their miseries.

Jonson seeks to become unaffected by the cycles, but Herrick's acceptance of this natural order leads him to advise a grief-stricken lady to stop mourning for her husband on the grounds that it is

141

unnatural to grieve without end (H-259). Though her cheeks have been "long drown'd with sorrows raine," she should "now appeare / Like to the peeping-spring-time of the yeare." Since to continue grieving beyond the proper season would be to violate the natural order, her winter must give way to spring: "Upon your cheek sate *Ysicles* awhile; / Now let the Rose raigne like a Queene, and smile."

This sensitivity to the natural cycle of the seasons shapes Herrick's view of history. As he suggests in his comment on the succession of kings, history follows a cyclical pattern analogous to that of the seasons and the rotation of the day: "As oft as Night is banish'd by the Morne, / So oft, we'll think, we see a King new born" (H-80). His tendency to see history in the larger context of nature recalls the assumptions of Jean Bodin, Sir Walter Raleigh, and Hakewill, but most notably Le Roy, who began his history of the great empires by describing the "successiue alteration" of all things in the universe: "The Sunne . . . who rising and setting maketh the day and the night, by coming towards vs, and going from vs, causeth the yeres continually to be renewed, and . . . doth distinguishe . . . the fower Seasons of the sommer and winter, of the spring and harvest: In the which consisteth the vicissitude of life and death, and the change of all thinges."[9]

Because the cyclical pattern is repeated throughout the various ages, Herrick is inclined to find parallels between himself and men of former ages. Indeed, his many biblical and classical allusions reveal his sense of the similarity between his own situation and that of others in the past. *"His Lachrimæ or Mirth, turn'd to mourning"* (H-371) recalls Jeremiah's grief at the captivity of the Jews: "The joy of our heart is ceased; our dance is turned into mourning" (Lamentations 5:15). The implication is that Herrick's banishment into the "loathed West" is like the Jews' exile from Jerusalem. Before he was banished, he "co'd rehearse / A Lyrick verse," but now time

> Has laid, I see
> My Organ fast asleep;
> And turn'd my voice
> Into the noise
> Of those that sit and weep.

Not only does this change in Herrick's life remind him of the Jews' exile and the vicissitude that characterizes all life in general, but also these lines echo Job 30:31 ("My harp also is *turned* to mourning, and my organ into the voice of them that weep"). Like Job, Herrick is a good, righteous man who has been visited by cruel afflictions. But the historical parallel may also offer him some hope for an end to his grief. In accordance with the general pattern of the succession of opposites, Job's misery was eventually succeeded by joy. Perhaps after all these tribulations, Herrick's life too will end happily.

Through his allusions, Herrick will sometimes suggest both biblical and classical parallels within the same poem. His outraged attack on the "warty incivility" of Dean-bourn (H-86) incorporates Cicero's invective against Catiline and Jeremiah's bitter castigation of the sin-hardened people of Jerusalem who refused to receive the Lord's "correction" and return to Him (Jeremiah 5:3).

> O men, O manners; Now, and ever knowne
> To be *A Rockie Generation!*
> A people currish; churlish as the seas.

These allusions suggest that Herrick is disturbed by more than mere lack of breeding or manners; his countrymen's "incivility" includes corruption and sinfulness. Herrick presents himself as the new Cicero or Jeremiah of his age, attacking the corruption that surrounds him just as they did in the past. The cyclical nature of history forms a bond between past and present and allows Herrick to draw on classical as well as Hebraic wisdom.

Herrick's conception of the cyclical pattern of history specifically informs his interpretation of the Civil War. History is essentially an extension of nature in the realm of human affairs, exemplifying the same cyclical pattern as the seasons. Consequently, the Civil War is not for Herrick an example of chaotic disorder, but rather part of the natural order. He sees the Civil War and Charles I's virtual loss of his throne as exemplifying the cyclical vicissitudes that govern history. But because history follows the seasonal pattern of nature, Herrick hopes that the war will not last — peace will eventually return, and Charles I will be restored to the throne. Vicissitude and the cycles are sources of hope for Herrick, not despair.

His poem *"Farwell Frost, or welcome the Spring"* (H-642) clearly reveals the extent to which he views this war in natural terms. The renewal of spring after a violent, destructive winter promises that peace will naturally succeed war. Herrick describes the north wind in military terms as the *"Northern Plunderer"* who has stripped the "trees, and Fields, to their distresse, / Leaving them to a pittied nakednesse." But despite the ravages of this winter season, spring has come again, just as after a "frantick Storme" there "succeeds a breeze / That scarcely stirs the nodding leaves of Trees." It seems as certain that peace will be restored as that spring has followed winter.

> So when this War (which tempest-like doth spoil
> Our salt, our Corn, our Honie, Wine, and Oile)
> Falls to a temper, and doth mildly cast
> His inconsiderate Frenzie off (at last)
> The gentle Dove may, when these turmoils cease,
> Bring in her Bill, once more, *the Branch of Peace.*

Thus Herrick has faith that Charles may regain his rightful rule. Though the land is "Sick . . . to'th'heart" in this war, he hopes that "that golden Age" will "come again, / And *Charles* here Rule, as he before did Raign" (H-612).

Richard Lovelace's suggestively political poem "The Grasshopper" also describes the Civil War in terms of the seasonal cycle, but this poem offers an interesting contrast to Herrick's *"Farwell Frost"* in the attitude that the poet takes to the cycles of history. The tranquil summer in which the grasshopper flourished, symbolic of the period of Charles I's reign before the war, has now given way to winter. The "Sharp frosty fingers" (l. 15) and winter storms recall Herrick's metaphors in *"Farwell Frost."*[10] But although the cycle of the seasons provides Lovelace with an analogy for England's recent political history, unlike Herrick he does not find consolation in the return of spring. Rather than suggesting that the storms of winter will eventually be replaced by a verdant spring, he turns instead to friendship that will create a lasting summer that contrasts with the transient one of nature.

> Thou best of men and friends! we will create
> A genuine summer in each other's breast,
> And spite of this cold Time and frozen Fate,
> Thaw us a warm seat to our rest. (ll. 21–24)

In his attitude toward the cycles Lovelace is closer to Jonson than to Herrick, since he seeks an alternative to what he sees as threatening cyclical vicissitude. The grasshopper, swinging "upon the waving hair / Of some well-filled oaten beard" (l. 1), is caught up in the cycles and thus is a victim of them. In contrast, Lovelace distances himself from the natural and political vicissitudes, creating with his friend a perpetual summer, an "everlasting day" (l. 36), and a private kingdom that is not subject to the cyclical changes of day and night or of the seasons.

One of the most interesting ramifications of these poets' placing the Civil War within the cyclical pattern is that the enemy—the rebels who are attacking the divine right of Charles I to rule—become as much a part of the natural order as Charles I himself and the traditions he stands for. Despite the seeming disorder of the war, the devastation England has experienced is like the winter storms that trees and fields undergo each year before the coming of spring. By drawing a parallel between the ravaging force of the enemy and that of the north wind, Herrick emphasizes that the Puritan rebellion is an integral (even essential?) part of the natural order rather than a violation of it. This view does much to undermine the conventional belief that since the monarch is divinely appointed, any attempt at revolution is a sin. Because the king and his rule are subject to the temporal cycles, there can be no assurance of permanent Royalist rule. Even if Charles I were restored to his throne, he could not hope to retain his power continuously. Though Herrick and Lovelace were staunch Royalists, their views of history sharply qualify the Royalist assumption of the king's divine right to rule, for once the king is placed within this particular cyclical order, revolution becomes natural and indeed perhaps expected.

Like ordinary people, even like Herrick himself, kings are part of nature—mere trees that are subject to the natural cycle of life leading to death.

> ALL *things decay with Time:* The Forrest sees
> The growth, and down-fall of her aged trees:
> That Timber tall, which three-score *lusters* stood
> The proud *Dictator* of the State-like wood:
> I meane (the Soveraigne of all Plants) the Oke
> Droops, dies, and falls without the cleavers stroke.
>
> "All *things* decay and die," H-69

Ultimately there is little difference between the "Soveraigne" (the rightful, true king) and the *"Dictator"* (the tyrant or usurper of the throne). The fall from power or death comes naturally to all. In this curiously prophetic poem (Charles I was killed the year after *Hesperides* appeared), Herrick implies that violence and the execution of the king do not really violate the natural order but only precipitate the end that would eventually come about in the due course of time.[11]

Because the Civil War is part of the cyclical order of history, Herrick does not consider it unique but finds parallels between it and historical events in the past. Herrick sees Prince Charles arriving at Exeter (H-756) as a new Sulla, who promises to conquer the populace army just as the Roman leader did during the civil war in his time. Similarly, when the king comes to Hampton Court, the poet addresses him as *"Great Cesar,"* *"Great Augustus"* (H-961), in the hope that he will bring peace to England as his Roman counterpart did to his own country. And to insure a like success, Herrick promises to reenact the classical rituals, offering to sacrifice "a thousand thighes / Of Beeves."

Herrick's belief that the Civil War is part of the cyclical pattern of history includes a sense that Divine Providence may be behind this war. In *"Farwell Frost, or welcome the Spring"* (H-642) not only does he place the war within the context of the succession of the seasons, but through biblical allusions he also implies that the Civil War is actually a punishment for the sins of England. Having spoiled "Our salt, our Corn, our Honie, Wine, and Oile," it has brought about the very devastation that God had promised would afflict the Israelites if they served false gods.

> And it shall come to pass, if ye shall hearken diligently unto my commandments which I command you this day, to love the *Lord* your God, and to serve him with all your heart and with all your soul, That I will give *you* the rain of your land in his due season, the first rain and the latter rain, that thou mayest gather in thy corn, and thy wine, and thine oil. . . . Take heed to yourselves, that your heart be not deceived, and ye turn aside, and serve other gods, and worship them; And *then* the *Lord's* wrath be kindled against you, and he shut up the heaven, that there be no rain, and that the land yield not her fruit; and *lest* ye perish quickly from off the good land which the *Lord* giveth you.
>
> Deuteronomy 11:13–14, 16–17

This providential explanation of the war is strengthened by the poem's concluding reference to the dove that brought the olive branch of peace after Noah's flood, for the implicit comparison of the war to the Flood suggests that this war too constitutes God's punishment of sin. In keeping with his faith in the alternation of opposites as well as with his sense of the parallel, Herrick hopes that God will eventually restore peace as He did in the past. Behind the cycles of history, the seasons, and the vicissitudes of God-created nature lies a providential order.[12]

In *"Upon the troublesome times"* (H-596), however, Herrick seems much less optimistic about the restoration of peace, for he fears the cycle will not renew. These "Times most bad" are

> Without the scope
> Of hope
> Of better to be had!

Although they have survived "Some storms," he fears that this is the final one from which there is no escape:

> . . . we must all
> Down fall,
> And perish at the last.

Perhaps this is not just another war, another instance of the vicissitudes that characterize history, but rather the Apocalypse in which all will perish. What Herrick seems to fear most is that there will be no renewal.

Promises of Renewal: Ceremony and Poetry

Herrick's poetry is preoccupied with the problem of renewal and the continuation of the cycle. As we have seen, Sir Francis Bacon finds the cyclical pattern of history a result (and an image) of sinful error, and he seeks to replace the cycles with progress. Jonson similarly associates the cycles with vice and corruption. Despairing of man's ability to change the course of history, he tries to transcend the cycles and become unaffected by them. Herrick's attitude, however, is much closer to that of Hakewill, Le Roy, or Browne, who see in cyclical vicissitudes a confirmation of God's order in the universe. Herrick's poems reveal an acceptance of cyclical flux, of war and pain, even of death; and, consequently, his impetus toward transcendence is not nearly as strong as Jonson's. Indeed, Herrick is far more concerned with insuring the renewal of the cycles than with escaping them. As Thomas Whitaker so rightly has recognized, art for Herrick "offers momentary imaginative transcendence of the temporal—that life may spring again. The escape of art leads back to the world of nature."[13]

This desire to perpetuate the cyclical order lies behind Herrick's emphasis on ritual and ceremony. Most of Herrick's ceremonial poems are linked to or commemorate a part of the cycle, and they usually assume an awareness of the larger process. "Corinna's *going a Maying*" (H-178) celebrates spring as a time of renewal, rebirth, fertility; and the speaker urges Corinna to participate in this natural order, just as the birds and flowers and the rest of nature do. As usual, Herrick's concern with spring and youth takes account of the rest of the process including death. The cycle can no more be stopped than the sun can be arrested in its progress through the day. Even in May and in youth, Herrick reminds us that we are decaying and that night comes on apace.[14] His interest in this poem is not that we (like Donne) stop time or (like Jonson) transcend it, but that we participate in its cycle. Similarly, "*The Hock-Cart, or Harvest home*" (H-250) sets the rites of harvest within the context of the seasonal cycle. These rites are essentially linked to the renewal of the spring. Just as the harvest leads on to the renewal of the cycle with the next spring, so the festivity is for the purpose of enabling the labor to "spring againe." In order to insure that the cyclical process will continue, it is important that these rituals be properly performed with an awareness of their meaning.[15]

Even his many ceremonies concerning death treat it as part of the natural order, the cycle of life. His rites for burial are based on an acceptance of death as part of nature, as much a part of it as birth or marriage is. And although in *Hesperides* Herrick typically refrains from offering Christian promises of an afterlife, the flowers strewn on the graves (H-912) and the tears he asks the virgins to shed, which will cause the flowers to "flourish" (H-343), perhaps bespeak a hope latent in these poems that man as a flower will also renew, if these rites are properly performed. Meanwhile, the ceremonies must be carried out so the ghost will rest calmly. Invoking the classical commonplace, he asks the earth to rest lightly on the corpse, as if it were only sleeping until the proper time to awake.

The numerous "sacrifice" poems that appear throughout *Hesperides* are also linked to Herrick's cyclical concerns, for they represent his interest in keeping the cycle going. The speaker in these poems promises to give sacrifices to the "gods" if they will bless him with gifts or protect him from harm (see, for example, H-302, H-303, H-325, and H-360). Such sacrifices are not merely thanks for divine aid but in a sense insurance that it will continue. Herrick's concern with these ceremonial sacrifices is a recognition that the renewal of life and its cycles depends on God, regardless of whether He is conceived of monotheistically or polytheistically. There is a necessary reciprocity: we must offer good things to the gods so that we will receive benefits in return. As Herrick explicitly states in *His Noble Numbers:*

> Gods Bounty, that ebbs lesse and lesse,
> As men do wane in thankfulnesse.
> "Gods Bounty," N-76

Just as Herrick performs sacrifices to insure renewal and the continuation of life, so he invokes charms to ward off evil. These charms often seem to be merely primitive folk superstitions—a curious mixture of folk, pagan, and Christian. One *"Spell"* (H-769) uses "Holy Water" and "the *Saints-Bell*" as well as "Sacred Spittle," meal, and oil. Similarly, his *"Ceremony upon Candlemas Eve"* (H-980) incorporates folk superstitions into a Christian festival.

Indeed, the poems throughout *Hesperides* show an interesting mingling of classical or pagan and Judaeo-Christian elements.[16] For example, King Charles I is described within the same poem as both Caesar and a type of Christ (H-161). Herrick's recurrent definition of man as a flower or plant whose fragile life is very brief probably has a biblical as well as a classical source.[17] And his insistence in *"To be merry"* (H-806) on seizing the pleasures of today combines echoes of Solomon with the traditional *carpe diem* theme:

> Lets now take our time;
> While w'are in our Prime;
> And old, old Age is a farre off:
> For the evill evill dayes

> Will come on apace;
> Before we can be aware of.

The final lines of this poem present an interesting adaptation of Ecclesiastes 12:1 ("Remember now thy Creator in the days of thy youth, while the evil days come not, nor the years draw nigh, when thou shalt say, I have no pleasure in them"). Transforming the original passage by placing it in the seemingly alien context of a *carpe diem* poem, Herrick seems to imply that enjoying this life and its pleasures *is* remembering God.[18] His sense of religion is hardly ascetic.

In "Corinna's *going a Maying*" (H-178), biblical allusions, "Mattens," and "Beads" keep company with Aurora, Flora, and Titan, and Herrick stresses the naturalness of this relationship. Again, *"The Sacrifice, by way of Discourse betwixt himselfe and* Julia" (H-870) combines classical, Hebraic, and Christian elements in the ritual. As in the ancient Hebrew religion, a "holy Beast" is offered for a "Trespasse-offering," but the participants in this ceremony wear Christian "Surplices," and the sacrifice is offered to "the gods" rather than to the Judaeo-Christian God who is one. Similarly, Herrick's prayer *"To the Genius of his house"* (H-723) is addressed to a classical, pagan genius, but the blessing of "living water" he asks for recalls the gift Christ said God would give: "he would have given thee living water" (John 4:10).

Herrick is typically eclectic, and the basis for his eclecticism is, I suggest, his belief that all these religions share a sense of the cyclical order, which their rituals affirm and seek to perpetuate. Furthermore, the cyclical nature of history — that various civilizations and religions in different times have similarly perceived this order — allows Herrick to draw parallels. The cyclical pattern links present and past, classical and Christian. Although he is certainly aware of the differences among these religions, he emphasizes their basic similarity and harmony — whether pagan, Jewish, or Christian, all recognize the fundamental order of the universe. This order, Herrick insists, is essentially religious. As "Corinna's *going a Maying*" makes clear, to ban or outlaw what are essentially religious celebrations of the natural, God-created order (as the Puritans did when they outlawed "pagan" celebrations and "papist" rituals) is a sin. In this sense, much of *Hesperides* should be seen as a subtle attack on what Herrick believed were the tendencies and values of Puritanism in seventeenth century England.[19]

These ceremonies commemorating or insuring the continuation of the cyclical process reveal Herrick's basic acceptance of the cyclical order of time. In contrast to Jonson, Herrick insists on his involvement in this process, for the order provides a certain stability and comfort. What most disturbs Herrick is the ending of the cycle. Both nature and history manifest a cyclical pattern of regeneration: winter gives way to spring; the disorder of war is succeeded by a restoration of peace and a renewal of life. But human beings, though they experience cyclical changes, have only one cycle of life. It is for this reason that Herrick advises them to seize the pleasures of the day:

> Let us now take time, and play,
> Love, and live here while we may;
> . . . .
> For, once dead, and laid i' th 'grave,
> No return from thence we have.
>
>   "*To* Sappho," H-691

Such poems as these do not really deny a spiritual immortality to human beings. Rather they are primarily concerned with *this* life and with the pleasures of the natural world, and Herrick's regret is for the individual's inability to renew naturally and to continue to enjoy life. In nature decay is inevitable, but so is renewal. In this respect nature's general pattern represents an ideal. The land revives in the spring; the moon and the seas "wain; / But they fill up their Ebbs again" (H-336). By contrast, man like "a Lilly lost" "Nere can repullulate, or bring / His dayes to see a second Spring." He is cut off from this natural renewal. In "To A. L. Persuasions to Love," Carew similarly distinguishes between human beings with their single cycle and other things in nature, which have a capacity for renewal:

> The snake each year fresh skin resumes,
> And eagles change their aged plumes;
> The faded rose each Spring receives
> A fresh red tincture on her leaves:
> But if your beauties once decay,
> You never know a second May. (ll. 73–78)

Ironically, most of the flowers to which Herrick compares men and women are perennial flowers—tulips, roses, violets, daffodils, even lilies—and there is a disturbing discrepancy between the poet's insistence on the seeming finality of the flower's death and his choice of such flowers.[20] Although the individual lily or rose dies, another springs up in its place the next year. The same might be said of human beings, but curiously Herrick refrains from offering this consolation. Perhaps because he himself never married and never had children, Herrick does not suggest that a person can find "a second Spring" through procreation, though such an extension of life could be seen as analogous to the regeneration inherent in perennial flowers. Moreover, figurative renewal through progeny does not adequately compensate for personal death. Instead, what Herrick wants is for the individual to have the assurance of renewal that the species as a whole and nature more generally have.

Man's inability naturally to "repullulate" is, for Herrick, the crucial problem, and his poetry is essentially concerned with providing solutions. What he desires is not so much stasis or transcendence of cyclical flux as the assurance of renewal, the regeneration of life that nature in its larger aspect so effortlessly possesses.[21] In *Hesperides* he offers several different ways to attain this renewal.

Some of the "metamorphosis" or "how" poems (in which Herrick presents a mythological explanation of how certain flowers came to be) reveal one way in which the finality of death can be remedied. Typically, these flowers were originally girls who were unfortunate in love and died and were then turned into flowers. Herrick's explanation of "*How* Pansies *or* Hearts-ease *came first*" (H-391), for example, offers this metamorphosis as a remedy:

> Frollick Virgins once these were,
> Over-loving, (living here:)
> Being here their ends deny'd
> Ranne for Sweet-hearts mad, and dy'd.
> Love in pitie of their teares,
> And their losse in blooming yeares;
> For their restlesse here-spent houres,
> Gave them *Hearts-ease* turn'd to Flow'rs.

By allowing these girls a continued life as pansies, Love compensates for their tears and early death. Similarly, the wallflower was a maid who died trying to meet her lover and was turned into a flower by Love out of pity. Although at first it might seem that these girls have been transformed into even more ephemeral things, paradoxically their metamorphosis is a remedy for death, since as flowers they are assured of renewal every spring. Despite the apparent fragility, these flowers actually have more permanence than the maids did. But this kind of metamorphosis does not really carry much weight for Herrick. It is clearly fanciful and thus does not provide any assurance for man that his life will renew.

Ceremony provides a more convincing regeneration, though indeed the immortality it offers is also limited. People are resurrected in the memory of those who remember them. When Herrick sails from Julia, he tells her to

> Give my dead picture one engendring kisse:
> Work that to life, and let me ever dwell
> In thy remembrance (*Julia*).
>
> > *"His sailing from* Julia," H-35

Julia's concern will enable him to live in her "remembrance" while he is absent. But memory is also able to perpetuate the life of the dead. He and Julia sing dirges for "the Saints now dead" who "deserve our best remembrances" (H-584). By performing the proper prayers and rituals, he can insure that these saints will remain alive in the memory of those performing the rites, and he promises Julia that she shall have the same rites when she dies. Whereas Donne's sense of the temporal process of decay leads him to exalt memory as the faculty that can take us back to truth and perfection, Herrick's cyclical view of time lies behind his quite different idea that memory performs a kind of resurrection for the dead whom we remember.

It is poetry, however, that most frequently gives Herrick hope for "repullulation." Poetry has a magical effect. As "Enchantments" (H-8), his poems possess the power to provide an alternative or antidote to the painful vicissitudes in life, even to the *"bad season[s]"* (H-612) in the cycles of history. Despite his political misfortunes, Charles I can reign as king in Herrick's verse (H-685). Not only is Maria firmly enthroned as queen in his poetry, but she can also find "rest" and respite in *"This Sacred Grove"* of *Hesperides* (H-265) from the political turmoils. Poetry has the power to renew our

vigor and spirits. As a "Care-charming-spel" (H-254), it is identified
with music and shares its power to "convert" the "consuming fire"
of a fever "Into a gentle-licking flame, / And make it thus expire"
(H-227). It cures pains and gives repose. Because of its effects on
the imagination, it can temporarily remedy the shortness of human
life by making

> . . . the frollick yeere,
> The Month, the Week, the instant Day
>   To stay
> The longer here.
>
> "*An Ode to Sir* Clipsebie Crew," H-544[22]

Stretching out the pleasurable pieces of time, poetry has the ability
to prolong life and can even renew youth in old age.

Herrick's belief in this power of poetry is perhaps best revealed
in "*His age, dedicated to his peculiar friend, Master* John Wickes" (H-
336). He imagines himself in his old age, "bruised on the Shelfe
/ Of Time," his "locks behung with frost and snow" (ll. 74–76),
sitting with his "old leane wife" by the fire, "foretelling snow and
slit, / And weather by our aches" (ll. 84–87). In the winter of his
life, besieged with aches and pains, he asks his young son, Iülus,
to read some of Herrick's own verses. Miraculously they renew his
youthful vigor and lust, making him "Flutter and crow, as in a fit
/ Of fresh concupiscence" (ll. 110–11). Poetry can "beget" (l. 101)
in man "a more transcendant heate" (l. 102) than even the famed
Helen of Troy was able to stir in old men. But the renewal that
poetry can effect in this life is, Herrick recognizes, only temporary,
for after Herrick experiences this splendid return of youth, the symbolic fire by which he and his (imaginary) wife are sitting dies, and
they finally go to bed "Farre more then night bewearied" (l. 152).

Although during a person's lifetime poetry can provide only a
partial, momentary regeneration, it does allow a more lasting one
after death by offering immortality both to the people who are
included in the poems and to the poet himself. Herrick's book itself
is immortal: it is "a plant sprung up to wither never, / But like a
Laurell, to grow green for ever" (H-240). It is a "Charm'd and
enchanted" pillar (H-1129), which is impervious to the historical
cycles that bring about the ruin of kingdoms. It will

> . . . withstand the blow
> Of overthrow:
> Nor shall the seas,
> Or *Outrages*
> Of storms orebear
> What we up-rear,
> Tho Kingdoms fal,
> This pillar never shall
> Decline or waste at all.
>
> *"The pillar of Fame,"* H-1129

Since poetry outlasts the fall of kingdoms as well as the death of men, it allows Herrick's cycle to renew so that he will not "lye forgot" in the grave "And piece-meale rot / Without a fame in death" (H-211). Though time "cut'st down all," scarcely leaving any "Memoriall," Herrick "*trust*[s] *to Good Verses,*" as the title of H-201 declares, for he has faith that "Numbers sweet, / With endless life are crown'd" (H-201). Significantly, this poem, *"To live merrily, and to trust to Good Verses,"* modeled on Ovid's *Heroides* 15.76, is far more optimistic about the power of poetry than its original. That the poet Tibullus is dead and only a handful of ashes remains seems to Ovid to far outweigh the immortality of poetry. Indeed, he turns to question the assumption that the poets are the care of the gods—what good does it do since they live only briefly and die as trivially as other people? Herrick, however, transforms Ovid's rather bitter poem into an affirmation of poetry's ability to attain "endless life," though he clearly recognizes the limitations of the immortality poetry offers—it is an extension of fame, a preservation of memory, a figurative but not a literal resurrection.

Elsewhere Herrick places even less emphasis on the fact of the poet's death. In *"Poetry perpetuates the Poet"* (H-794) he claims that poetry provides the "Repullulation" he so much desires:

> Here I my selfe might likewise die,
> And utterly forgotten lye,
> But that eternall Poetrie,
> Repullulation gives me here
> Unto the thirtieth thousand yeere,
> When all now dead shall re-appeare.

It gives him the renewal, the second spring, which will last until the Apocalypse when all the dead will be resurrected. Herrick's version of the immortalizing function of poetry differs from Jonson's primarily in that whereas Jonson emphasizes poetry's power to hold people "up and even" above time and its vicissitudes (*Forest* XII, "Epistle to Elizabeth Countesse of Rutland," l. 42), Herrick stresses poetry's ability to give "Repullulation." The difference in these versions of poetic immortality reflects the divergent attitudes of Jonson and Herrick toward time and its cycles. Jonson desires transcendence, but Herrick seeks renewal. Since for Herrick the cycles do not endanger a person's stability or virtue, he does not share Jonson's overriding concern to remain superior to time, untouched by its flux.

Herrick does place a temporal, Christian limitation (albeit in terms of the Platonic year) on the classical belief in the immortality poetry can provide, but within these limits his faith in poetry is strong. Poetry can provide renewed life not just for himself but also for the people he includes in his poems. Repaying the debt he owes his dead father for having given him "Mortall" life, Herrick gives him "a life immortall from my Verse" (H-82). Though Herrick recognizes limits and bounds, his basic desire seems to be to break through them, to extend his own existence and that of the good people he immortalizes in his poetry. Near the end of *Hesperides* he writes:

> The bound (almost) now of my book I see,
> But yet no end of those therein or me:
> Here we begin new life; while thousands quite
> Are lost, and theirs, in everlasting night.
>
> *"On his Booke,"* H-1019

Though they have reached the end of the cycle, they will have a kind of second spring. Poetry figuratively allows the resurrection that nature denies human beings, but this new life is offered to only a few, just as salvation is only granted to the chosen.

Indeed, Herrick actually effects a religious transformation of the classical idea that poetry is able to provide immortality. His conception of poetic immortality has strong Judaeo-Christian overtones, which are often overlooked. Just as God writes down people's names in the book of life, Herrick inscribes men and women in his book of poetry. "While others perish," Sir Thomas Heale's "life [is] decreed / Because begot of my *Immortal* seed" (H-869). To another friend he writes, "Looke in my Book, and herein see, / Life endlesse sign'd to thee and me" (H-906). Herrick's insistence on the importance of his inscribing these good people in *Hesperides* not only derives from the classical belief in the immortalizing power of the poet—the belief that Jonson had made central to his poetry—but, more interestingly, it also recalls numerous passages from both the Old and New Testaments. Daniel prophesies an apocalyptic time when there will be terrible trouble, but God's chosen people will be "delivered, every one that shall be found written in the book" (Daniel 12:1). The book of Malachi also mentions "a book of remembrance," which will include all those "that feared the *Lord*" so that "they shall be mine, saith the *Lord* of hosts, in that day when I make up my jewels; and I will spare them, as a man spareth his own son that serveth him" (3:16–17). In the Old Testament this "book of remembrance" is a promise of life, a promise that God will "spare" or redeem those who are inscribed in it, but in the New Testament this book of life becomes clearly associated with Christian immortality. Those whose names are in this book are assured of a life beyond the grave. As Jesus says, "He that overcometh, the same shall be clothed in white raiment; and I will not blot out his name out of the book of life, but I will confess his name before my Father, and before his angels" (Revelation 3:5). It is this book of life that will be used on the Day of Judgment. In his vision John sees "the dead, small and great, stand before God; and the books were opened: and another book was opened, which is *the book* of life: and the dead were judged out of those things which were written in the books, according to their works. . . . And whosoever was not found written in the book of life was cast into the lake of fire" (Revelation 20:12, 15).

Herrick conceives of his poetry as a "book of life" in which the chosen few are remembered and "crowned" with endless life; the rest perish as the grass or as a flower and, cut off from spring's renewal, are doomed to lie in oblivion in an endless night. In *"To his Friend, Master J. Jincks"* (H-859), he places his friend "here among my righteous race" where he shall "live for ever, with my Just." His phrase recalls David's remark in Psalm 14:5 that "God is in the generation of the righteous," and the implication of Herrick's words is that God is actually behind Herrick's choice of the righteous. Herrick has divine sanction for giving them immortality. As for those not granted this remembrance, "The bastard Slips

may droop and die / Wanting both Root, and Earth." Echoing
Solomon's remark "the multiplying brood of the ungodly shall not
thrive, nor take deep rooting from bastard slips, nor lay any fast
foundation" (Wisdom of Solomon 4:3), Herrick implies that those
who shall perish without a name in his verse are the "ungodly,"
whereas the people he immortalizes are actually pious, righteous,
and God-fearing. In the Old Testament as in Herrick's verse, the
wicked person who sins against God is threatened with being blotted
out of the Lord's book. "His remembrance shall perish from the
earth, and he shall have no name in the street" (Job 18:17), but
"the righteous shall be in everlasting remembrance" (Psalms 112:6).

Herrick thus gives religious sanction to his poetry. *Hesperides*
records "the Generation of my Just" (H-664). His book is a "Testament" (H-977) and a *"Psalter"* (H-604), and the "crowne of life"
(H-224) he gives the chosen few suggests the "crown of life" Jesus
promises to those who have been "faithful unto death" (Revelation
2:10). Herrick actually canonizes these people. Penelope Wheeler
"a Saint shall be, / In Chiefe, in this Poetick Liturgie" (H-510).
His book presents "A stock of Saints; where ev'ry one doth weare
/ A stole of white" (H-545). This is certainly a Christianized version
of the classical belief in poetic immortality, and Herrick's emphasis
on his ability to make saints constitutes a rather subtle counterattack
on the Puritan rejection of Catholic saints and images as objects
of idolatrous worship. *Hesperides* itself is a *"white Temple* of my
Heroes," "Beset with stately Figures (every where) / Of such rare
Saints-ships," filled with "Statues" and *"eternall Images"* (H-496).
Some of these metaphors and analogies are, of course, self-con-
sciously fanciful or whimsical. Indeed, much of the wit of *Hesperides*
derives from the apparent discrepancy between his short, slight
lyrics and the large claims Herrick makes for them. Nevertheless,
behind the at times playful wit lies a serious view both of his role
as a poet and of the power of poetry.

In his conception of his own poetry, Herrick thus combines the
classical notion of the immortalizing power of the poet with the
biblical idea of being inscribed in the book of life and the Catholic
idea of canonizing saints. All are ways of renewing man's life,
enabling him to extend his life beyond the limits of its brief cycle.
Herrick's view of the cyclical pattern of time underlies his blending
of these different traditions, but there is also a teleological note,
for he implies that poetic immortality eventually leads to Christian

salvation. As an Anglican priest as well as a priest of poetry, Herrick seems sure that those he selects for remembrance are those to whom God also will grant eternal life. The resurrection he gives anticipates the final one, and the crown of life poetry offers foreshadows the one that Christ will offer to his saints. Moreover, Herrick wittily argues that his efforts in poetry will ultimately earn him a place in heaven:

> After thy labour take thine ease,
> Here with the sweet *Pierides.*
> But if so be that men will not
> Give thee the Laurell Crowne for lot;
> Be yet assur'd, thou shalt have one
> Not subject to corruption.
>
> *"The mount of the Muses,"* H-1123

As the place he will rest after his "labour[s]" in poetry, heaven is identified with Parnassus, and Herrick envisions God giving him the "incorruptible" crown (I Corinthians 9:25), as if it were at least in part a reward for his poetic achievement. In his Christian transformation of the classical ideal of the immortalizing power of poetry, Herrick differs from Jonson, who in his poetry usually observes what he assumes to be rather firm boundaries between the secular and the sacred. Herrick's belief that poetry can lead to salvation is analogous to Bacon's faith that science can lead to the apocalyptic redemption of mankind. Both Herrick and Bacon invest seemingly secular pursuits (science, poetry) with religious significance, and both writers suggest that human beings through these pursuits work toward their own redemption.

From Hesperides *to the Christian Consolation of* Noble Numbers

The combination of classical and Judaeo-Christian elements, which distinguishes Herrick's conception of the immortalizing function of his poetry and is evident throughout *Hesperides,* also characterizes his *Noble Numbers,* whose very title page with its quotation from Hesiod's *Theogony* exemplifies this mixture. Herrick probably intended these two collections of poetry to be read as complementary, much as Browne's *Hydriotaphia* and *Garden of Cyrus* together form a whole.[23] Indeed, a particularly suggestive parallel between *Hes-*

perides and *Noble Numbers* hints at their close relationship: both have an essentially cyclical structure. In general *Hesperides* moves from youth to age and ends with the persona's death and burial, and the promise of immortal life through his poetry. *Noble Numbers* is similarly structured. After several introductory poems corresponding to those at the opening of *Hesperides,* it begins with the birth of Christ, moves toward his crucifixion and burial, and concludes with his resurrection from the grave.[24] The shaped poem of the cross (N-268) parallels *"The pillar of Fame"* (H-1129), and each in its own way offers the promise of immortality. Both *Hesperides* and *Noble Numbers* emphasize the cyclical order and offer hope for the renewal of the cycle for man.

Herrick presents Christ's life as fitting into the classical cyclical pattern. Moreover, the basic tenets of Christianity exemplify this order. The paradox that Christ's crucifixion gave human beings eternal life harmoniously blends with the classical notion that vicissitude characterizes life: pleasure follows pain (N-45), things of worth are brought forth with tears (H-257), and *"Crosses* [in both secular and religious senses] *doe still bring forth the best events"* (H-275). Apparently, Christianity does not abolish the old cyclical pattern of history but follows it. The idea that everything has its season and that *"New things succeed, as former things grow old"* appears even in Herrick's *"Ceremonies for Candlemasse Eve"* (H-892):

> Down with the Rosemary and Bayes,
>   Down with the Misleto;
> In stead of Holly, now up-raise
>   The greener Box (for show.)

Interestingly, this succession is described in political terms: though "Holly hitherto did sway," it is now time for "Box" to "domineere." But Box, too, though "youthfull" now, will by Easter be "Grown old" and must "surrender. . . his place, / Unto the crisped Yew." The yew in its turn is replaced by the birch, and so forth, and Herrick concludes: "Thus times do shift; each thing his turne do's hold." The ceremonies associated with Christian festivals confirm the cyclical order. Because Herrick presents Christianity as fitting so thoroughly into this cyclical pattern, which is the natural order of the universe, he tends to diminish the miraculous and paradoxical aspects of Christianity. What to Browne would be paradox is to

Herrick merely the succession of opposites or the cyclical, seasonal order. Perhaps it is Herrick's overriding concern with the cyclical pattern of nature and history—which shapes even his conception of religion—that has led a number of his readers to feel that his spirit is essentially classical or pagan.

Not only are there correspondences between *Hesperides* and *Noble Numbers* that reflect parallels between pagan and Christian traditions, but Herrick also suggests an almost typological relationship between these two collections of poems.[25] *"The Argument of his Book"* (H-1), which opens *Hesperides*, suggests a sense of progression from *Hesperides* to *Noble Numbers*, for, after cataloguing the subjects he will cover in *Hesperides*, he concludes:

> . . . I sing (and ever shall)
> Of *Heaven*, and hope to have it after all.

Just as his poetry ultimately brings him to heaven, so *Hesperides* clearly leads to *Noble Numbers*.

Many concerns and motifs in *Hesperides* look foward to more explicitly Christian ones in *Noble Numbers*. Although there is an intermingling of classical, Hebraic, and Christian elements in both works, the proportion changes. In *Hesperides* the classical and to a lesser extent the Old Testament allusions predominate, but in *Noble Numbers* the emphasis is much more specifically Christian. Herrick has a sense of the differences as well as similarities among the classical, Hebraic, and Christian. Though eclectic, he is not really a syncretist. As the relationship between *Hesperides* and *Noble Numbers* suggests, a direction toward the future distinguishes his view of the cycles from the classical one, which is characterized by a sense of endless, directionless repetition.

Hesperides foreshadows *Noble Numbers* in interesting ways. The many sacrifices and offerings in *Hesperides* anticipate the crucifixion of Christ, the ultimate sacrifice to which *Noble Numbers* builds. Moreover, in *Noble Numbers* Herrick tends to emphasize the spiritual significance of the sacrifices, whereas in the preceding work much more attention is given to the literal and physical details. In fact, in his poem *"To God"* (N-103) he confesses the inadequacy of any literal sacrifice; it is impossible to make restitution for even half of God's "loane." Not only are the sacrifices of *Hesperides* typical of the great sacrifice of Christ, but also Julia is sometimes wittily presented in terms that associate her with God and even with Christ. In his poem on "Julia's *Petticoat*" (H-175), Herrick is so taken by her petticoat that he follows it as the Israelites followed the "pillar of a cloud" in which the Lord appeared to lead them out of Egypt (Exodus 13:21):

> That Leading Cloud, I follow'd still,
> Hoping t'ave seene of it my fill;
> But ah! I co'd not: sho'd it move
> To Life Eternal, I co'd love.

The clothes she wears are humorously compared to the form in which God appeared to his people, and Herrick's persona in this poem worships her with a devotion similar to that with which Herrick worships God in *Noble Numbers*. In *"The Rainbow: or curious Covenant"* (H-687) Herrick compares Julia to God when He made a covenant with man after the Flood. Herrick's "eyes, like clouds, were drizling raine" apparently because of Julia's displeasure. But his sadness is dispelled when the "gentle Beams from *Julia's* sight" produce a "curious Rainbow," which Herrick interprets as "the Covenant, that she / Nor more wo'd drown mine eyes, or me."

In a number of the Julia poems biblical allusions associate her with Christ. When Julia dispenses alms, the "wafer Dol'd by thee, will swell / Thousands to feed by miracle" (H-350). Her miracle is like Christ's miracle of the loaves and fishes (Matthew 15:32–38). Julia preserves Herrick from corruption (H-327) and even brings redemption. Like Christ, she must "appease / Love for our very-many Trespasses" (H-539): "For our neglect, Love did our Death decree, / That we escape. *Redemption comes by Thee.*" Not only is Julia wittily treated as a type of Christ, but Herrick's response to Christ as he worships at his sepulcher recalls his very similar response to Julia. Toward the end of *"To his Saviours Sepulcher: his Devotion"* (N-269) Herrick exclaims, "Ravisht I am! and down I lie, / Confus'd, in this brave Extasie." These lines are interestingly anticipated in a poem upon Julia's voice (H-68), where Herrick promises that at next hearing her sing he will "lye / Entranc'd, and lost confusedly." Indeed, his devotion to Julia in *Hesperides* looks forward to his devotion to Christ in *Noble Numbers*, where Christ is his "Maiden-Saviour" (N-270), the recipient of his deepest love.

Perhaps most important, Herrick's emphasis on poetic immortality in *Hesperides* foreshadows the eternal life that Christ offers to humanity and that becomes the ultimate means of "repullulation" in the *Noble Numbers*. The ever-flourishing "Plantation" in which he places the "chaste spirits" he immortalizes (H-392) offers a foretaste of heaven, the true paradise; and the "City . . . of *Heroes*" Herrick creates, "whose firm foundation laid, / Shall never shrink" (H-365), is a type of the New Jerusalem where the saints will possess the crown of life Herrick figuratively offers in his poetry. Between *Hesperides* and *Noble Numbers* there is in general a shift of emphasis from the resurrection he offers in *Hesperides,* which is mainly in memory and in poetry, to the resurrection that Christianity offers.[26] As Herrick says, only Christianity offers the promise of a complete resurrection.

> That *Christ* did die, the *Pagan* saith;
> But that He rose, that's the *Christians* Faith.
>
> *"The Resurrection,"* N-247

Christianity can offer people a second spring that is not limited by time. As Herrick recognizes, even poetry's immortality has its limits, for it is bound by the apocalyptic end of the world: though poetry will "superlast all times," it will finally "turn to dust" when the "whole world die[s]" (H-405). Just as Herrick wishes to extend life beyond death, so he also desires his immortality to last beyond this apocalyptic limit. Desiring an even more complete resurrection than poetry can provide, he turns to Christianity for the final solution to the problem of "repullulation."

The Christian belief in resurrection dominates *Noble Numbers,* where Herrick firmly asserts his faith that he will be resurrected and will live with Christ eternally (N-78). Significantly, he links Christ with the renewal of nature. At Christ's birth December turns to May (N-96), and the symbolic blood of his circumcision makes "here / Spring Tulips up through all the yeere" (N-97). His effect on nature suggests his similarly regenerative effect on human beings. Though poetry is a partial cure for pain, sickness, and even death in *Hesperides,* God provides the only complete cure. With God there is "All saving health" (N-17), and Herrick crawls to Christ for "curing *Balsamum*" (N-129): "To all our wounds, here, whatsoe're they be, / *Christ* is the one sufficient *Remedie*" (N-221).

But Herrick does not establish an antithesis between his faith in poetry and his faith in God. In *"His wish to God"* (N-115) he asks to spend the "remnant" of his days "Reading Thy Bible, and my Book." Perhaps Herrick is simply calling the Bible his book. But there is a certain ambiguity in this line, for he may also be referring to his own book of poetry. If so, he betrays no discomfort about making his poetry a companion piece to the Bible. Moreover, as his poems inscribing good men and women in his book of life suggest, poetic immortality quite naturally leads to Christian salvation. In a prayer *"To God"* (N-262) he even asks God to give him his *"Lawrell"* so that Herrick will be "Thy *Poet,* and Thy *Prophet Lawreat."*

Christianity provides the ultimate opportunity for people to enjoy a second spring, enabling them to have the regeneration that nature inherently possesses but without the eventual decay and death. Far from being a *contemptus mundi* wish to escape from this world, Herrick's longing for immortality reflects his desire for his spring to renew, and it is prompted by the love of life that pervades his entire poetry. Though he sees death as natural and inevitable and therefore accepts it calmly, he is always filled with regret at the idea of losing life and its pleasures.[27] Rather than seeking simply to escape the natural, temporal cycles, he desires to rise again as the flowers and plants do at the spring.

For Herrick, Christianity most surely fulfills this desire with its promise of resurrection at the "great Aprill" of the world (H-763; cf. S-4). It is significant that Herrick describes even the Apocalypse in terms of the renewal of nature and the seasons rather than as a time of destruction and damnation. His deep concern with the cyclical order of nature radically shapes his conception of the Apocalypse and Christian immortality. When the dead are buried, their bodies are sown in the earth like seeds to rise again at the final great spring. In *Noble Numbers* he treats this resurrection as if it were quite natural.

> For each one Body, that i' th' earth is sowne,
> There's an up-rising but of one for one:
> But for each Graine, that in the ground is thrown,
> Threescore or fourescore spring up thence for one:

So that the wonder is not halfe so great,
Of ours, as is the rising of the wheat.

"The Resurrection, possible, and probable," N-208

For Herrick, ultimately the Resurrection is merely another part of the providentially ordered cycles of nature, though he realizes that with the Resurrection cyclical time will cease, absorbed into an eternity where there is no spring (N-229). But what is even more curious is that Herrick suggests that the rising of wheat from a "Graine" should arouse more wonder and admiration than the Christian resurrection of man from the grave. This poem demonstrates particularly well the extent to which Herrick is fascinated with the immediacy of the present and the processes of nature. Perhaps the cycle of nature is the most miraculous of all God's works.

Notes

1. See, e.g., Claude J. Summers, "Herrick's Political Poetry: The Strategies of His Art," in *"Trust to Good Verses": Herrick Tercentenary Essays,* ed. Roger B. Rollin and J. Max Patrick (Pittsburgh: University of Pittsburgh Press, 1978); Claude J. Summers, "Herrick's Political Counterparts," *SEL* 25 (1986), 165-82; and Leah S. Marcus, "Herrick's *Hesperides* and the 'Proclamation made for May,'" *SP* 76 (1979), 49–74.

2. On Herrick's treatment of man as part of nature, see Roger B. Rollin, *Robert Herrick* (New York: Twayne, 1966), pp. 40–46.

3. *The Complete Poetry of Robert Herrick,* ed. J. Max Patrick (New York: Doubleday, 1963). I am indebted to Patrick's notes, which indicate many of the biblical and classical allusions in the poems. I will identify all poems subsequently referred to by Patrick's "H-," "N-," and "S-" numbers.

4. Thomas Carew, "To A. L. Persuasions to Love," in *Minor Poets of the Seventeenth Century,* ed. R. G. Howarth (New York: Dutton, 1969), p. 65.

5. Ronald Berman, "Herrick's Secular Poetry," *ES* 52 (1971), 20–30, has argued that Herrick, like Sir Thomas Browne, has a "figural" habit of mind and sees a larger meaning behind natural objects such as flowers.

6. For example, Collingwood, *Idea of History,* has described the Greek view of history as emphasizing a pattern of "catastrophic changes from one state of things to its opposite" (p. 22).

7. Le Roy, *Of the Interchangeable course,* pp. 5v, 6r. This pattern of the succession of opposites is even apparent in Herrick's ordering of the poems in *Hesperides.* See Richard L. Capwell, "Herrick and the Aesthetic Principle of Variety and Contrast," in a special issue entitled "Essays in the Renaissance in Honor of Allan H. Gilbert," *SAQ* 71 (1972), 488–95.

8. Hakewill, *An Apologie,* sig. C1v.

9. Le Roy, *Of the Interchangeable course,* pp. 3r, 2r.

10. Richard Lovelace, "The Grasshopper," in *Minor Poets,* ed. Howarth, p. 259.

11. It is interesting to note that in his sense of the naturalness, and therefore the inevitability, of the Civil War and the fall of monarchs, Herrick anticipates the comment of the republican James Harrington (cited in my first chapter): "The *dissolution of the late Monarchy was as natural as the death of a man*" (*Oceana,* p. 46).

12. In the poem "*To Doctor* Alablaster" (H-763), Herrick's version of Daniel's description of the Apocalypse stresses the cyclical pattern of history, clearly implying that God is behind this order. The divinely inspired Alablaster

> . . . dost foretell
> When this or that vast *Dinastie* must fall
> Downe to a *Fillit* more *Imperiall.*
> When this or that *Horne* shall be broke, and when
> Others shall spring up in their place agen.

Herrick's sense that God's providence directs the cycles is quite traditional. See, e.g., Le Roy, *Of the Interchangeable course,* Bk. I; Holinshed, comp., *Chronicles,* vol. 1, preface; Raleigh, *History of the World,* preface; and Hakewill, *Apologie,* sig. C1v and pp. 45–46.

13. Thomas R. Whitaker, "Herrick and the Fruits of the Garden," *ELH* 22 (1955), 33.

14. Even Herrick's "*An Epithalamie to Sir* Thomas Southwell *and his Ladie*" (H-149A) ends with Herrick's vision of their eventual death when they will be "to the Barn then born / Two, like two ripe shocks of corn" (ll. 169–70).

15. On Herrick's ceremonial poetry, see Whitaker, "Herrick and the Fruits of the Garden," pp. 16–33; A. Leigh DeNeef, "Herrick's 'Corinna' and the Ceremonial Mode," *SAQ* 70 (1971), 530–45; DeNeef's fuller study, "*This Poetick Liturgie*": *Robert Herrick's Ceremonial Mode* (Durham: Duke University Press, 1974); Robert H. Deming, "Robert Herrick's Classical Ceremony," *ELH* 34 (1967), 327–48; and Deming's *Ceremony and Art: Robert Herrick's Poetry* (The Hague: Mouton, 1974).

16. On the mingling of classical and Christian elements in Herrick's poems, see Deming, *Ceremony and Art;* S. Musgrove, "The Universe of Robert Herrick," *Auckland Univ. College Bulletin,* no. 38, English Series, no. 4 (1950), 28–30; and especially A. B. Chambers's two articles, "Herrick and the Trans-shifting of Time," *SP* 72 (1975), 85–114, and "Herrick, Corinna, Canticles, and Catullus," ibid., 74 (1977), 216–27.

17. See Job 14:1–2: "Man *that is* born of a woman is of few days, and full of trouble. He cometh forth like a flower, and is cut down: he fleeth also as a shadow, and continueth not." Also Job 14:7–10: "For there is hope of a tree, if it be cut down, that it will sprout again, and that the tender branch thereof will not cease. Though the root thereof wax old

in the earth, and the stock thereof die in the ground; *Yet* through the scent of water it will bud, and bring forth boughs like a plant. But man dieth, and wasteth away: yea, man giveth up the ghost, and where *is* he?" The second biblical passage, like Herrick's poems, compares man to a plant, but then separates him from nature's capacity for renewal.

18. Cf. the combination of the biblical with the classical *carpe diem* theme in "Corinna" (H-178); Patrick's notes to the poem clearly indicate such mingling.

19. In "Robert Herrick's Classical Ceremony," Deming concludes that Herrick's concern with the classical rituals represents his "devotion to an older . . . but suspect order of values he felt compelled to assert in the face of Puritan opposition" (p. 347). Leah S. Marcus, "Herrick's *Noble Numbers* and the Politics of Playfulness," *ELR* 7 (1977), 108–26, argues that his collection of religious poetry defends Anglican values and practices that the Puritans were attacking. In "Herrick's *Hesperides*" she shows that his poems of country festivity support the Royalist position. See also Miner, *Cavalier Mode*, pp. 160–62.

20. Chambers, "Herrick and the Trans-shifting of Time," p. 102, notes that the daffodil, which Herrick uses as an image of mutability and transience, in classical contexts had "the notable attribute of . . . immortality."

21. DeNeef, in *"This Poetick Liturgie,"* argues that Herrick's concern in *Hesperides* is "to create a realm of stasis, of immutability and transcendence" (p. 18).

22. In *"An Ode to Sir* Clipsebie Crew" (H-544), it is actually the combination of drinking wine and reading the poems of Anacreon and Horace that lengthens time, making even "The instant Day / To stay / The longer here" (st. 4). Wine and poetry are frequently linked in Herrick's verse, for both have the power to work on the imagination.

23. Chambers, "Herrick and the Trans-shifting of Time," has also argued that *Hesperides* and *Noble Numbers* are to be read as companion works.

24. John L. Kimmey, "Robert Herrick's Persona," *SP* 67 (1970), 221–26, shows that in both *Hesperides* and *Noble Numbers* the persona progresses from youth to death to immortality. But Herrick also suggests a parallel between the persona's progress in both works and Christ's in *Noble Numbers*.

25. The importance of typology in Herrick's poetry has not been examined fully, despite the intriguing suggestions of several scholars. Rollin, for example, has remarked in passing that there are "foreshadowings" of *Noble Numbers* in *Hesperides* (*Robert Herrick*, p. 134), and Berman ("Herrick's Secular Poetry") has observed that a typological habit of mind underlies Herrick's poetry.

26. This shift of emphasis is a general pattern. There are a few poems in *Hesperides* that are exceptions and clearly refer to the Christian faith in resurrection. See, for example, H-514 and H-549.

27. *"To his lovely Mistresses"* (H-634) provides a particularly good example. As many readers have noticed, the values of *Hesperides* are in this life. I would add that so are those of *Noble Numbers* to a surprising degree.

CHAPTER VI

John Milton: Providential Progress or Cyclical Decay

> So when the cherfulnesse of the people is so sprightly up . . . it betok'ns us not degenerated, nor drooping to a fatall decay, but casting off the old and wrincl'd skin of corruption to outlive these pangs and wax young again, entring the glorious waies of Truth and prosperous vertue destin'd to become great and honourable in these latter ages.
>
> *Areopagitica*

THROUGHOUT HIS LIFE JOHN MILTON was deeply concerned with history. When he argued for reformation of the church, for revision of divorce laws, and for the right of the people to execute a tyrant, he turned to history to explain the present errors that demanded correction. He wrote a *History of Britain*, believing that the past held valuable lessons for the present. Even his poetry testifies to this lifelong interest. Not only do the three major poems recreate episodes from biblical history, but also *Paradise Lost* concludes with an overview of history that extends from Cain and Abel into the seventeenth century.

Milton gave much thought to the shape history had taken, and like many others in the century he believed that history had been essentially cyclical. But whereas Robert Herrick found consolation in the cyclical order, Milton's response is much like Sir Francis Bacon's. Milton's study of the past leads him to the conclusion that people must break with the past rather than repeat the pattern of former ages. From the early prose to the late poems he consistently contrasts the cycles of the past with the path of progress that people can forge in the future.

There is, however, a difference between the view of history in the early works and the historical perspective that developed later. His first antiprelatical tract, *Of Reformation* (1641), exuberantly looks forward to England's future: God has delivered her from miseries

169

in the past so that He can prepare her "for greatest happinesse to come."[1] But in the Digression in the *History of Britain* Milton looks back to the Civil War period and finds that the English have not progressed to unprecedented glories; instead they have fallen into the same "confusion" as their ancestors (*CPW*, 5:i, 451). His experiences during the Civil War and Interregnum led Milton to revise his view of history, as he gradually lost faith in the people's willingness to change the shape of history. But before examining this change in attitude, it is necessary to define his basic idea of history's patterns and to explore some of the fascinating ways that it shapes his work.

Breaking Away from the Past

The patterns of history that Milton's prose defines underlie the poetry as well. He accepts the Christian view that history follows a linear course from Creation to the Apocalypse, but he believes that within this linear, teleological framework history has taken a cyclical course.[2] In the "revolution of time" (*Areopagitica*, *CPW*, 2:539) periods of virtue and purity are succeeded by corruption and decline. *Of Reformation* clearly defines this pattern in the history of religion and church discipline. Following the traditional Protestant interpretation of church history before the Reformation, Milton argues that in the early days the "Doctrine of the *Gospel*" was "refin'd" to a great "Spirituall height," but this early perfection soon decayed (*CPW*, 1:519). Indeed, Christianity was pure only for 100 or 200 years; the next 1,300 were characterized by corruption (*De Doctrina Christiana*, *CPW*, 6:117). When men during the Reformation began to recover the "*lost Truth*" (*Of Reformation*, *CPW*, 1:525), they had the possibility of reversing the process of decay. But the Reformation was succeeded by a relapse into old error, as prelacy and erroneous traditions were renewed in England. Thus religious history has exhibited a cyclical process of refinement, decay, renewal, and yet another decay.

Such a cyclical pattern, however, is not inevitable. As Milton insists in *Reason of Church-Government*, the state of religion depends not on fortune but on the condition of church discipline: "the flourishing and decaying of all civill societies, all the moments and turnings of humane occasions are mov'd to and fro as upon the axle of discipline. So that whatsoever power or sway in mortall things weaker men that have attributed to fortune, I durst with more confidence . . . ascribe either to the vigor, or the slacknesse of discipline" (*CPW*, 1:751). Since people can either perfect or corrupt discipline, these cycles are within human control. If people institute the true church discipline for which Milton argues, the church can flourish indefinitely and avoid cyclical decline.[3]

It is God's providence that offers people the opportunity to change the cyclical pattern. In *Defence of the People of England,* Milton compares the "criminal madness" of those in Parliament who voted to send more proposals to the king to that of the Roman senators who voted to send ambassadors to Marc Antony. In the natural course of events similar follies yield similar consequences. But God can alter this cyclical pattern, and it seems He has given the people of England a special dispensation: "their end would likewise have been the same, had not almighty God granted a different outcome, reducing the Romans to slavery but assuring us of our freedom" (*CPW*, 4:i, 332). Whereas Herrick believed that the Civil War was simply part of the cyclical pattern of history ordained by God, Milton sees it as a providential chance to transform the shape of history.

Milton's belief that people can break with the cyclical or degenerative pattern of the past provides the major impetus for his prose. In the divorce pamphlets, for example, he insists that the corruption that has accumulated during the past centuries can be reversed. During the Reformation at the time of Edward VI, the divorce laws were criticized but not reformed, and a period of degeneration followed. Now in what Milton sees as the second reformation, he is raising the divorce issue again. Although the parallel he draws between the first and second reformations might seem to suggest that England is repeating the cycle, he hopes that the pattern of reform followed by decline will be broken this time. He prays that *"this present renewing of the Church and Common-wealth . . . may be more lasting,"* and he encourages Parliament in the *"fair progress of your noble designes"* (*Judgement of Martin Bucer, CPW,* 2:437–38).

The antiprelatical and divorce treatises both assume that Parliament need only make certain reforms for progress to be insured. If Parliament gets rid of the traditions, laws, and errors that hinder the Reformation, England can advance. This is also the position that underlies *Eikonklastes,* in which Milton implies that because

Charles I tried to stop the Reformation, executing him removes a major obstacle to progress.

In many ways Milton's conception of history is similar to Bacon's, for both writers believe that history has followed a cyclical pattern that can be changed through man's efforts aided by God's providence. Milton's works, like Bacon's, are inspired by a desire to persuade people to break with the cyclical pattern of the past and begin a course of continuous progress. Although Bacon seeks a scientific revolution while Milton desires a religious and political one, both share the ideal of continuous progress and for both the end of progress is the redemption of mankind.

This belief that people (with God's help) can replace the cyclical pattern of the past with a future pattern of progress underlies Milton's sense of his own role in the pamphlets. Encouraging Parliament to make the necessary reforms, he sees himself trying to speed England's progress now that God has given this nation a special opportunity. Like Bacon, he gives hope, persuading people that the cycles of degeneration are not inevitable, and implies that like Christ he is offering in his defense of divorce a remedy for human misery (*Doctrine and Discipline of Divorce, CPW,* 2:241, 282–83). Fighting the passivity that stems from the view that "the worst situations . . . [are] unalterable" (*Defence of the People of England, CPW,* 4:i, 398), he defends deposing of kings as a way to change life for the better.

Although Milton's prose radiates his hopes for present and future progress, it also betrays his sense of what the dangerous alternative is. Throughout his work Milton contrasts the ideal of progress to the possibility of decay, of going back to a previous condition. Aiming to spur England's advancement, he wars against the forces that threaten to arrest progress, to lead England back to a former condition, or to revive the errors of the past and thus bring about cyclical decay.

Because Milton's hopes for progress are defined against his fear of cyclical relapse, his prose works are animated by this idea of the contrasting patterns of history. *Of Reformation,* for example, argues against the prelates who, undoing the achievements of the Protestant Reformation, "have brought us back" to our earlier condition of ignorance, tyranny, and "Popish blindnesse." The *"Ceremonies"* the English church retains are "dangerous earnest of sliding back to *Rome"* (*CPW,* 1:548, 526, 527). Milton prays that God will not allow the prelates to effect the return to the darkness that preceded the Reformation: "O let them not bring about their damned *designes* . . . to *re-involve* us in that pitchy *Cloud* of infernall darknes" (p. 614). The *Animadversions* and *Reason of Church-Government* similarly pit England's hopes for progress against the danger of returning to the old papal error.

Perhaps *Areopagitica* most clearly defines Milton's idea of the two patterns of history, his commitment to progress, and his desire to prevent cyclical decay.[4] This famous defense of liberty of the press is not only an eloquent paean for the human ability to discover and possess truth. But it is also Milton's manifesto of his ideal of progress and a definition of the grim alternative version of history.

Since licensing threatens to halt the progress of truth, Milton's attempt to dissuade Parliament from passing the licensing act aims to insure that England attain "the utmost prospect of reformation" rather than stay at this intermediate level and "pitch our tent here" (*CPW*, 2:549). But Parliament seems bent on hindering the nation's progress. England is at a crossroads, faced with a choice between further progress and relapse into old error, and Milton repeatedly contrasts the potential for unlimited advancement with the threat of regression. Tracing its history, he argues that prepublication licensing was invented by the Roman Catholics "to obstruct and hinder the first approach of Reformation" (p. 507). The Reformation managed to triumph over the papist attempt to suppress the light of truth, but its achievements were limited in England, for the reforms were soon succeeded by the growth of episcopal tyranny. Now in 1644, with the bishops ousted, England has yet another chance to advance the Reformation, but it seems that the presbyters are little better than the bishops they replaced. Although England can now progress beyond all Europe in liberty, Milton fears Parliament will instead choose to inflict "a second tyranny over learning" (p. 539). In its attempt to reinstitute licensing, Parliament is following the example of the Catholic Inquisition, aiming to halt the second reformation of religion in England, repeating the error of the past, and thus threatening England with cyclical decline into the tyranny, darkness, and ignorance that Milton identifies with papacy. Milton's fear that the cycle is repeating itself emerges clearly in his description of the present condition, as he stresses the word "again": "But now the Bishops abrogated and voided out of the Church, as if our Reformation sought no more, but to make room for others into their seats under another name, the Episcopall arts begin to bud again, . . . liberty of Printing must be enthrall'd again under a Prelaticall commission of twenty, the privilege of the people nullify'd, and which is wors, the freedom of learning must groan again, and to her old fetters; all this the Parliament yet sitting" (pp. 541–42).

In contrast to this picture of the repetition of error, Milton envisions England as a strong man rousing himself after sleep or an eagle moulting to renew itself. Although these two images of England's renewal may seem to suggest a cyclical pattern, Milton's emphasis in these images is on growth, vision, the purgation of error and tradition, and there is no sense that decline will follow. In this hopeful vision perfectibility displaces cyclicality.

The Ideal of Progress

Perhaps one of the most basic ways in which Milton's ideal of progress shapes his poetry and prose is in his fondness for the traditional Judaeo-Christian metaphor of life as a journey, with its strong linear and teleological associations. We immediately think of *Comus* (the lady must travel through woods of danger and sensuality to her home), *Paradise Regained* (the spirit of God leads Christ into the wilderness), and *Samson Agonistes* (the poem opens with Samson asking to be led "a little further on" and ends with him attaining his climactic, heroic end).[5] But the image of the journey also informs the prose works.

In *Of Education* Milton defines the end of learning ("to repair the ruins" of the Fall [*CPW*, 2:366]) and then proceeds to establish the proper path for reaching it. Whereas other plans take a long time and often fail to achieve their goal, his is "of time farre shorter, and of attainment farre more certain, then hath been yet in practice" (p. 364). The image of the journey pervades nearly every page of this work. In the usual method of teaching the arts, students first become "stuck" on the "Grammatick flats & shallows." Then they are "transported under another climat to be tost and turmoild with their unballasted wits in fadomles and unquiet deeps of controversie." Finally they go "their severall wayes" (p. 375). Opposed to these dangerous, stormy, and badly directed journeys, which often end in shipwreck, Milton offers "the right path of a vertuous and noble Education; laborious indeed at the first ascent, but else so smooth, so green, so full of goodly prospect" (p. 376). The purpose of lectures is to "lead and draw them in willing obedience," and Milton presents the whole plan of education as a delightful journey in which students proceed smoothly forward by steps from the easiest subjects, "most obvious to the sence," to the most difficult and abstract (pp. 374, 384–85, 387). His ideal of progress along a linear path that leads to a clearly defined goal is remarkably similar to the ideal that shapes Bacon's prose.

This preference for linear, progressive movement is reflected both in Milton's proleptic poetic method and in the ways his poems end. Not only do the epic similes in *Paradise Lost* often point forward to a later event in the fable, but also the structure of Milton's poems tends to be proleptic.[6] Even the endings of the poems are characteristically forward-looking. *Lycidas* concludes with the "uncouth Swain" anticipating "fresh Woods, and Pastures new" (11. 186, 193). Though Adam and Eve look back to Paradise, they begin mankind's journey through history with the "World . . . all before them" (*PL,* XII, 646). *Samson Agonistes* points to the future as Manoa advises Israel to "lay hold on this occasion" (1. 1716) for deliverance that Samson has provided. In *Paradise Regained* Christ's quiet return to his mother's house might seem to suggest that he has made little progress, that he is returning to and in the same condition he left, but the brief epic has in fact revealed Christ's growth in understanding, and the angelic choir looks forward to his future work: "on thy glorious work / Now enter, and begin to save mankind" (*PR,* IV, 634–35). Although to the unilluminated eye Christ may seem no different than when he left his mother's house, we know that he already has entered his destined path. What appears to be a cyclical return is in fact progress.

Like Bacon, Milton contrasts linear progress either to circular, repetitive movement or to wandering. Both writers tend to link the repetitive, cyclical pattern with error, custom, and tradition. When people rely on tradition, they perpetuate error, impede progress, and succumb to a cyclical pattern of decline. In his polemical writing, Milton chooses to argue in such a way that his readers *"may come the speediest way to see the truth vindicated"* rather than losing themselves *"in the labyrinth of controversall antiquity"* (*Animadversions, CPW,* 1:664). Bacon similarly had advocated the direct open path, condemning the proud, tradition-bound philosophers who wander in labyrinths. In *Eikonoklastes* and his *First Defence* of the English people, Milton follows a linear sequence as he refutes his opponents' arguments in the order in which they appear in the original work.[7] In contrast to his own method of sure progression to an end Milton presents Salmasius as "set whirling" by "foolish trifles" so that he does not know "what should at any time be said 'first or later or in conclusion'" (*First Defence, CPW,* 4:i, 326). A similar association between error and circular movement appears in the *Second Defence of the English People,* where Milton refuses to waste time repeating what he has said before: "Must I always tread the very same orbit and repeat what I have said so many times before, at the croaking of any buffoon? I will not do it!" (*CPW,* 4:i, 632). Whereas his opponent "barricade[s] the path to him who would proceed directly" or regresses, "having returned now to your former ways" (*Defence of Himself, CPW,* 4:ii, 723, 751), Milton claims that he will steadily advance; he will not "delay or interrupt the smooth course" of his writing (*History of Britain, CPW,* 5:i, 4).

People must resist the temptation to wander or stray from the path. Comus imitates his mother Circe, luring "weary Traveller[s]" who forget their "native home" once they interrupt their journey (ll. 64, 76). The Lady, too, is faced with the threat of not reaching the end of her journey. It is significant that she becomes vulnerable to Comus once she stops to rest, "wearied out / With this long way" (ll. 182–83), and the brothers become lost when they leave the path, stepping "to the next Thicket side / To bring [her] Berries" (ll. 185–86). Satan in *Paradise Lost* similarly tries to stop people from following their appointed path. Like the Leviathan that deceives the seafarers into believing he provides firm ground on which to anchor, Satan tempts people to trust in him, thus preventing them from reaching their true harbor. The fallen angels will later continue this pattern, assuming new names of pagan gods and corrupting "Mankind . . . to forsake / God thir Creator" (I, 368–69). Though God is man's proper "Guide" (Adam would have "begun / My wand'ring" unless God had led him to Eden [VIII, 311–12]), Satan is like the *ignis fatuus,* "a wand'ring Fire" that "Misleads th' amaz'd Night-wanderer from his way / To Bogs and Mires . . . There swallow'd up and lost" (IX, 634, 640–42). In *Samson Agonistes* the Chorus believes that women assume this Satanic function, drawing man awry, steering him on to shipwreck (ll. 1040–45).

Embodying evil and error (which comes from the Latin word

"to wander"), the fallen angels' activities are characteristically end-less, circular, wandering. After the council in Hell, they "Disband, and wand'ring, each his several way / Pursues," full of "restless thoughts" (*PL*, II, 523–24, 526). Others sit "apart," contemplating theological problems, and find "no end, in wand'ring mazes lost" (ll. 557, 561). Here we see the Baconian association of error, rest-lessness (which comes from lacking a proper end or goal), wan-dering, and the isolation that is the consequence of pride. In later ages the fallen angels' followers, vain men who build their hopes of fame and glory on "vain things," will similarly "wander" in the limbo of fools, finding no rest (III, 448, 458).

Unlike the other fallen angels, Satan in his journey to the new world does pursue a definite path, but his voyage parodies the proper journey of the virtuous person, and once he reaches the earth his motion becomes circular. He "compasses" the earth, "cir-cles" the equinoctial line three times, and "revolves" his thoughts (IX, 59–86). In *Paradise Regained* he is perhaps even more clearly an enemy of the providential pattern of progress, as he tries to prevent Christ from successfully undertaking his journey to "at-tain" the "promis'd Kingdom" (I, 265). Many of Satan's tempta-tions seek to persuade Christ to repeat the actions of his prede-cessors,[8] to perpetuate the cyclical pattern of history. For example, as Christ recapitulates the journey of the Israelites in the wilderness, Satan wants him to succumb to the same distrust of God's ability to provide, but Christ must avoid repeating the errors, must perfect the imperfect types. When Satan offers Christ Parthia, he assumes that since David gained his kingdom through military might, Christ also will need force to gain his kingdom. Satan thus fails to recognize the necessary progress from physical to spiritual, from type to antitype. Indeed, Satan throughout *Paradise Regained* endorses the cyclical view, believing that history inevitably repeats itself.[9] Given Milton's commitment to progress, it is entirely appropriate that Satan should be associated with the pattern of history that Milton throughout his work identifies with error and the enemies of truth. Moreover, Satan's own action in the poem is repetitive.[10] He is compared to a "swarm of flies" that keeps returning to the wine-press or the "surging waves" that continually "renew" their "as-sault" against the rock (IV, 15, 18–19). The image of the waves is a traditional figure for cyclical vicissitude, but both images suggest the futility of such cyclical, nonprogressive movement. Paradoxically, this cyclical motion is essential static.

Milton dislikes stasis. If the "waters" of truth "flow not in a perpetuall progression, they sick'n into a muddy pool of conformity and tradition" (*Areopagitica, CPW,* 2:543). This description of truth as a river or fountain contrasts interestingly with Donne's most characteristic version of this biblical metaphor and thus reflects the differences in their views of history. Donne insists on tracing the waters to their source. His emphasis on going back to the origins is the consequence of his view of history as a process of degeneration. Milton, however, with his faith in the possibility of perpetual growth and progress, finds the continuous forward progression of water a proper image for truth. The alternative is stagnation.

This ideal of progress is intimately connected with Milton's view of perfection as growth and change. As I suggested in the introduction, the idea of progress depends on a disposition to see change as good, rather than as a sign of imperfection or a deviation from original perfection. When Raphael tells Adam "God made thee perfet, not immutable" (*PL,* V, 524), he suggests that perfection does not preclude the possibility of change. Distinguishing between perfection and immutability, Raphael corrects Adam's mistaken notion that perfection is static. Indeed, Milton here implies that change may be essential to perfection. His definition of perfection as including change may well be related to the idea of an infinite universe, which developed in the late sixteenth and seventeenth centuries. In this newly expanded universe change as well as infinity was sometimes seen as an expression and, indeed, a celebration of the Creator.[11] Although Milton does not embrace the idea of an infinite universe, he is affected by the new, positive attitude toward change. Milton assumes that Adam's ability to change is not a liability but rather a mark of special dignity and of God's generosity. Thus Milton's notion of perfection is radically different from the older view that perfection requires stasis, a view that we have seen reflected in Ben Jonson's tendency to distrust the temporal world of change and to find value only in what is permanent, eternal, unchanging. Unlike Jonson, Milton embraces change as potentially good.

The Garden of Eden in *Paradise Lost* embodies a far from static perfection. Although some critics have criticized Milton's paradise as dull and fixed, others have felt that the elements suggestive of

change and mutability make it less than ideal. But both sets of
critics are judging his paradise in terms of a different conception
of perfection than Milton's. Even before the Fall, there are showers,
and though the climate is temperate, the "meridian heat" (V, 369)
is hot enough to force Adam and Eve to rest at noon. Adam and
Eve have an almost unlimited variety in their food (VII, 542).
Perhaps most important, the garden itself is characterized by lux-
uriant growth that must be pruned.[12] Pruning makes the garden
flourish, furthering rather than restraining growth. The plants
grow "Luxurious by restraint" (IX, 209), just as Adam and Eve
will if they obey the one prohibition.[13]

So much does God favor growth and change that he even incorporates progress into the scale of creation. Although every creature is assigned to its proper sphere, each "aspire[s]" to the next
higher level and body can work up to spirit, as Raphael's speech
to Adam explains.

> *O Adam,* one Almighty is, from whom
> All things proceed, and up to him return,
> If not deprav'd from good, created all
> Such to perfection, one first matter all,
> Indu'd with various forms, various degrees
> Of substance, and in things that live, of life;
> But more refin'd, more spiritous, and pure,
> As nearer to him plac't or nearer tending
> Each in thir several active Spheres assign'd,
> Till body up to spirit work, in bounds
> Proportion'd to each kind. So from the root
> Springs lighter the green stalk, from thence the leaves
> More aery, last the bright consummate flow'r
> Spirits odorous breathes: flow'rs and thir fruit
> Man's nourishment, by gradual scale sublim'd
> To vital spirits aspire, to animal,
> To intellectual, give both life and sense,
>
> . . . .
> . . . time may come when men
> With Angels may participate, and find
> No inconvenient Diet, nor too light Fare:
> And from these corporal nutriments perhaps
> Your bodies may at last turn all to spirit,
> Improv'd by tract of time, and wing'd ascend
> Ethereal, as wee, or may at choice

>Here or in Heav'nly Paradises dwell;
>If ye be found obedient. . . . (V, 469–85, 493–501)

Far from being a fixed hierarchy, Milton's chain of being, in which everything derives from the "one first matter" that comes from God, contains the potential for creation to ascend eventually to God. With the Fall, Adam and Eve destroy this possibility of natural ascent, but God offers humanity yet another opportunity for progress through grace and Christ's redemption.[14]

Milton seems even more radically committed to change than Bacon. As we have seen, Bacon's ultimate aim is for science to enable human beings to regain the perfection that existed before the Fall, and thus he shares Donne's assumption that perfection existed in the beginning of time. The tendency to define future happiness in terms of an Edenic state that existed in the beginning of time is, of course, central to much Renaissance and seventeenth-century thought. And Milton is not unaffected by such thinking. Much like Bacon, he maintains that the purpose of learning is to "repair the ruins of our first parents" (*Of Education, CPW,* 2:366) and that the linear progressive journey of the human race through time and history is ultimately circular since it ends with the regaining of Paradise. Christ shall "bring back / Through the world's wilderness long wander'd man / Safe to eternal paradise of rest" (*PL*, XII, 312–14). Nevertheless, as Raphael's speech to Adam indicates, Milton is less bound than most of his contemporaries to the assumption that the original state is the most perfect that could exist. With his sense that unfallen man, "Improv'd by tract of time," could have eventually progressed to an even better condition, Milton implies that absolute perfection did not exist at Creation and that it can only be reached through the process of time and change.

Moreover, whereas Bacon assumes that all human efforts should lead to a state of rest and stasis (the Sabbath), Milton's heaven (the goal to which human beings aspire) is characterized not just by rest but also by change and variety.[15] In *Reason of Church-Government,* his description of the saints' happiness includes variety as well as order: the "effluences of sanctity and love" in the heavenly saints are not "confin'd and cloy'd with repetition of that which is prescrib'd"; instead, our happiness will "orbe it selfe into a thousand vagancies of glory and delight, and with a kinde of eccentricall equation be as it were an invariable Planet of joy and felicity" (*CPW,*

1:752). This description of perfect happiness incorporates both change and constancy; while the movement may seem generally circular, it is in fact "eccentricall," avoiding the repetitiveness of truly circular motion. Here the wanderings ("vagancies") are orderly and delightful, not deviations from the proper path, and they anticipate the rivers' "mazie" wanderings in the Garden of Eden, which do not have the usual negative connotations.[16] In *Paradise Lost* heaven is similarly characterized by change. Raphael explains that there is time and motion in heaven as well as on earth (V, 580–82). Although the angels often stand "in Circles" (V, 631), their "Mystical dance" involves "mazes intricate, / Eccentric, intervolv'd, yet regular / Then most, when most irregular they seem" (V, 620, 622–24). Heaven also has its evening for "change delectable" (V, 629), as if sheer lack of variety would be cloying. Even angels need "Grateful vicissitude" (VI, 8).

God's preference for growth rather than stasis is evident not only in His creation of a universe that incorporates change in a positive way, but also in His successive creations. Whereas Donne with his degenerative view of history suggests that God created all things at once in their perfection, Milton's God is characterized by his continual creativity. Only after the Fall of the angels does He create the world human beings will inhabit. Indeed, the exaltation of the Son, the act that precipitates Satan's rebellion, is the supreme example of God's creativity and of the principle that change can be for the better.

> This day I have begot whom I declare
> My only Son, and on this holy Hill
> Him have annointed, whom ye now behold
> At my right hand; your Head I him appoint;
> And by my Self have sworn to him shall bow
> All knees in Heav'n, and shall confess him Lord. (V, 603–8)

"This day" and "now" emphasize newness, the break with the past, and God's announcement that all "shall bow" similarly divides future behavior from the pattern set in the past. Milton's position that Christ was not exalted from the beginning insists on God's disposition to effect successive changes in time. Moreover, it allows the poet to contrast God's endorsement of change with Satan's dislike of anything new.

Satan likes things the way they were, believing that the exaltation of the Son destroys rather than perfects the hierarchy in heaven.[17] Though Donne labeled Satan the first innovator, Milton portrays him as conservative or reactionary—Satan is essentially against change. As Satan says to one of his companions:

> . . . new Laws thou see'st impos'd;
> New Laws from him who reigns, new minds may raise
> In us who serve, new Counsels, to debate
> What doubtful may ensue. . . . (V, 679–82)

Satan's dislike of "new" things appears again in his rejection of the "new" doctrine that all things (including himself) were created by Christ.

> That we were form'd then say'st thou? and the work
> Of secondary hands, by task transferr'd
> From Father to his Son? strange point and new!
> Doctrine which we would know whence learnt: who saw
> When this creation was? remember'st thou
> Thy making, while the Maker gave thee being?
> We know no time when we were not as now. (V, 853–59)

Satan supports tradition, custom, and error, not new doctrines, which Milton associates with truth. Far from being revolutionaries, Satan and the other rebellious angels reject progress, desiring to return to the old ways and conditions that have been superseded, and thus the fallen angels embody the characteristics Milton gives his opponents in his polemical prose.[18]

Primitive Christianity provides Milton with the best sanction for this view that the new is usually desirable, an improvement over the old. Whereas Herrick finds that Christianity affirms the cyclical order, Milton and Bacon assume that Christianity opposes the cyclical idea of history. Milton suggests that from its inception Christianity asserted that the old could be superseded by the new, suggesting a progressive view of history.[19] Since it taught new doctrines, Christianity itself was first accused of "noveltie" (*Eikonklastes*, *CPW*, 3:534; *Animadversions*, *CPW*, 1:703). The change from the Old Testament law to the gospel is essentially a progressive movement from "bondage" to "freedom," from the physical to the spiritual, from infancy or "childhood" to "manhood" (see, e.g., *Treatise of*

Civil Power, CPW, 7:259). Christ abrogated the ceremonial law of the Old Testament, showing that the old traditions had become outmoded and erroneous. Unlike Donne, who often sees the change from childhood to maturity as a process of decline into greater sin, Milton typically defines it as a growth and progress, a movement toward fulfillment and perfection. And the state of childhood, incomplete in itself, looks toward its future purpose or end. "THE MOSAIC LAW WAS . . . INTENDED FOR THE ISRAELITES ALONE. . . . ITS AIM WAS TO MAKE THE ISRAELITES HAVE RECOURSE TO THE RIGHTEOUSNESS OF THE PROMISED CHRIST, THROUGH A RECOGNITION OF MANKIND'S, AND THEREFORE THEIR OWN DEPRAVITY. ITS AIM, ALSO, WAS THAT ALL WE OTHER NATIONS SHOULD AFTERWARDS BE EDUCATED FROM THIS ELEMENTARY, CHILDISH AND SERVILE DISCIPLINE TO THE ADULT STATURE OF A NEW CREATURE, AND TO A MANLY FREEDOM UNDER THE GOSPEL" (*De Doctrina Christiana, CPW,* 6:517). Those who seek to return to the bondage of the Old Testament are thus countering the pattern of progress that God has sanctioned.

Indeed, it is not God but human beings who condemn things for being new. God Himself chose to teach mankind by progressive revelations disclosed in various ages. Milton's belief in progressive revelations and his association of God with change contrast sharply with the far more conservative position represented, for example, by Richard Baxter, who insists in his *Church-History* that our own "actual experience" shows that "God doth not give New Revelations to the world . . . since the Scripture times"; He is not continually "changing or adding to his Laws."[20] For Milton, even God's regeneration of mankind includes the idea of newness; Milton's definition in *De Doctrina* stresses that regeneration is not simply a restoration of a former state: "This is how supernatural renovation works. It restores man's natural faculties of faultless understanding and of free will more completely than before. But what is more, it also makes the inner man like new and infuses by divine means new and supernatural faculties into the minds of those who are made new" (*CPW,* 6:461). And God's creativity leads to man's, as regeneration yields "NEW LIFE AND GROWTH" in which people "BRING FORTH GOOD WORKS FREELY AND OF THEIR OWN ACCORD" (*CPW,* 6:477, 479).

Milton's endorsement of change and newness even shapes his conception of his own poetic aims of surpassing his predecessors, of outdoing and even criticizing the traditions and conventions with which he works. Although as a humanist he admires the classical models, he insists throughout *Paradise Lost* that he will outdo the classical epic poets. Jonson, too, had hoped to surpass his predecessors. Despite his sense that history is inevitably cyclical, he apparently believed that the individual person might be able to progress beyond the achievements of the past. But Milton goes further. In *Paradise Regained* he boldly announces that his poem will add to the biblical account of Christ's temptation, recording deeds "unrecorded left through many an Age" (I, 16). Milton implies he has received a new revelation. Divine inspiration can give him illumination, allowing him an understanding unpossessed by all who have gone before him. Thus he rejects the inspiration not just of the nine muses (*PL*, VII, 6) but specifically of "Dame Memory" (*Reason of Church-Government*, *CPW*, 1:820), a muse excessively tied to the past. We are far from Donne's exaltation of memory as the surest means to bring us back to perfection and God.

Convinced that what is new is good and that God favors new creations rather than clinging to old ways, Milton can dismiss his opponents' charges that his ideas are wrong because they are new. Rejecting the Remonstrant's argument that he must be wrong because no one has contradicted episcopacy in England before, Milton claims in *Animadversions* that "the renovating and re-ingendering Spirit of God" has come down among the English to perform a new creation; the defenders of episcopacy thus are perversely rejecting God's "new creature" thinking it is an "upstart noveltie" (*CPW*, 1:703). Since God's creative, progressive spirit is behind the reformation of the church, Milton sometimes sees the Reformation as a new creation, not simply (as Donne believed) a restoration of the perfection of primitive Christianity. Unlike some defenders of the Reformation, such as John Foxe, who believed the primitive church embodied the perfection the Reformation sought to restore, Milton comes to distrust any attempt to idolize the purity of the early church. "The rule of perfection" should not be what "was don in the beginning" (*Tetrachordon*, *CPW*, 2:667). The pattern for church discipline must be taken, not from a time in the past, but from the Scripture as interpreted by the illumination of God's spirit.[21] In this respect Milton's position is much like that of Martin

Luther, who refused to see "any historical period, person, or event as normative."[22]

Milton's attitude toward change and the new and his belief that antiquity is not necessarily a test or mark of truth were to some extent shared by Smectymnuus, the five Puritan divines who like Milton argued against episcopacy. Joseph Hall, the defender of episcopacy, whose *Episcopacie by Divine Right Asserted* (1640) and *An Humble Remonstrance* (1640) sparked the Smectymnuan controversy, had insisted that people should not change institutions "which long use, and many Lawes have firmly established."[23] Assuming that "Antiquity" is "the rule" (p. 8), he attacked those who wanted "to introduce new formes of administration, and rules of Divine worship" (p. 9; italics mine). Like Donne, Bishop Hall opposes innovations; words like "new," "novelty," and "innovation" are terms of opprobrium. But in *An Answer to a Booke Entituled An Humble Remonstrance* (1641), Smectymnuus shows less reverence for antiquity as well as a sense that what was good in the past may no longer be so in the present: "those things which to former Ages have seemed *Necessary* and *Beneficiall* may to succeeding generations prove not *Necessary* but *Noxious.*"[24] *An Answer* interestingly anticipates Milton's argument that Christianity itself demonstrated that the new could indeed be better than the old: "the Iewes might have pleaded against Christ the Antiquity of more then so many hundred years, and thus the Heathens did plead against the Christian religion" (p. 19).

Like Milton, Smectymnuus suggests in this passage that change can be good, but *Answer* actually reveals rather conflicting attitudes towards antiquity and the new. Despite the rejection of Hall's arguments for custom, tradition, and antiquity, Smectymnuus argues as often from antiquity as from Scripture, insisting that the "first Antiquitie" is "best" (p. 27), and quoting Tertullian's comment that "whatsoever is first is true; but that which is latter is adulterous" (p. 27). "Innovation" becomes for them, too, a term of insult. Where Hall had accused the opponents of episcopacy of being innovators, Smectymnuus now labels the defenders of episcopacy innovators. *Answer* concludes by firmly rejecting the new: "Let us avoide those novelties of words, according to the Apostles prescript and keepe the ole termes, . . . and the words will bring us to the faith of our first Apostles, and condemne these new Apostates, new faith and phrases" (p. 92). This recommendation reveals a conservatism that is in ways closer to Hall and Donne than to Milton. We can see how revolutionary Milton is in his attitude toward change and newness, and in his resistance to the idealization of antiquity that seems to have been deeply ingrained in this culture that so often sought in the ancient past its patterns of reform for the present.[25] And we can thus understand why Milton eventually distinguishes himself from the Presbyterian clergy, who were more tied to the rule of the past than Milton.

Repeatedly, Milton defends the new against those who want to rely on precedent and custom. He defends extemporary prayer rather than repetition of a fixed liturgy, because "God every morning raines down new expressions into our hearts" (*Eikonoklastes*, *CPW*, 3:505). Rejecting divinely sanctioned change and creativity, Charles I's attempts to enforce the liturgy of the Book of Common Prayer "imprison and confine . . . our Prayers [and] that Divine Spirit of utterance that moves them" (p. 505). At a time when many of his contemporaries were looking to the past for precedents to justify their present actions, Milton in *Tenure of Kings and Magistrates* exhorts the Parliament and Military Council to act "without precedent" in deposing the king "if it appeare thir duty" (*CPW*, 3:237). Parliament must be free to advance to new and wiser views. It must not be "so committed to its earlier beliefs ever after" as to "hesitate to adopt new measures . . . when God has granted them the understanding and the opportunity" (*First Defence*, *CPW*, 4:i, 525).[26] In *De Doctrina Christiana* Milton presents what he believes are new truths that should supersede the "conventional opinions" of the church, which are erroneous (*CPW*, 6:121). When he says that he does not "see how the Church can be more disturbed by the investigation of truth, than were the Gentiles by the first promulgation of the gospel" (pp. 9–11), he slyly implies that his doctrine supersedes the traditional church doctrine just as Christ's teachings did the Mosaic law. Moreover, he suggests that the church as a defender of old, erroneous traditions is as antagonistic to true religion as the Gentiles were. The established church, then, like Satan in *Paradise Lost*, becomes a reactionary enemy of the truth.

Not only does Milton's belief that people should progress beyond the achievements of the past make him distrustful of argument by precedent or examples from the past (bad examples may be invoked perhaps more easily than good ones).[27] It also probably underlies his tendency to draw negative parallels between his own age and

the past. Although Milton sometimes draws favorable parallels—
for example, between Fairfax and Scipio Africanus (*Second Defence,*
CPW, 4:i, 669)—most frequently his historical parallels suggest that
England is in danger of repeating the cyclical pattern of the past
rather than progressing beyond the old mistakes. *Areopagitica* discerns the similarity between the Presbyterians in Parliament and
the bishops they ousted: both desire to impede the progress of truth
by licensing books. The Digression in the *History of Britain* draws
a lengthy parallel between Britain after the Romans left and England during the Civil War, which results in a damning indictment
of the English. In both periods "the like defects, the like miscar-
riages notoriouslie appear'd, with vices not less hatefull or inex-
cusable" (*CPW,* 5:i, 443), causing them to lose the opportunity God
had given them for liberty.

Milton draws on the popular, conventional identification between
England and Israel, but most frequently these parallels are unfa-
vorable. They represent either a warning for England not to repeat
the errors of the Israelites or else sharp criticism for her already
having done so. He hopes that England will not repeat the error
of the Jews in the wilderness who asked God for a king (*Tenure of*
Kings and Magistrates, CPW, 3:236). Though England has been delivered from the bondage of Charles I's tryanny, Milton fears she
will once again choose a monarchy: "we shall like those foolish
Israelites, who depos'd God and *Samuel* to set up a King, *Cry out*
one day *because of our King,* which we have bin mad upon; and then
God, as he foretold them, will no more deliver us" (*Eikonoklastes,*
CPW, 3:580). In *First Defence,* England's desire to return to the
bondage of kingship recalls the "sin" of the Israelites "who were
overcome with longing for their former captivity in Egypt and were
at length destroyed by God in countless disasters of all sorts" (*CPW,*
4:i, 532). Milton's sense of the danger of following the pattern of
the past is yet again evident in the *Readie and Easie Way:* "if lastly,
after all this light among us, the same reason shall pass for current
to put our necks again under kingship, as was made use of by the
Jews to returne back to *Egypt* and to the worship of thir idol queen,
because they falsly imagind that they then livd in more plentie and
prosperitie," then "our condition . . . will bring us soon . . . to those
calamities which attend alwaies and unavoidably on luxurie" (*CPW,*
7:462). Like Israel, England prefers bondage and idolatry to liberty

and true worship, and such vices, Milton contends, always bring on a cyclical decline into adversity.

Behind all these parallels lies Milton's belief that people to progress must abandon the patterns of the past.[28] When Milton does invoke parallels in a favorable light, he usually emphasizes the progress the present has made over the past. England's valorous deeds are comparable to those of Greece and Rome, but they are even greater since England's adversary was not merely a political tyrant but an enemy of true religion (*Second Defence, CPW,* 4:i, 548–52). Similarly Milton's program of education is like the ancient schools of Pythagoras, Plato, Isocrates, and Aristotle, but it "shall exceed them" since "this institution . . . shall be equally good both for Peace and warre" (*Of Education, CPW,* 2:408).

It is Christian typology, however, that perhaps best incorporates the essentially progressive spirit of Christianity and rejects the cyclical repetition of past patterns. Typology admits a parallel with a person, action, or event in the past, but it stresses the forward movement of history and the superiority of the present to the past, as later antitypes fulfill and surpass the figures that foreshadow them. *Paradise Regained* clearly illustrates the crucial difference between the view of history that emphasizes parallels and that which stresses a typological, progressive relationship between historical persons or events. Satan sees Christ as paralleling biblical and classical figures from the past (Adam, Moses, David, Job, Hercules) and tempts him to imitate these types literally, to repeat the actions of past figures rather than to pass beyond them. Bound to the view that man is doomed to repeat the example of the past, Satan bases his temptations on the assumption that Christ must follow the same patterns as his predecessors.[29] But Christ must reject this cyclical view of history. He must progress beyond the limitations of types such as Adam and David, avoiding their errors and progressing to a spiritual understanding of his role.

Christ in *Paradise Regained* embodies Milton's ideal of progress. As Christ overcomes the temptations of appetite, distrust of God, and pride that Adam and Eve succumbed to, he refuses to repeat the errors of the past. Resisting Satan's invitations either to identify himself with inferior types or to imitate exactly the noble types of Moses and Elijah, he advances beyond the best the past can offer.[30] With the defeat of Satan in each successive temptation, Christ grows in knowledge and illumination. He must resist believing that the past offers examples of the best that can be achieved. And Christ himself offers the supreme evidence to human beings that progress is possible.[31]

Disillusion: History and the Limits of Education

Although *Paradise Regained* provides a pattern for progress, the poem also reflects a certain skepticism about the likelihood of the people actually achieving it. When Christ tells Satan that the time has not yet come for him to deliver the Israelites, he criticizes their seemingly innate preference for bondage and idolatry rather than liberty, and this judgment parallels Milton's indictment of the English people.

The earlier part of Milton's career is marked by his faith in progress, but from the 1640s he comes increasingly to suspect that people are more likely to fall back to the ways of the past than to advance. The possibility of decline presents an insistent and ever more likely danger. Milton's growing disillusion is evident in the prose of the 1640s and 1650s,[32] and it profoundly affects the major works published at the end of his life.

The seeds of disillusion lie in his view that the alternative to progress is cyclical decay. As we have seen, this view is present even in the earliest antiprelatical tracts. The divorce treatises (1643–45), though still hopeful for reform, continue to warn against returning to the old ways of error. Milton argues that although the gospel gives Christians more liberty than the Old Testament gave the Jews, the current restrictions on divorce are a throwback to the older bondage—indeed, seventeenth-century divorce laws are even more confining than those in the Mosaic law. Parliament now has the opportunity to enable England to make great progress, but *Judgement of Martin Bucer* betrays Milton's anxiety that England will ignore his advice. Indeed, in the "Post-Script" he worries that this work may not even be allowed to be published: the old "ecclesiastical thraldom . . . begins afresh to grow upon us" (*CPW*, 2:479). This specter of cyclical decline appears again in *Tetrachordon*, where the expectation of *"glorious changes and renovations both in Church and State"* is countered by the fear that if Parliament rejects his *"sound argument and reason,"* the *"end"* will be *"that all good learning and knowledge will suddenly decay"* (*CPW*, 2:583–85). Moreover, his description of the two "steps" in the decline of a nation reveals a suspicion that England may be on the verge of decay rather than growth. "In every common wealth when it decayes," people first come to live only according to outward law not inward virtue, as Rome did in Horace's time. The "next declining" consists in "crooked interpretations" of the law — "To both these descents the Pharisees . . . were fall'n" (*CPW*, 2:639). Milton's rhetorical tactic, of course, is to stimulate in his audience a desire to avoid repeating the errors of the Romans and Pharisees and thus to avert decay, but the passage also reveals his sense that decline is indeed possible.

England's failure to reform the divorce laws and the sharp criticism that he received for his views on divorce may have contributed to his fear that England was likely to decline. This fear pervades the *Areopagitica* (1644), in which Milton's warnings comprise an important part of the argument. What emerges from this defense of liberty of the press is a sense of the cyclical pattern of history and a fear that this pattern will continue instead of being replaced by a new pattern of progress.

Despite their tardiness in abolishing error and advancing truth, the execution of Charles I offered the English people a unique chance to break with their past and establish a godly and free commonwealth, but still there were obstacles. Now, however, the impediments seemed to lie with the people rather than with the laws or institutions. Instructing the people to continue "in the glorious way wherin Justice and Victory hath set them," Milton in *Tenure of Kings and Magistrates* (1649) argues against those who earlier had participated in deposing Charles but now reveal their "feare of change" by pitying and defending the king (*CPW*, 3:194). *Eikonoklastes* finds that the "degenerate" majority, ready to idolize Charles I as a martyr, are more inclined to return to the past than to take advantage of the opportunity for liberty that the execution of the king has provided (*CPW*, 3:344). Those who want to restore the monarchy would either bring England back to her former state of bondage or "put [England] back to a second wandring over that horrid Wilderness of distraction and civil slaughter" at a time when they were at the point of entering into the promised land (p. 580).

Milton's fear that England will fail to realize his ideal of progress helps explain the fact that his two defenses of the English people are also admonitions to his country. Though written to vindicate England's actions to Europe, the *Defences* are as concerned to warn

England of the dangers of backsliding as they are to defend her acts and encourage her progress. Toward the end of *First Defence* (1651) he addresses the English, warning them against choosing to return to their past condition at a time when the future holds so much promise: "for you to wish to resist your destiny and return to slavery [by choosing a king] after your freedom had been won by God's assistance and your own valor, after you had performed so many brave deeds and made so memorable an example of this most powerful king, would be not simply a shameful act, but an ungodly and a criminal act!" (*CPW*, 4:i, 532).

Although, as this passage implies, the linear course of progress is the pattern God favors, God's hand is also descernible in the cycles of degeneration. When at the end of *First Defence* Milton advises the English to avoid becoming debauched in peace, he suggests that whereas God rewards virtue with opportunities for progress, decay is His appropriate punishment of vice: the English will "find that God's hatred of you will be greater than was . . . his kindly grace towards you above all peoples now on earth" (p. 536). Even when God has elected a nation for a glorious destiny, that nation can still bring about its decline. Like Jonson, Milton assumes that cyclical decay results when men abandon the rule of reason. But where Jonson suggests that this is a natural pattern, explainable simply through secondary causes, Milton's providential interpretation of history leads him to stress God's role in shaping history.

Milton's fear of relapse is even stronger in the *Second Defence of the English People* (1654). His praise of Oliver Cromwell for accepting the title of protector rather than seeking the name of king contains an implicit warning that Cromwell should not violate the liberty he had defended by becoming the very thing he had overthrown. The danger of repeating the pattern of the past perhaps seems even more imminent in the people, for they are falling back into the same vices—"avarice, ambition, and luxury"—that the Royalists had (*CPW*, 4:i, 680–81). And since slavery to these appetites corrupts a nation and makes it a victim of political tyranny, Milton warns that imitating the Royalists' vices will bring on the Puritans a fate similar to the one that attended their oppressors. Either they will be overthrown by the Royalists who were their enemies, or they will be subdued by others who have "the same patience, integrity, and shrewdness which were at first your strength" (p. 681). Their chance for liberty once missed, they will not be delivered again. God will transfer the opportunity to another nation. Milton's sense of urgency accounts for the impatient, strident tone: "You, therefore, who wish to remain free, either be wise at the outset or recover your senses as soon as possible" (p. 684). The clarity of his vision of England's failure suggests that by 1654 Milton felt that cyclical relapse was a likelier possibility than progress.

By early 1660 England was clearly relapsing in both politics and religion. Despite Milton's efforts in *Treatise of Civil Power* (1659) and *Likeliest Means to Remove Hirelings* (1659), the church was still corrupted by the practice of tithes, and civil force continued to violate the freedom of people's religious practice. Moreover, after the death of Cromwell and the brief, ineffectual reign of his son, England was preparing to welcome back the exiled Charles II, fulfilling the prophetic warnings that Milton had been offering with increasing insistency for nearly twenty years. *Readie and Easie Way* (1660) is Milton's last attempt before the return of Charles II to arrest the cyclical course history was taking. Once again, he castigates England's "unsound humor of returning to old bondage," her desire "to fall back, or rather to creep back . . . to thir once abjur'd and detested thraldom of kingship" (*CPW*, 7:355–57). Though pessimistic about the English people's attraction to servitude, Milton suggests that only "a few main matters now put speedily into execution, will suffice to recover us, and set all right" (p. 387). Milton's proposals for the commonwealth represent desperate expediencies rather than his considered ideals.[33] Whereas earlier he had encouraged speedy and glorious progress, now Milton merely tries to stop imminent decline, "to stay these ruinous proceedings," which would hurry the English to "a precipice of destruction" (*Readie and Easie Way* [2d ed.], *CPW*, 7:463).

Milton felt that England was about to destroy the possibility of progress and immerse herself once again in the cycles of error. Moreover, once the cyclical pattern was reinstituted, she would never be able to regain her present height. If the people "return to kingship" and find the "old incroachments" again, they may have to "fight over again all that we have fought . . . but are never like to attain thus far as we are now advanc'd, to the recoverie of our freedom, never likely to have it in possession, as we now have it, never to be voutsaf'd heerafter the like mercies and signal assistances from heaven in our cause, if by our ingratefull backsliding we make these fruitless" (*CPW*, 7:357–58). At the state of greatest advancement in her history, England is also precariously on the point of losing all. Like Christ on the pinnacle in *Paradise Regained,* she is being tempted to cast herself down, but her temptation clearly comes from within. In a sense Christ's standing on the pinnacle embodies the hopes Milton had for England, but the miraculous nature of Christ's feat sets off the frailty of man, who seems by nature disposed to fall. Although even in *Readie and Easie Way* Milton insists that the English, like Adam and Eve, still can avoid falling into old error, he seems to have lost nearly all confidence that they will.

Ultimately England's refusal to seize the providential opportunity for progress points to a failure of education, which Milton sees as essential to progress. The word's etymology suggests advancement. His tract on education emphasizes continual linear progress in the course of a person's training and implies that one of the main purposes of education is to enable a nation to attain greater achievements. In *Paradise Lost* we see that God Himself is an educator, sending Raphael and Michael to teach Adam and Eve, "informing" the Israelites "by types / And shadows" (XII, 232–33), giving them the Law to prepare them for progress—its "purpose [is] to resign them in full time / Up to a better Cov'nant, disciplin'd / From shadowy Types to Truth" (XII, 301–3).

One of the major functions of education is to enable people to learn from the past. Because history reveals a pattern in which like errors and vices are followed by like consequences, we can see parallels between the present and the past. In *Eikonoklastes* Milton points to this educative function of history: "We may have learnt both from sacred History, and times of Reformation, that the Kings of this World have both ever hated, and instinctively fear'd the Church of God"; and those who tried to suppress the true church "have drawn upon themselves the occasion of their own ruin." Thus what happened to Charles I recalls Pharoah's punishment for persecuting the Israelites (*CPW,* 3:509–10). We can learn not only to see similarities between past and present but, more important, to avoid the errors of the past. As we have seen, Milton's polemical prose repeatedly invokes past examples only to exhort England not to follow them.

In the major poems the heroes must learn similar lessons. In *Paradise Lost,* for instance, the "Divine Historian" Raphael (VIII, 6–7) gives Adam (who is supposed in turn to teach Eve) the example of Abdiel, the faithful angel who stands loyal though surrounded by evil and error, as well as the example of Satan, the angel whose disobedience is punished. At the end of his account of the war in heaven, Raphael warns Adam to remember the example of Satan and refrain from repeating it; it is characteristic of Milton's view of history to place more emphasis on the need to avoid repeating the bad examples from the past than on the desirability of imitating good examples:

> . . . let it profit thee to have heard
> By terrible Example the reward
> Of disobedience; firm they might have stood,
> Yet fell; remember, and fear to transgress. (VI, 909–12)

But Adam and Eve fail to remember: "still they knew, and ought to have still remember'd / The high Injunction not to taste that Fruit" (X, 12–13). Their failure recalls that of the brothers in *Comus* who forget the Attendant Spirit's injunction to seize the sorcerer's wand. Despite the long history they are given, Adam and Eve repeat Satan's error. Although Milton believes that people are able to progress through education, that they can learn the lessons of history and avoid repeating the errors of their predecessors, he has come to see that people typically fail to profit from these lessons.

Paradise Lost reveals Milton's diminished faith in the actual accomplishments of education. Many scholars have stressed the importance of education in *Paradise Lost* and the poem's didactic function. Christopher Hill has argued that the poem teaches "a different type of political action from those which . . . failed so lamentably" in the English Revolution, and he sees Milton as still hopeful about reform.[34] I would suggest, however, that in an important sense *Paradise Lost* demonstrates the failure of education and thus a pessimism about the likelihood of political reform. Despite the lengthy efforts of Raphael, Adam and Eve forget the lessons his history teaches. Satan himself provides the supreme example of someone who cannot learn from his past errors. "Untaught" by the outcome of his "Vain War with Heav'n" (II, 9), he persists in believing that he can defeat God. Indeed, all the fallen angels share this incapacity, which is perhaps most vividly depicted in Milton's description of their eating the fruit that turns to ashes in their mouths:

> . . . oft they assay'd,
> Hunger and thirst constraining, drugg'd as oft,
> With hatefullest disrelish writh'd thir jaws
> With soot and cinders fill'd; so oft they fell
> Into the same illusion. (X, 567–71)

Their punishment perfectly fits their error: they are doomed to repeat their mistake, unable to learn from experience.

Though the Fall shows Adam and Eve failing to profit from the lessons Raphael presents, in the last two books Adam is given another chance. Michael educates him in human history, and, as has frequently been noted, Adam here progresses in understanding.[35] By the end of Michael's account, Adam has undergone conversion, becoming the first Christian. The last two books, however, indicate Milton's loss of faith in education in yet another sense.

The vision of history's vicissitudes reveals that though Adam's understanding may grow, people in general do not learn from history. In Book XI Adam witnesses the unjust kill the just as Cain murders Abel; the sober sons of God yield up their virtue to lascivious women; warriors repeat Cain's sin on a large scale, strewing fields with corpses and gaining fame through military conquest; and the people turn from war to luxury and riot. Throughout these scenes in Book XI Adam sees violence alternate with lust, and we remember that Adam and Eve feel these two impulses immediately after the Fall. This sense of the repetitive pattern of human experience is even stronger in Book XII, where Michael's narration shows history dominated by a recurrent pattern of decline and degeneration. For a time after the Flood, men are more virtuous "while the dread of judgment past remains / Fresh in thir minds" (ll. 14–15), but ambitious Nimrod gains "Dominion undeserv'd / Over his brethren" (ll. 27–28), and the cycle of sin and punishment begins once again. After the flood—as before—the world degenerates "from bad to worse" (l. 106). But once again history seems to begin anew when God, "wearied" with the people's sins, selects His chosen nation, and Abraham, exemplifying Milton's ideal, breaks with the past and leaves his false "Gods, his Friends, and native Soil" (l. 129) to journey to an unknown land, founding a new nation. But despite Abraham's rejection of false traditions, Israel, the chosen nation, tends to repeat the pattern of the past, succumbing to sinfulness and idolatry. Although God works toward the redemption of mankind through Christ and thus history reveals God's progressive movement from types and the flesh to truth and the spirit, the history Milton offers shows little sense of human progress. Corruption is, if anything, worse after the crucifixion of Christ. Good people are still persecuted; and whereas in earlier ages God directly intervened in history to save virtuous men such as Enoch from their enemies, now the good person can expect only "inward consolations" as a recompense in this world (l. 495). After the Apostles, history shows even further degeneration as the few true worshippers are persecuted and the great majority persist in their idolatrous rites. And so the world will continue, "To good malignant, to bad men benign" (l. 538) until the Day of Judgment. Milton's failure to mention the Reformation tends to negate even further any possible sense of human progress. Adam's response at the end of Michael's narration of "salvation history" is hope and faith in God's providence. However, his hopefulness derives from his assurance that at the apocalyptic end of time evil will be confounded and the virtuous few rewarded with "eternall Bliss" (XII, 551)—not from any sense that mankind will progress in goodness throughout history.

In fact, Michael's history has revealed that instead of progressing, people continue to repeat the vices of the past—they seem caught in a cyclical repetition of error.[36] There are indeed good individuals, but they seem unable to change the course of history, to effect progress rather than cyclical decline. When Enoch tried to reason with the people, they "seiz'd" him "with violent hands" (XI, 669). Noah "set" before the wicked "the paths of righteousness," but they refused to change their "ways" (XI, 812–16). Milton, too, had tried to teach his countrymen, with similar results. In *Paradise Lost* Milton explains to England why she lost her opportunity for political freedom and what is necessary to gain liberty.[37] But he seems to have little hope of improving a nation and persuading it to progress in virtue. He stands at the end of a long line of good, indeed inspired men sent by God, who have defended virtue though surrounded or even killed by evil people—none have been able to reform his countrymen. Although for Milton there is always the possibility of breaking with the precedent of the past, it seems unlikely that England will do so. The individual (Adam) may advance in understanding, but Milton's overview of history in the final books of *Paradise Lost* reveals that nations do not learn from the past.

In the *History of Britain* as well as *Paradise Lost* we see Milton's reservations about education. Although he probably began writing the *History* toward the end of the period 1645–47 and by 1649 had drafted the first four books, Milton actually composed the *History* over a number of years, and he probably continued to revise it until it was finally published.[38] His publication of the work in 1670 suggests that he offered it as representing his mature views. Recounting Britain's history from the time of the Romans to the Norman conquest, he shows that his country has gone through a number of cycles in which subjection to a foreign people was followed by liberty, which itself allowed the growth of vice and the attendant corruption of the people that made them once again subject to conquest and bondage.[39] We see a long history in which people repeat the mistakes of their predecessors. The Northumbrians succumb to "all the same vices which *Gildas* alleg'd of old to have ruin'd the *Britans*"; and the Saxons become "as wicked as the *Britans* were at their arrival, brok'n with luxurie and sloth" (*CPW*, 5:i, 256, 259).

The Digression extends this vision of the cyclical pattern of history into the seventeenth century as Milton draws a parallel between the Britains after the Romans left and England during the Civil War period. Originally intended to open Book III, the Digression was published only after Milton's death as the *Character of the Long Parliament and Assembly of Divines* (1681). While it may well reflect Milton's disillusion in early 1648 when the first Civil War was over and a new form of government had not yet been established, I would suggest that it also embodies his final and considered view of the English people.[40] During both the time after the Romans' departure and the Civil War, the English were given an opportunity for freedom, but their vices and "the ill husbanding of those faire opportunities" (*CPW*, 5:i, 443) caused them to destroy their chances for liberty. More than an invective against the Long Parliament and the Westminister Assembly, the Digression exposes England's inability to deserve and maintain freedom, and the vices he attacks are the same ones he warns against in the *Second Defence* and *Readie and Easie Way*. Moreover, the *History* as published in

1670 suggests the parallel between seventeenth-century Englishmen and the ancient Britons, even though it is not developed at length. The parallel would be at least as appropriate after the Restoration as before, for England had willingly returned to the bondage of monarchy.[41]

In emphasizing the historical parallels, Milton suggests that the English still have not learned from their mistakes. But he insists at the opening of Book III that in writing this history, he is giving England another chance to learn about herself: "we may be able from two such remarkable turns of State, producing like events among us, to raise a knowledg of our selves" (*CPW*, 5:i, 129–30). Such self-knowledge presumably could cause England to reform her vices and thus arrest this cyclical course of history and make progress possible. But the Digression clearly indicates that Milton has so little faith in the character of the English that he is skeptical about their changing. By their very nature, conditioned by the climate, the English people are courageous but not wise or virtuous: "For Britain . . . as it is a land fruitful enough of men stout and couragious in warr, so is it naturallie not over fertil of men able to govern justlie & prudently in peace; . . . civilitie, prudence, love of the public more than of money or vaine honour are to this soile in a manner outlandish; grow not here but in minds well implanted with solid & elaborate breeding" (p. 451).

Milton's disillusion did not prevent him from trying to teach his countrymen. In the year before his death (1673), he reprinted *Of Education* and published his tract *Of True Religion, Haeresie, Schism, and Toleration*, which concludes with a call to England to "amend our lives with all speed" (*CPW*, 8:440). That he continued to argue for reform, however, does not mean that he expected it. The Old Testament prophets, too, had persisted in warning the Israelites even when it was clear to them that these warnings would not be heeded.

In his *History of Britain* Milton grimly suggests that the English people may well be "unteachable" (*CPW*, 5:i, 451).[42] In *Paradise Regained* Christ expresses a similar view when he says that the Israelites, despite their suffering and captivity, have not reformed their vices. If he were to free them now, the idolatrous "captive Tribes" would only return to their idolatry. At length, however, God "may bring them back repentant and sincere" (III, 414, 435).

It would take an act of grace to make either the Israelites or the English worthy of being delivered.

Samson Agonistes: *The Progress of the Hero and the Failure of the People*

Like so many of Milton's works, *Samson Agonistes* is concerned with deliverance from the bondage that Milton typically associates with the cyclical repetition of error and sin. No one knows with certainty when Milton wrote this poem. But, published near the end of his life, it draws together many of the concerns we have been exploring. With his idea of tragedy as "the gravest, moralest, and most profitable of all other Poems" (preface to *SA*, p. 549), Milton offers the "example" (*SA*, l. 166) of Samson from which we can learn. The crucial issues are: What is Samson an example of? What lessons are we expected to learn?

The poem presents Samson in two ways. He is both the special, unique individual and the representative of Israel. And since, as scholars have observed, Israel seems to parallel England, Samson's two roles have quite different implications for England. As a hero, chosen and marked by God, raised as Nazarite, Samson is set apart from the rest of the Israelites.[43] Thus he holds much the same relation to Israel as Israel (the chosen people) does to the Gentiles. Samson also separates himself from the Israelites as he condemns them for rejecting the opportunities for deliverance he offered them. The men of Judah seem as much his enemies as the Philistines, since they hand him to the enemy to protect their land (ll. 256–57). Refusing to accept responsibility for Israel's continued servitude, Samson indicts

> . . . *Israel's* Governors, and Heads of Tribes,
> Who seeing those great acts which God had done
> Singly by me against their Conquerors
> Acknowledg'd not, or not at all consider'd
> Deliverance offer'd. (ll. 242–46)

In this sense Samson's relationship with the Israelites parallels Milton's with the English.

In another way, though, Samson represents Israel. His bondage parallels the servitude of the Israelites; his decline from glory reflects theirs. Implying an analogy between Samson's life and Israel's history, the Chorus finds in Samson's fallen condition an opportunity to consider the shape and meaning of history. "Fall'n" from "the top of wondrous glory" to the "lowest pitch of abject fortune" (ll. 167, 169), Samson's career illustrates for the Chorus the cyclical wheel of fortune; he is a "mirror of our fickle state" (l. 164). The Chorus's understanding, however, is limited and does not represent Milton's view.[44] Although the Chorus discerns a pattern in human life, it wrongly suggests that the fall from great height suggests either the inevitability of cyclical decline or the arbitrary fickleness of God:

> God of our Fathers, what is man!
> That thou towards him with hand so various,
> Or might I say contrarious,
> Temper'st thy providence through his short course,
> Not evenly. . . . (ll.667–71)

The special people that God has "elected, / With gifts and graces eminently adorn'd / To some great work" (ll. 678–80) seem especially vulnerable to sharp changes of fortune.

> . . . toward these, thus dignifi'd, thou oft,
> Admidst thir height of noon,
> Changest thy count'nance and thy hand, with no regard
> Of highest favors past
> From thee on them, or them to thee of service. (ll. 682–86)

The Chorus can only see an inexplicable, arbitrary, unjust vicissitude in Samson's decline and, by implication, in Israel's also.[45]

But Samson readily has acknowledged his responsibility for his fall—his own weaknesses have led to his decline as Israel's have led to her servitude. The poem corrects the Chorus's view of history, suggesting (as *Paradise Lost, Paradise Regained,* and the *Second Defence* did) that physical or political bondage results from and is God's punishment of inner slavery, submission to one's passions. That people themselves are responsible for cyclical decline indicates that such cycles are not inevitable. Milton thus undercuts the Chorus's view of the pattern of life, showing that God's just providence and human responsibility lie behind its order.

For all the similarities between Samson and Israel, there is a crucial difference in their histories. Samson after his decline undergoes a regeneration that we do not see Israel experience. When the poem begins, Samson is fallen. The cyclical decline has occurred in the past, and *Samson Agonistes* itself presents a pattern of progress that provides the alternative and antidote to decline. As readers have frequently noted, Samson himself progresses in patience, wisdom, and understanding. He begins abject, confined, in darkness. He ends illuminated, possessed of renewed strength and inner liberty. The opening lines in which Samson asks to be led "a little onward" by "thy guiding hand" (l. 1) suggest the progress Samson will make with God's help, and the image of the linear journey contrasts with the endless, circular movement at the mill where Samson is working at the opening of the poem. As Samson progresses from weakness to strength, blindness to illumination, despair to confidence, he becomes an example of how human beings can break the cyclical pattern. Through his encounters with Manoa, Dalila, and Harapha, he overcomes his weaknesses and learns to avoid past errors. The Chorus sees Samson repeating mistakes others have made and (like Satan in *Paradise Regained*) assumes that the pattern will always be the same: "wisest Men / Have err'd, and by bad Women been deceiv'd; / And shall again, pretend they ne'er so wise" (ll. 210–12). But the poem celebrates the individual's ability to free himself from the past, to change.

Manoa, Dalila, and Harapha each represent a weakness in Samson, and in resisting the temptations they offer, Samson demonstrates his ability to conquer the inner flaws that led to his downfall. Manoa embodies not just a concern with fame but also the belief that man can control events. He thinks it is in his power to free his son, to ransom him, but we see that only God can deliver him. Samson must learn that the people may not properly value heroic acts and, more important, that God not man ultimately controls the outcome of events, though the individual still retains choice and responsibility. By the end of the poem Samson acts under God's guidance, not simply on his own impulse. In the encounter with Dalila, Samson conquers his former enslavement to sexual passion as he resists her offers. And with Harapha he overcomes inordinate pride and gains confidence that God is still with him, even in captivity.[46]

In resisting Dalila, however, we perhaps most clearly see Samson's progress, for he shows his ability to alter his former pattern, to avoid repeating the past. When he married Dalila, he had not learned from his past experiences. The woman of Timna had earlier betrayed him, persuading him to tell her a secret and then revealing it to his opponents. The same pattern occurred with Dalila—he revealed a secret and she betrayed him to the Philistines. Failing to learn, though "warn'd by oft experience" (l. 382), Samson seems bound to repeat the same mistakes. But the encounter with Dalila shows that Samson *can* break with the past. In rejecting her offers of sensuality, he diverges from his former behavior and thus embodies the paradigm for progress that Milton endorses. When at the end the Semichorus describes Samson as a phoenix reviving from its ashes, the image suggests not merely a restoration of former glory but also a new creation.

If Samson represents Milton's ideal of progress, the Israelites show the failure of people to alter the pattern of their lives. Samson's indictment of Israel's refusal to accept his offers for deliverance prompts the Chorus to list previous examples of deliverers "contemn'd":

> Thy words to my remembrance bring
> How *Succoth* and the Fort of *Penuel*
> Thir great Deliverer contemn'd,
> The matchless *Gideon* in pursuit
> Of *Madian* and her vanquisht Kings:
> And how ingrateful *Ephraim*
> Had dealt with *Jephtha*, who by argument,
> Not worse than by his shield and spear
> Defended *Israel* from the *Ammonite*,
> Had not his prowess quell'd thir pride
> In that sore battle when so many died
> Without Reprieve adjudg'd to death,
> For want of well pronouncing *Shibboleth*. (ll. 277–89)

The repetition of error demonstrates how firmly Israel is fixed in the cyclical pattern. Time after time, she has failed to take advantage of opportunities for liberty. Samson's final act of heroism once again gives Israel an opportunity for deliverance, and many readers have seen in this ending Milton's optimism: Israel can achieve the kind of progress Samson has.[47] Manoa says that all Israel needs is to "Find courage to lay hold on this occasion" (l. 1716). Such a reading of Israel's possibilities depends on our identification of

Samson with Israel. But, as we have seen, the figure of Samson also contrasts with Israel, and partly because of this contrast the final implications of the poem are far from optimistic as they concern Israel. Biblical history shows that Israel failed once again to seize the occasion, and the corrupt Danites eventually vanished from history.[48] Milton would have expected his audience to know this outcome. Thus the ending is in an important way ironic— though Samson has progressed and Israel has the opportunity, the audience knows, as Manoa and the Chorus cannot, that she will not use it to advance. It seems that education succeeds in the individual but fails for the masses—Israel does not learn, though "warn'd by oft experience" (l. 82).[49]

In *Samson Agonistes*, and indeed in all the major poems published late in Milton's life, only the individual actually fulfills the ideal of progress Milton had entertained for England. The true hero is the one who successfully breaks with the past. Behind Milton's well-known shift of interest to the individual, to the paradise within,[50] lies his changing view of history—his gradual loss of faith in the ability of the people to learn from the past and to change their lives.

Just as in the prose, so in *Samson Agonistes* Milton suggests a parallel between Israel and England. Like Israel, England has rejected its opportunity for liberty, and Israel's inability to learn from history suggests the similar failure of the English, which Milton exposes in the *History of Britain*. Although he indeed assumes an educative role in *Samson*, the lessons are not encouraging. The example of Samson teaches the way of progress; the example of Israel shows the more common rejection of progress, the refusal to stop the cycle. Perhaps England may learn to imitate Samson, but Milton's final sense of progress as an individual achievement suggests that *each* person must undergo this transformation to produce a reformed nation. Mass regeneration seems unlikely. Even if the English were to change and become worthy of liberty, God might not give them another chance for deliverance.

It is interesting that the lesson Israel and England must learn is quite different from the one Samson needs to learn. Israel must learn to seize the offer of liberty when it comes. In his prose Milton similarly had exhorted England to take advantage of the providential opportunity to break with the cyclical pattern of the past. Urging the people to act, he criticized their tendency to delay reform, to hesitate in the way, to be slow in removing obstacles to progress. But Samson needs to learn patience. He must wait for illumination from God. And he must accept that no matter what heroic act he performs, if Israel is undeserving of freedom, she will remain in bondage.

Even in his youth, Milton had recognized the value of patience. Sonnet VII ("How Soon Hath Time") betrays his anxiety that he has yet to produce the "bud or blossom" that comes with "ripeness" (ll. 4, 7), and he clearly feels the pressure of time, which has already stolen twenty-three years. Some twenty years later, in Sonnet XIX ("When I Consider..."), Milton is still concerned that his "one Talent" remains "Lodg'd with me useless" (ll. 3–4). His gift for great poetry has gone unfulfilled while he has been engaged in prose polemics. Both sonnets show that Milton is disturbed by his tardiness, but his conclusion in both is to remain patient.[51] His advice to himself is quite different from that which he gives the English people. Resigning himself to God's time, he recognizes in Sonnet VII that he cannot force progress:

> Yet be it less or more, or soon or slow,
>   It shall be still in strictest measure ev'n
>   To that same lot, however, mean or high
> Toward which Time leads me, and the will of Heav'n.
>   (ll. 9–12)

Again in Sonnet XIX he must learn to react to delays with "patience" (l. 8); and though thousands are called to "speed / And post o'er Land and Ocean without rest," he may be one of those whose calling is simply to "stand and wait" (ll. 12–14). Though Milton is disturbed by the delay in his poetic achievements, these poems imply that the temptation for him is to precipitous, premature action. The conclusion Milton reaches for himself—that he must be patient and wait for the fulness of God's time—becomes in the major poems the virtuous individual's proper response to the vicissitudes of human history.[52] Whereas the mass of people typically refuse to seize the opportunities God gives them, the danger for Milton and his heroes lies in haste.

Milton's pictures of history in *Paradise Lost*, *Paradise Regained*, and *Samson Agonistes* portray the repetition of error, and the lesson the heroes in these poems learn is the one Milton had already

grasped on a personal level in the sonnet on his twenty-third birth-
day—that man cannot force progress. Michael's history in the last
two books of *Paradise Lost* teaches Adam that Christ's redemption
of mankind does not mean that rapid progress will follow. Although
the individual can advance and achieve the paradise within, the
majority of people will either remain the same or degenerate further. One of the most important truths Christ comes to recognize
in *Paradise Regained* is that the course of history cannot be rushed.
Satan repeatedly tempts him to act before the proper time—to
deliver mankind immediately.[53] Advising Christ to grasp "Occasion's forelock" (III, 173), Satan's temptation embodies the desire
Milton had earlier to free his country from bondage. Once again
we see that the individual's mistake is to act before the "due time"
(*PR*, III, 182). Even in the *Nativity Ode* Milton knew that despite
his longing for the apocalyptic restoration of the golden age, history
must run its full course: "But wisest Fate says no, / This must not
yet be so" (ll. 149–50). And in *Paradise Regained* it is Simon and
Andrew, not Christ, who make the mistake of believing that the
perfection that had been prophesied is about to be fulfilled: "Now,
now, for sure, deliverance is at hand, / The Kingdom shall to *Israel*
be restor'd" (II, 35–36). Milton had harbored similar hopes for
progress, but his experience of history had gradually altered his
expectations.

England's turmoils during the mid-seventeenth century thus
yielded a generalization that previous history confirmed: people
prefer the well-trodden way. To the end of his life, Milton retained
his ideal of progress and his dislike of mere cyclical repetition of
the past. He always felt that the people could and should change
the shape of history. Nevertheless, he came to share Jonson's view
that because most people are ruled by their appetites rather than
reason, the cyclical pattern would probably characterize history
until the Apocalypse. While God may give nations the opportunity
for progress, most fail to take advantage of it. Whereas Bacon's
works, late as well as early, resound with confidence in man's ability
to achieve progress, Milton's observation of the English people
radically diminished his faith in the possibility of changing the
course of history. Shifting his faith in progress from the realm of
history to the life of the individual, he concluded that progress is
possible only for the special individual. The good person may try

to change the course of history, but he cannot make a recalcitrant people progress.

Notes

1. *Of Reformation,* in *Complete Prose Works of John Milton,* ed. Don M. Wolfe, 8 vols. (New Haven: Yale University Press, 1953–82), 1:615. I have used this Yale edition for the prose, hereafter referred to as *CPW.* All references to Milton's poetry are to *Complete Poems and Major Prose,* ed. Merritt Y. Hughes (New York: Odyssey Press, 1957).

2. Arguing that the Christian view of history is essentially linear and contrasts with the Greco-Roman view of temporality as cyclic, C. A. Patrides sees Milton as a proponent of this linear view of history. See *Grand Design of God,* pp. 84–90, and *Milton and the Christian Tradition* (Oxford: Clarendon Press, 1966), ch. 8. Laurie Zwicky, "Kairos in *Paradise Regained:* The Divine Plan," *ELH* 31 (1964), 271–77, also emphasizes Milton's belief in the linear Christian view of history. However, Michael Fixler in *Milton and the Kingdoms of God* (London: Faber and Faber, 1964), p. 67, observes that Milton as a historian accepted the cyclical theory. Both views are in a sense correct, but neither fully encompasses the complexity of Milton's ideas. Although Patrides among others places the Christian linear view of history in opposition to the cyclical, the providential view of history often combines the cyclical and linear. For one explanation of this combination, see Edward Tayler, *Milton's Poetry: Its Development in Time* (Pittsburgh: Duquesne University Press, 1979), introduction.

3. Fixler, *Milton and the Kingdoms of God,* p. 89, recognizes that in *Of Reformation* Milton apparently hoped that "reformation would free England permanently from the cyclical revolutions of the past." See also Mary Ann Radzinowicz, *Toward "Samson Agonistes": The Growth of Milton's Mind* (Princeton: Princeton University Press, 1978), p. 75.

4. Thomas Kranidas, "Polarity and Structure in Milton's *Areopagitica,*" *ELR* 14 (1984), 175–90, discusses the pattern of "contrasts between public and private, Greek and Latin, true praise and flattery, unity and diversity" (p. 176). Though Kranidas does not discuss the contrast between cyclical and progressive patterns of history, this important polarity also contributes to the structure of *Areopagitica.*

5. An important version of the journey is the Exodus myth, which John Shawcross finds central in *Paradise Regained, Samson Agonistes,* and especially *Paradise Lost;* see "*Paradise Lost* and the Theme of Exodus," *Milton Studies* 2 (1970), 3–26.

6. See James Whaler, "The Miltonic Simile," *PMLA* 46 (1931), 1034–74; and Tayler, *Milton's Poetry,* chs. III and V. See also Christopher Ricks, *Milton's Grand Style* (Oxford: Clarendon Press, 1963), pp. 118–19, 132;

and Arnold Stein, *Heroic Knowledge* (1957; rpt. Hamden, Conn.: Archon Books, 1965), pp. 36ff.

7. Wolfe, in introduction, *CPW,* 1:118, notes that answering the opponent point by point was a common method of arguing.

8. See Fixler, *Milton and the Kingdoms of God,* pp. 234, 269; Barbara Kiefer Lewalski, *Milton's Brief Epic: The Genre, Meaning, and Art of "Paradise Regained"* (Providence, R.I.: Brown University Press, 1966), pp. 181, 195.

9. See Barbara Lewalski's article, "Time and History in *Paradise Regained,*" in *The Prison and the Pinnacle,* ed. Balachandra Rajan (Toronto: University of Toronto Press, 1973), p. 66.

10. Lewalski, "Time and History in *Paradise Regained,*" p. 68, points out that Satan's returning "again and again only to be repulsed as many times" is the counterpart of his view of the "repetitiveness of . . . history."

11. Murray Roston, *Milton and the Baroque* (Pittsburgh: University of Pittsburgh Press, 1980), defines the baroque as reflecting and celebrating this new sense of the universe, and he argues that *Paradise Lost* is essentially baroque. On the development of the idea of an infinite universe, see Koyrè, *From the Closed World.*

12. Arguing that perfection in Paradise implies continuous and fruitful motion, Joseph H. Summers, in the *Muse's Method: An Introduction to Paradise Lost* (London: Chatto and Windus, 1962), ch. III, esp. pp. 73, 86, recognizes the connection between Milton as a celebrator of change and his rejection of static being as an ideal. Ricardo J. Quinones, *The Renaissance Discovery of Time* (Cambridge, Mass.: Harvard University Press, 1972), observes that "Milton seems more open to change" than Dante, Petrarch, Spenser, and Shakespeare, "in whose quest for permanence one can detect the horror they experience in their changeful existences" (p. 461).

13. See Barbara Kiefer Lewalski, "Innocence and Experience in Milton's Eden," in *New Essays on "Paradise Lost,"* ed. Thomas Kranidas (Berkeley: University of California Press, 1969), p. 92; she also argues that Adam and Eve grow in understanding during the Edenic portion of *Paradise Lost* (pp. 99–100).

14. Milton's suggestion that man naturally could have risen to God if he had not fallen should make us hesitant to believe that Milton saw the Fall as fortunate. See Virginia R. Mollenkott, "Milton's Rejection of the Fortunate Fall," *Milton Quarterly* 6 (1972), 1–5. Though Earl Miner, in "*Felix Culpa* in the Redemptive Order of *Paradise Lost,*" *PQ* 47 (1968), 43–54, suggests that Milton accepts the paradox of the fortunate Fall, he stresses that the Fall is fortunate only for a very few and that there will be a long period of waiting "before the fall can possibly be felt to be fortunate" (p. 48).

15. In "Time and History in *Paradise Regained,*" Lewalski explains that Milton departs from tradition in depicting heaven as characterized by change (p. 51).

16. For a discussion of Milton's use of words in the original meanings, stripped of their usual negative associations, see Leland Ryken, *The Apoc-*

alyptic Vision in "Paradise Lost" (Ithaca: Cornell University Press, 1970), pp. 58–74; Ricks, *Milton's Grand Style*, pp. 109–17; Arnold Stein, *Answerable Style: Essays on "Paradise Lost"* (Minneapolis: University of Minnesota Press, 1953), pp. 66–67.

17. Joan Webber, *Milton and His Epic Tradition* (Seattle: University of Washington Press, 1979), recognizes that "in announcing the begetting of the Son, God reveals himself as a creative, active, living force, while Satan, unwilling to risk his own status, attempts to freeze the hierarchy" (p. 120).

18. Satan's support of tradition, custom, and error recalls Milton's portrayal not only of prelacy but of Charles I. Joan S. Bennett, "God, Satan, and King Charles: Milton's Royal Portraits," *PMLA* 92 (1977), 441–57, demonstrates Milton's parallels between the monarchy of Charles I and Satan's tyranny.

19. Tuveson, *Millennium and Utopia*, has noted that "the germ of a concept of progress is implicit in the nature of the Christian religion," even though "the Christian idea contains elements alien to the idea of secular progress as we have come to know it" (pp. 6–7). See also Nisbet, *History of the Idea of Progress*, ch. 2, where he argues that the early Christian philosophers from Eusebius to St. Augustine contributed to the development of the idea of progress.

20. Baxter, *Church-History*, p. 468.

21. As Radzinowicz explains (*Toward "Samson Agonistes"*), Milton realized that parts of the Bible had been lost or corrupted, so he placed preeminent authority on the internal scripture of the Holy Spirit rather than on the written word. Moreover, he believed that men "may progressively discover the truths always latent in the text" (pp. 278–79).

22. Headley, *Luther's View of Church History*, p. 163.

23. Joseph Hall, *An Humble Remonstrance* (London, 1640), p. 19.

24. Smectymnuus, *An Answer to a Booke Entituled An Humble Remonstrance* (London, 1641), p. 20. Cf. also Richard Hooker, who half a century earlier had similarly argued (though against quite different opponents— the English Calvinists who wanted a more thorough reform of the English church) that we should not be tied to the practices of antiquity and that changes in church discipline may be not only necessary but desirable (*Laws of Ecclesiastical Polity*, Bk. III, ch. x).

25. Even John Lilburne, the Leveller, insisted that he wanted to restore the old liberty, rather than create something new. See, e.g., *The Legal Fundamental Liberties of the People of England* (London, 1649), and *Englands New Chains Discovered* (London, 1648).

26. It is interesting to note William Prynne's quite different attitude toward change in his criticism of the Independents for their unwillingness to bind themselves in the future to their present beliefs; see *A fresh discouery of some prodigious new Wandring-Blasing Stars, & Firebrands, stiling themselves New-Lights* (London, 1645), pp. 47–48.

27. Z. S. Fink, *The Classical Republicans*, 2d ed. (Evanston: Northwestern University Press, 1962), pp. 94–95, notes that though "Milton looked to

classical precedents in political theory," in his pamphlets he declared that his country was acting without precedents and did not need them.

28. In *A Defence* Milton praises England for not following the example of Israel, who asked for a king (*CPW*, 4:i, 354). Michael McKeon, *Politics and Poetry in Restoration England: The Case of Dryden's Annus Mirabilis* (Cambridge, Mass.: Harvard University Press, 1975), has argued that in the seventeenth century "there were few revolutionaries whose desire for a new start did not envision, as a foundation for the future, a return to the past" (p. 264). Milton, it would seem, is one of those few.

29. See Lewalski, "Time and History in *Paradise Regained*," p. 69.

30. See Lewalski, *Milton's Brief Epic*, p. 195.

31. Lewalski points out in "Time and History in *Paradise Regained*" that by fulfilling the types Christ "has made novelty and re-creation possible—new men, new lives, in a new kingdom whose history need not be sterile repetition but can be marked by significant and unique events" (pp. 72–73).

32. Arthur E. Barker, *Milton and the Puritan Dilemma, 1641–1660* (Toronto: University of Toronto Press, 1942), traces in the prose the development of Milton's disillusion in the English people and in the imminent establishment of Christ's kingdom. Fixler, *Milton and the Kingdoms of God*, p. 106, sees that Milton loses his apocalyptic fervor and unlimited optimism after the anti-episcopal tracts.

33. See William Riley Parker, *Milton: A Biography*, 2 vols. (Oxford: Clarendon Press, 1968), 1:543. See also Don M. Wolfe, *Milton in the Puritan Revolution* (New York: Thomas Nelson and Sons, 1941), pp. 297–310.

34. Christopher Hill, *Milton and the English Revolution* (New York: Viking Press, 1977), p. 348 and ch. 28.

35. See, e.g., H. R. MacCallum, "Milton and Sacred History: Books XI and XII of *Paradise Lost*," in *Essays in English Literature from the Renaissance to the Victorian Age, Presented to A. S. P. Woodhouse*, ed. Millar MacLure and F. W. Watt (Toronto: University of Toronto Press, 1964), pp. 159–60; Barbara Kiefer Lewalski, "Structure and the Symbolism of Vision in Michael's Prophecy, *Paradise Lost*, Books XI–XII," *PQ* 42 (1963), 25–35; Michael Cavanagh, "A Meeting of Epic and History: Books XI and XII of *Paradise Lost*," *ELH* 38 (1971), 206–22; and Tayler, *Milton's Poetry*, p. 80.

36. Balachandra Rajan, *The Lofty Rhyme: A Study of Milton's Major Poetry* (Coral Gables: University of Miami Press, 1970), p. 98, observes that Book XII reflects Milton's loss of confidence in progress, though some other critics have suggested that the last two books contain an element of progress (e.g., Shawcross, "*Paradise Lost* and the Theme of Exodus"). Georgia B. Christopher, *Milton and the Science of the Saints* (Princeton: Princeton University Press, 1982), discerns two patterns of history presented by the narrative of the final books of *Paradise Lost*. On the one hand, there is the increasing "clarity" and then "ever-widening proclamation of the word"; on the other, there are the "little cycles of degeneration and renewal," which actually trace "a large arc downward" (pp.

186–89). Thomas Amorose, "Milton the Apocalyptic Historian: Competing Genres in *Paradise Lost*, Books XI–XII," *Milton Studies* 17 (1983), 141–62, argues that in these books Milton offers an apocalyptic, prophetic vision of history that denies "the ultimate validity of the cyclical view of history" (p. 145).

37. See Hill, *Milton*, ch. 28–29 (pp. 341–412), on the political relevance of *Paradise Lost* and the parallels to England during the Revolution.

38. See French Fogle, introduction to *History of Britain*, CPW, 5:i, pp. xxxix, xliii.

39. Although Patrides, *Milton and the Christian Tradition*, pp. 257–59, sees only the providential view in the *History of Britain*, J. A. Bryant, Jr., "The Evolution of Milton's Conception of History" (Ph.d. diss., Yale University, 1948), finds that the *History* embodies a cyclical view of history (pp. 225ff.).

40. On the Digression as reflecting Milton's view in 1648, see Fogle, introduction to *History of Britain*, pp. xxxix–xl; and Sir Charles Firth, "Milton as an Historian," in his *Essays Historical and Literary* (Oxford: Clarendon Press, 1938), p. 64. Fogle, in his preface to the Digression (printed separately at the end of vol. 5, pt. 1), pp. 423–25, sees this disillusion as temporary and the conclusions as inconsistent with Milton's writings in the 1640s. But I would suggest that the conclusions do not really contradict what we see in Milton's other prose, especially the later works. Since there is no clear evidence to the contrary, it is reasonable to suppose that Milton worked on this Digression later than 1648 and that, consequently, it also reflects the disillusion of his later years.

41. Firth, "Milton as an Historian," p. 100, suggests that because the parallel would not have been relevant in 1670, Milton omitted the Digression. Though Fogle (preface to the Digression, CPW, 5:i, 410) admits that the seventeenth century was more adept than ours at drawing parallels, and so it might have been relevant, he also concludes that Milton was responsible for omitting the Digression as irrelevant, inartistic, and inconsistent with his views (p. 426). The Digression, however, is a more general indictment of England that might well seemed dangerous to a censor, for Milton clearly implies that monarchy is bondage.

42. Fogle (preface to the Digression, p. 424) sees this conclusion as uncharacteristic of Milton, probably because he dates these statements in 1648. But it is possible that they are later additions; they certainly fit with the disillusion about education reflected in the later works.

43. Anthony Low, *The Blaze of Noon: A Reading of "Samson Agonistes"* (New York: Columbia University Press, 1974), pp. 40–43, discusses Samson's isolation from all the other characters.

44. See John Huntley, "A Revaluation of the Chorus' Role in Milton's *Samson Agonistes*," *MP* 64 (1966), 132–45.

45. Denis Saurat, *Milton: Man and Thinker* (1944; rpt. London: J. M. Dent and Sons, 1946), p. 198, believes that Samson represents the fallen Puritan party and that the Philistines are the Royalists triumphing in debauchery. More recently, Radzinowicz and Hill have argued for Milton's

view of the contemporary relevance of his Samson story. Radzinowicz, *Toward "Samson Agonistes,"* p. 92, suggests that the hero's fall mirrors the fall of the elect; Hill, *Milton,* pp. 435–37, sees Samson as a symbol of the revolutionary cause and, specifically, of the army.

46. Low, *Blaze of Noon,* pp. 162–63, sees Harapha as Samson's parodic double; Radzinowicz, *Toward "Samson Agonistes,"* p. 52, finds that "all the encounters with external characters symbolize encounters of Samson's own cast of inner personalities. He faced in the Chorus his own self-doubt; in Manoa, his own self-tenderness; in Dalila, his own appetency; and in Harapha, his own aggression."

47. See, e.g., Radzinowicz, *Toward "Samson Agonistes,"* pp. 87–108.

48. See Northrop Frye, "Agon and Logos: Revolution and Revelation," in *Prison and the Pinnacle,* ed. Rajan, pp. 157–58.

49. In "Irony as Tragic Effect: *Samson Agonistes* and the Tragedy of Hope" (in *Calm of Mind: Tercentenary Essays on "Paradise Regained" and "Samson Agonistes" in Honor of John S. Diekhoff,* ed. Joseph Anthony Wittreich, Jr. [Cleveland: Case Western Reserve University Press, 1971]), John T. Shawcross argues that *Samson* is tragic because the hero is simply one of a long line, none of whom liberates Israel (pp. 295–96) and because the people "do not realize that deliverance comes only of the individual self" (p. 297). See also Barbara K. Lewalski's view, in *"Samson Agonistes* and the 'Tragedy' of the Apocalypse," *PMLA* 85 (1970), 1050–62, that the tragic conclusion is "that in the fallen world the deliverers whom God raises up achieve no lasting liberations because they are constantly betrayed by the people's corruption and their own sinfulness" (p. 1061).

50. See, e.g., Barker, *Milton and the Puritan Dilemma;* Fixler, *Milton and the Kingdoms of God;* and George M. Muldrow, *Milton and the Drama of the Soul: A Study of the Theme of the Restoration of Man in Milton's Later Poetry* (The Hague: Mouton, 1970). Miner has argued that in Milton's major poems "the public mode has been made completely inward, and man's soul becomes the issue in the most public of forms, the heroic poem" (*Restoration Mode,* p. 507).

51. Tayler, *Milton's Poetry,* p. 124, has observed that "the principle of Milton's poetic being seems to have been delay, deferment of the full release of those powers."

52. Paul R. Baumgartner, "Milton and Patience," *SP* 60 (1963), 203–13, discusses the emphasis on the Christian virtue of patience in Milton's later works. See also William O. Harris, "Despair and 'Patience as the Truest Fortitude' in *Samson Agonistes,"* in *Critical Essays on Milton from ELH* (Baltimore: Johns Hopkins University Press, 1969), pp. 277–90; and Stanley Fish, "The Temptation to Action in Milton's Poetry," *ELH* 48 (1981), 516–31.

53. See Zwicky, "Kairos in *Paradise Regained,"* p. 271, and Tayler, *Milton's Poetry,* p. 155.

CHAPTER VII

John Dryden: Providence, Progress, and the Cycles of History

Wit's now ariv'd to a more high degree;
Our native Language more refin'd and free.

Epilogue to *Conquest of Granada*, Part II

Not ill they Acted, what they cou'd not spoil:
Their Setting-Sun still shoots a Glim'ring Ray,
Like Ancient *Rome*, Majestick in decay.

"To Mr. *Granville*, on his Excellent Tragedy,
call'd *Heroick Love*"

JOHN DRYDEN'S POSITION as both poet laureate and historiographer royal reflects the remarkably close interrelationship between poetry and history in his literary career. In *Life of Plutarch* he remarked that reading histories had "always" been his "most delightful Entertainment,"[1] and he often claimed for himself the role of historian in poetry as well as prose. Not only did he write biographies (*Life of Plutarch, Life of Lucian,* and *Life of St. Francis Xavier*), which he considered the third "species" of history, but Dryden might well have ranked himself, as he did Lucan, "rather among Historians in Verse, then Epique Poets."[2]

There were, of course, recognized differences between poetry and history and consequently between the roles of poet and historian. The poet, maker of fictions, was not to be tied to the same standards of historical accuracy and verisimilitude as the historian, who, as Jean Bodin had insisted, was committed to giving an exact record of events. Bodin distinguished the historian from both the rhetorician and the philosopher when he criticized those historians who, "acting like rhetoricians or philosophers, break off the thread of the completed narrative" and interpose their moral "judgments" or make "rhetorical flourishes."[3] In separating history from rhetoric, truth from pleasure—"it is practically an impossibility for the man who writes to give pleasure, to impart the truth of the matter also" (*Method*, p. 55)—Bodin would seem to have established an unbridgeable gulf between history and poetry, between the historian and the orator/poet. "By no means can it happen that one and the same man fills the office of good orator and that of good historian" (*Method*, p. 45). But for all of Bodin's undeniable influence on historians and on history-writing, poetic practice throughout the seventeenth century continued to insist on the relationship between poetry and history. There was a long-established tradition, still vital in Dryden's time, that linked poetry with history: both were believed to teach moral lessons by example, even if the historian (according to Bodin) should not explicitly obtrude those lessons but rather should allow the judicious reader to infer them from his narrative. Despite Bodin's strictures, which were aimed at historians, many poets did indeed hope to be both good orators and good historians. The late sixteenth and early seventeenth centuries had produced a good deal of historical poetry and drama. One notes, to cite only a few, Samuel Daniel's *Civil Wars*, William Shakespeare's history plays, and Ben Jonson's *Sejanus* and *Catiline*. Much as history-writing in the course of the seventeenth century tended to focus increasingly on contemporary history rather than on a distant past, so Dryden's poetry was concerned with contemporary English political history in an unprecedented degree as he asssumed the role of poet-historian.

Recently it has been suggested that Dryden's role as historian was merely a guise, a rhetorical strategy of deception that acted as cover that allowed him to present covertly what were partisan, political arguments.[4] We have rightly been made aware of the subtle strategies of his art. Dryden was undoubtedly more partisan in many of his poems than traditional scholarship has recognized, and he frequently engaged in polemic. He had strong political convictions and believed that the poet should try to shape or influence political affairs. Nevertheless, his claim to be poet-historian is more than merely a ruse. As Earl Miner has remarked, "The historical provides the center upon which his poetry turns."[5] Though it may seem somewhat paradoxical, it was indeed possible for a person to have a firm political point of view, even to be allied with a party, and still to consider himself a judicious historian. Dryden's persistent interest in history led him to formulate certain views of history or interpretations of the pattern of human existence that profoundly affected his entire literary achievement. Throughout his career he strove to discern and articulate these patterns of history—in poetry, drama, and prose. It was Dryden's deep interest in history, his desire to discover its patterns, and his insistence on setting England's contemporary political events and figures within a larger historical context that made his often political poetry so effective and gave it unusual weight. His larger understanding of history, his sense of patterns that had been repeated in different ages and countries, lifted his political poetry above the merely "occasional" or partisan—it gave his poems a greater scope and significance and kept them from being tied too narrowly to the present.

In virtually all of his work Dryden reveals the seventeenth-century faith in the value of having a comprehensive view of the whole of human history in which the present must be placed to be properly understood. His historical perspective is complex. Both the cyclical idea of history and the idea of progress appear frequently in his works, and late in his life he even occasionally echoes the idea of decay that was popular in John Donne's time. Moreover, although Dryden was influenced by the increasing secularization that characterized the century, he also inherited the providential view that history reflects God's purposes and is shaped by His guiding hand. Because he voices so many views of history current during the seventeenth century, Dryden is an appropriate figure with which to conclude this book.

Each of the three ideas of history's pattern that we have discussed (cycles, progress, and decay) finds explicit statement in Dryden, but often they tend to merge in his writing. We have already seen that the basic ideas of history, though seemingly distinct or even contradictory, could appear in various combinations—a writer's general "view of history" might include more than one theory of history. It is striking, however, to find in a single writer all three ideas of history's pattern, as well as both providential and secular explanations of causation in history. With what Dryden called his "Skeptical" approach to truth,[6] his reluctance to take anything on "trust" ("Defence of the Epilogue," in *Works*, 11: 203), he refrained from accepting uncritically any of the traditional ideas of history's shape. Scrutinizing them repeatedly, particularly with respect to England's contemporary political scene, Dryden fashioned a view of history that at times resembles those of his predecessors but is distinctly his own. He continued throughout his life to reevaluate the pattern of England's history, and the conclusions he reached in the 1690s were quite unlike the hopes with which he began the Restoration.

The Cyclical View

Remaining popular in England well into the eighteenth century, the cyclical view of history in its various manifestations was the dominant theory of history in the seventeenth century. Herrick felt that the cyclical order united nature and history. Ben Jonson observed that cyclical degeneration inevitably attends the subservience to appetite and passion that has always characterized the majority of mankind. Even Bacon and Milton, who hoped for progress in the future, still concluded that the cyclical pattern accurately described the past.

As we might expect, the cyclical idea of history forms an important part of Dryden's view. The restoration of Charles II suggested to Dryden, as it did to Milton, a return to a former state. Both men saw Charles II's resumption of the throne in cyclical terms, but their attitudes differed sharply. For Milton the Restoration signaled England/Israel's return to bondage, a cyclical relapse into old error. But Dryden, like other Royalists, viewed this change as a return to order, peace, and sanity after the madness of the rebellion. That Charles II arrived in England during May encouraged Dryden to link the king's return with the renewal of spring after winter's devastation. In this association he recalls Herrick, who long before the war's end had found hope for the future in the analogy between the cycles of nature and those of England's political history.

As the title of *Astraea Redux* suggests, with the restoration of monarchy the classical goddess of justice has come back to England, having fled during the iron age of the Civil War. It was not unusual for poets to praise Charles II's restoration as signaling the return of the golden age.[7] Indeed, the tendency to interpret the Restoration as a cyclical renewal of a former, ideal state is apparent throughout the correspondence between Charles II, the House of Commons, and General George Monk that immediately preceded the king's return and that the earl of Clarendon records in his

History of the Rebellion and Civil Wars in England. But for Dryden, 1660 marks the return of not just the golden age before the war but the golden age of Augustan Rome, which itself was seen as a revival of the idealized happiness of Saturn's reign.[8] In this poem as in his later works, Dryden places contemporary events in England within a larger complex historical framework, thus giving the political "occasion" of the poem a significance that reaches far beyond the present moment. Behind *Astraea Redux* lies the idea that history repeats itself. Dryden envisions England attaining glories like those of Rome as he compares Charles to Augustus, in whose age both "arms and arts" flourished:

> Oh Happy Age! Oh times like those alone,
> By Fate reserv'd for Great *Augustus* Throne! (ll. 320–21)

In the works written soon after Charles's return, Dryden elaborates upon this cyclical view, in which the disorder of the rebellion is followed by the renewal and regeneration that he believes accompany the restoration of monarchy.[9] When Charles was in exile, wit and religion were also banished. But now the church has been "restor'd" ("To His Sacred Majesty," l. 48). Although the arts were "buried . . . under the ruines of Monarchy," "we see reviv'd Poesie lifting up its head" ("An Essay of Dramatick Poesie," in *Works*, 17:63).[10] Even Walter Charleton's work restoring Stonehenge to its true founders, the Danes, exemplifies this same cyclical pattern and is itself part of the greater restoration of "free-born *Reason*" to its proper supremacy after the long "Tyranny" of Aristotle ("To My Honored Friend, Dr. Charleton," ll. 1, 3).

At this point in his career Dryden tends to focus on this single cycle of England's history and the way it is mirrored in other areas—art, religion, and philosophy. Events during the late 1670s and early 1680s, however, suggested that England was repeating this cycle. The restoration of peace and true monarchy, which he had hoped would be permanent, was being threatened by the Popish Plot and the efforts to exclude James, the duke of York, from succession to the throne. For Dryden, these political turmoils recalled those of the Civil War: the people again were seeking to usurp the king's power. But even were these troubles to lead to another war, Dryden had faith that eventually England would once again recline "on a rightfull Monarch's Breast" ("The Medall," l. 322).

Dryden was interested not only in the alternation between rebellion and stable monarchy but also in the larger cycle: the rise and fall of empires. His plays explore the issues of rebellion, usurpation, foreign conquest, and the ultimate end to which these disorders can lead—the fall of kingdoms and empires. We find rebellion or usurpation, followed by the restoration of the rightful ruler, in such plays as *Secret Love* and *Marriage A-la-Mode*. But it is primarily the heroic dramas that focus on the great cycles of history.[11]

Conquest of Granada portrays a weak king, Boabdellin, who has allowed factions to grow at home and thus is a prey to Abdallah, who seeks to usurp his throne. As in so many of his works, Dryden sets the specific political situation within a larger historical framework, for we learn that Boabdellin himself is not the lawful king but one of a series of "*Moorish* Tyrants" who have ruled Granada (Pt. II, I.i.2). Once part of Spain, Granada has been under possession of the Moors for 800 years, and now King Ferdinand of Spain seeks to restore the true old religion and dominion. We see in this play a pattern similar to the one that pervades the poems: after years of rule under heathen, factious, and untrustworthy governors, Granada is "At once to freedom and true faith restor'd: / Its old Religion, and its antient Lord" (Pt. II, I.i.26–27).

But the restoration of Granada to Spanish rule also involves the fall of the Moorish empire. As an explanation of what is happening to the Moors, Ferdinand presents the cyclical idea of history:

> When Empire in its Childhood first appears,
> A watchful Fate o'resees its tender years;
> Till, grown more strong, it thrusts, and stretches out,
> And Elbows all the Kingdoms round about:
> The place thus made for its first breathing free,
> It moves again for ease and Luxury:
> Till, swelling by degrees, it has possest
> The greater space; and now crowds up the rest.
> When from behind, there starts some petty State;
> And pushes on its now unwieldy fate:
> Then, down the precipice of time it goes,
> And sinks in Minutes, which in Ages rose. (Pt. II, I.i.5–16)

Though small and "tender" in its "Childhood," an empire grows stronger and larger until it reaches maturity. But its glory cannot last. Eventually it falls—in part because in the biological cycle that determines the lives of nations as well as men maturity leads to old age and death; in part because the aging empire must give way to a young "state," which in its turn seeks power and territory. The fall of one empire is precipitated by the rise of another, and the cycles continue. The same view of cyclical history lies behind *Indian Emperour*, which shows Cortez precipitating the fall of Montezuma's empire as Spain extends her territory westward into the New World.[12] Dryden's sense that empires grow slowly but sink in "Minutes" is very similar to the position of Bodin, who observed that though states only gradually arrive at their "full perfection," usually they fall "all at once" by their own weight or by civil wars or, more commonly, by "the enemies violence." Only a few are allowed a more gentle decline, "by age growing old."[13]

Many of Dryden's heroic plays and tragedies explore the causes for the fall of empires, and they suggest that more is involved than old age or the growth of a rival state. In *Aureng-Zebe* the opening scene announces that the Mogul empire is threatened with ruin by the emperor's three sons, each of whom is fighting to gain the throne. Throughout this play, and indeed many others, Dryden insists that nations fall because the rulers are swayed by passion.[14] Jealous of his single loyal son because they love the same woman, the emperor spitefully makes his ambitious, rebellious son, Morat, his successor. As Arimant recognizes, the only one who can save the "sinking State" (I.104) is the loyal son, Aureng-Zebe, who in contrast to his father and brothers is ruled by reason: he is "temp'rate" and "by no strong passion swayed, / Except his Love" (I.102–3). Even when wrongly cast out from succession, Aureng-Zebe is not controlled by selfish passions: his primary concern is "to secure the State" (III.233). And when this wise man receives the crown at the end of the play, Dryden suggests that India's fall has been averted.

The political lesson here is a commonplace—empires fall when men are prey to passions and appetites rather than reason—and we recall Jonson's similar view in *Sejanus* and *Catiline*. But for all the similarity, there is an important difference. Jonson insists that in their corrupt obsession with satisfying their base appetites, Sejanus, Catiline, and Tiberius reflect the nature of the Roman peo-

ple. Jonson's position is that empires fall when the people are slaves
to their passions. But Dryden's emphasis is different. He locates
the state's stability in the ruler, not in the mass of people, the mob,
suggesting that the health of a nation depends on the wisdom of
its ruler, rather than on that of the people, in whose rational control
he has little faith. Repeatedly his plays show how rebellions occur
and empires are lost because the king is ruled by his passions.

In *All for Love*, Antony, whose army had gained him kingdoms,
loses them all once he is consumed by illicit passion for Cleopatra.
As he confesses,

> . . . While within your arms I lay,
> The World fell mouldring from my hands each hour. (II.295–96)

But it is with Cleopatra herself, the queen of Egypt, that we see
even more clearly how the fate of an empire depends on its ruler.
When Alexis, the queen's eunuch, says that she "might preserve"
Egypt if she would give Antony up to his enemy (I.79–81), he is
warning that her love for this Roman will bring about the ruin of
her country. Through the course of the play we watch her lose her
kingdom for Antony. The fate of Egypt, "Queen of Nations" (V.72),
depends on Cleopatra. And just as she, slave to her passion, has
"Sunk, never more to rise" (V.46), so by the end of the play Egypt,
vanquished by Rome, "from her ancient seat, / Is sunk forever in
the dark Abyss" (V.72–73). Empires may be "well lost" for love,
but they are lost nonetheless.

Indian Emperour similarly links the collapse of an empire with its
ruler's abandonment of reason. Montezuma's fall is at least in part
the result of his passion for Almeria. Wanting to preserve Mexico's
independence, he refuses Cortez's first offer of peace. But when
Montezuma rejects the second offer, he is swayed not simply by
heroic ideas of honor but also by his passion for Almeria. His first
reaction is to praise "with reason" Cortez's generosity (III.i.57),
but Almeria quickly convinces Montezuma that accepting peace
would be shameful. He follows her advice rather than listening to
his rational instinct, which is seconded by his youngest son, Guy-
omar, who throughout the play is associated with reason and who
prefers peace at "any terms" (III.i.73) to a war they cannot possibly
win. Montezuma yet again accedes to Almeria, when he agrees to
revenge her brother's death by killing Cortez. Because Cortez had

saved Montezuma's life, the emperor should spare his noble enemy. But he decides to conquer the "few Sparks of Vertue which remain" (III.iv.130) and execute Cortez. By following Almeria's counsel and his "head-long passion" (III.iv.131), he brings bloodshed, famine, and devastation on his land. Earlier Montezuma had heard the prophecy that one day when his foes were in his power he would have a chance "to save thy sinking State" (II.i.56), but overcome by his passions, he is unable to "take that opportunity" (II.i.61).

These plays of the 1660s and 1670s reflect a deep preoccupation with a cyclical view of history. They offer implicit advice to rulers on how to avoid bringing disaster on their countries, and the often ominous warnings would not have been irrelevant to England. Nevertheless, despite their emphasis on the ruler's responsibility for the health of the state, there also occasionally surfaces a darker sense that cyclical decline may be inevitable. If all great empires finally collapse, what will happen to England, now full of prosperity and imperialistic dreams?

The assumption behind the cycles of history portrayed in these plays is that "mankind . . . [is] the same in all ages, agitated, by the same passions, and mov'd to action by the same interests" (*Life of Plutarch,* in *Works,* 17:270). Dryden's version of this classical idea that human nature is always the same (a belief he shares with Jonson) emphasizes the cause-effect relationships that make history intelligible. Because "there is a natural connection" between "humane causes" (*Works,* 17:271), history assumes the characteristics of a science.[15] From the observation of human actions and passions, the scientist-historian can draw the connections between effects and their natural causes. Dryden is not alone in his disposition to view the study of history as a science. We find in the historian John Rushworth, for example, a similar tendency to speak in scientific terms of the prudence one gains from reading history. Insisting on the need for princes to read history, Rushworth writes: "It is hard for the *Pilot* to escape, unless he hath first discovered those shelves and Rocks, upon which others have been split: What is that we call *Prudence,* or *Policy,* but a *Systeme* of *Observations* and *Experience* deducted from other Mens Principles, Practices, Purposes, and Failings?"[16] For Dryden, too, history becomes instructive precisely because the uniformity of human nature insures that the same cause and effect relationships will be repeated. History "informs the understanding by the memory: It helps us to judge of what will happen, by shewing us the like revolutions of former times" (*Life of Plutarch*, in *Works*, 17:270). By emphasizing the similarity between different times, this cyclical view leads to the representation of human history as a series of parallels that the observer can trace: "nothing can come to pass, but some President of the like nature has already been produc'd, so that having the causes before our eyes, we cannot easily be deceiv'd in the effects, if we have Judgment enough but to draw the parallel" (*Works*, 17:271). This conception of the universality of human nature and the corollary of the cyclical pattern of history underlie the classical and Renaissance theory that history teaches precepts by means of examples and lead Dryden to use historical example and parallel in his works.[17]

Political events in the early 1680s spurred Dryden to discern historical parallels that would illuminate England's problems. In *Absalom and Achitophel* Dryden, claiming to be a "Historian" ("To the Reader," in *Works*, 2:4), suggests a parallel between Shaftesbury and Monmouth's roles in the Popish Plot and Absalom and Achitophel's rebellion against King David. But there were also other appropriate parallels. Collaborating with Nathaniel Lee, he wrote the play *Duke of Guise* (acted, December 1682), which concerned the plot of the Holy League in France a century earlier, a plot that seemed remarkably similar to the one that threatened to shake England's established monarchy. A little over a year later, he again warned England of this parallel when at the king's command he translated Louis Maimbourg's *History of the League*. In this *"Parallel"* history has repeated itself so exactly that "the Features are alike in all, there is nothing but the Age that makes the difference, otherwise . . . 1584 and 1684 have but a Century and a Sea betwixt them, to be the same" (preface to the *History*, in *Works*, 18:7).

In drawing these parallels, Dryden was not merely a dispassionate observer but rather assumed a political position that allied him with the king's party. Steven Zwicker has recently argued that Dryden adopted the "pose of historical disinterestedness," the "guise of amateur and historian because such positions gave him a freedom of movement and a cover" for polemical, partisan arguments.[18] Dryden's use of history is indeed often polemic, not detached or disengaged. Consequently, there seems to be a contradiction between Dryden's insistence on the objectivity of the scientist-historian and the engagement of the polemicist. I would suggest, however, that it is not simply a case of Dryden being dishonest, of

Dryden tricking his reader. We see a similar apparent contradiction in a number of seventeenth-century historians who asserted their objectivity and impartiality at the same time that they wrote from a particular political (or religious) position. To cite just one example, Richard Baxter insisted he was a good, truthful historian, and he is described on the title page of his *Church-History of the Government of Bishops and their Councils* (1680) as "A Hater of False History." Baxter had a great respect for accuracy and impartiality—he criticized the historian Peter Heylyn for Anglo-Catholic bias and he praised those like Gilbert Burnet, Rushworth, and Thomas Fuller who, following Bodin's recommendations, cited and even printed the records, parliamentary acts, and other writings that were their sources. And yet Baxter wrote his church history to show that the elaborate episcopacy of the Anglican church was a "degeneration" from the apostolic time when each church had its own bishop. For all their differences, Baxter, like Dryden, insisted on his impartiality and objectivity while he argued a position of which he hoped to persuade his readers. Like many others, he believed he could see and present "the truth," though "the truth" varied greatly from writer to writer.

Bodin had set high standards when he insisted that the historian in pursuit of truth should be "free from all bias."[19] He defined an ideal of objectivity and dispassion that the historians who followed him took seriously, but it was an ideal not easy to attain, as Bodin himself confessed when he remarked that "it is somewhat difficult to be free from all emotion" (*Method,* p. 44). Though there is a real difference between the extremes of "disinterested" history and "polemic," the exact line between the two often was difficult to draw. History-writing in the seventeenth century frequently did have a point of view. It was not coldly, scientifically detached but often offered implicit (and sometimes not so implicit) lessons or conclusions, which tended to support a particular political or religious position with which the historians were themselves aligned. Despite their increasingly conscious attempts at impartiality, accuracy, and responsible, critical use of source materials, many seventeenth-century English historians did ultimately feel that their histories taught pointed lessons. Rushworth (supporter of the parliamentary cause in the conflict with Charles I) condemned those historians who "intermingle their Passion with their Stories." Writing what Bodin called "bare history" (*Method,* p. 54), Rushworth scrupulously refrained from interposing "my own Opinion, or interpretation of actions," and yet in the prefatory dedication of his first volume of *Historical Collections* he declared that his history would show that the king's insistence on royal prerogative and disdain for Parliament and law had caused the Civil Wars.[20] On the other side, Clarendon, loyal supporter of the established monarchy, insisted on *his* objectivity and evenhandedness—"I shall perform the same [his account of the rebellion] with all faithfulness and ingenuity, with an equal observation of the faults and infirmities of both sides, with their defects and oversights in pursuing their own ends"[21]—yet his *History* (even the negatively charged word "rebellion" in the title) reflects his particular political point of view. For all the desire for impartiality and objectivity, the issues involved were often too pressing for a historian to maintain complete detachment. It is not simply that Baxter or Rushworth or Dryden was consciously lying or practicing accepted arts of disguise when he claimed to be an impartial, truthful historian. Rather, writers on both sides of a religious or political issue could be convinced that they had discerned the truth and that it was only their opponents who were the biased writers of false history. Though Dryden was usually arguing a political point of view, I would suggest that, like many of his contemporaries, he *believed* he was judicious. Indeed it was his wide reading of history, his understanding of the larger historical patterns that gave a special point and authority to his political views. He would not necessarily have felt a contradiction between his claim of impartiality and his alliance with a political party. Dryden very likely could have said what Rushworth, attacked for partiality by Royalists, did of himself as he defended the truth of his *Historical Collections:* "it is possible for an Ingenuous man to be of a *Party* and yet not *partial*."[22]

The cyclical view of history not only lies behind Dryden's interest in historical parallels, but it also forms the basis of the generally allusive mode of his prose and poetry. Whether the allusions are to biblical history, classical mythology, classical history, or later European history, they function by drawing parallels between different historical ages, persons, or events. In his dedication to *Don Sebastian* Dryden praises Leicester as a "second *Atticus*," who has preserved wisdom and virtue in the midst of his "mad" country's political "disturbances," and he closes with "the Words of *Cicero* to the first" (*Works*, 15:62, 60, 64), expanding the classical allusion into a historical parallel. This same literary technique of allusion operates in condensed form in his poetry. In *Astraea Redux* Charles II's exile recalls Jove's flight from Typhoeus in mythical history and David's banishment in biblical history. The English king's restoration parallels Augustus's ascension to the throne in classical history. Dryden's preoccupation with the repetitive, cyclical nature of history underlies his technique of locating his subjects within a historical framework through allusions that are, in fact, historical parallels.

The natural connection between causes and effects within the cycles permits the historian-poet not only to draw parallels but also to predict and advise. "Tho he cannot foresee accidents, or all things that possibly can come, he may apply examples, and by them foretell, that from the like Counsels will probably succeed the like events: And thereby, in all concernments, and all Offices of life, be instructed in the two main points, on which depend our happiness, that is, what to avoid and what to choose" (*Life of Plutarch*, in *Works*, 17:271). Polybius's virtue lies in his ability to draw the precepts from the examples: "It is wonderful to consider with how much care and application he instructs, counsels, warns, admonishes, and advises, whensoever he can find a fit occasion" ("The Character of Polybius and His Writing," in *S-S*, 18:33). In his praise of Polybius, Dryden is clearly rejecting Bodin's view that it is preferable for the historian to keep his comments out of his history.[23] If the "impartial" historian may directly give instruction, surely the lessons of history need not remain implicit in the work of the poet.[24]

In his poetry and prose Dryden himself assumes the role of adviser on the basis of historical examples and parallels. The dedication of his translation of the *History of the League* warns Charles II not to be too lenient with the rebels. The king should follow the example of Henry IV, who "fully vanquish'd" the rebels, and only then forgave and "receiv'd them all into Mercy" (*Works*, 18:5). In *Astraea Redux* Dryden counsels as well as praises Charles II when he describes the king's anticipated proclamation of forgiveness in terms of God's declaration of mercy to Moses. Dryden has been suspected of flattery in his dedicatory epistles and panegyrics because of the discrepancy between the actual contemporary people and the historic figures to whom they are compared. Much of the apparently hyperbolic praise, however, is the poet-historian's attempt to advise about future behavior on the basis of historical parallels rather than to commend past or present accomplishments.

Dryden's insistence on the importance of deriving counsel from historical examples implies that on the whole he avoids a pessimistic view of the inevitable repetition of history's cycles. Though he frequently proposes a cyclical view of history, he rejects the meaningless cycles of the ancients for whom the pattern of endless flux and reflux, rise and decline, virtually negated any constructive meaning in history.[25] If man is doomed to repeat the same processes and is incapable of altering the course of history, there is little reason for observing and drawing lessons from the cycles. Dryden, however, escapes the "directionless" quality of the classical cycles both through the Christian providential view of history and through a more modern conception of progress.

The Role of Providence

Dryden most lucidly expresses the providential approach to history in his digression on the epic in his *Discourse concerning . . . Satire*. In suggesting God's providential protection of man through guardian angels as the Christian poet's solution to the problem of finding an appropriate substitute for pagan epic machinery, he states all the essential elements of the eschatological view:

But 'tis an undoubted Truth, that for Ends best known to the Almighty Majesty of Heaven, his Providential Designs for the benefit of his Creatures, for the Debasing and Punishing of some Nations, and the Exaltation and Temporal Reward of others, were not wholly known to these his Ministers; else why those Factious Quarrels, Controversies, and Battles amongst themselves, when they were all United in the same Design, the Service and Honour of their common Master? But being instructed only in the General, and zealous of the main Design; and, as Finite Beings, not admitted into the Secrets of Government, the last resorts of Providence, or capable of discovering the final Purposes of God, who can work Good out of Evil as he pleases, and irresistably sways all manner of Events on Earth, directing them finally for the best, to his Creation in general, and to the Ultimate End of his own Glory in Particular: they must of necessity be sometimes ignorant of the means conducing to those Ends, in which alone they can jarr, and oppose each other. (*Works*, 4:20)

Behind the contours of history, behind the rise and fall of kingdoms, is God's hand punishing and rewarding nations. Such was the assumption of Milton, as well as historians such as Sir Walter Raleigh, Fuller, and Burnet. All events are part of a grand "Design," though man may not understand all the parts, and the entire course of history leads to an end that gives meaning and value to time.

The sense of history's design is apparent in many of Dryden's works. He suggests that history advances toward the final salvation of mankind, as he shows Christianity triumphing over the religion of the Mexican Indians (*Indian Emperour*), over Islam (*Conquest of Granada*), and over the pagan religion of Rome (*Tyrannick Love*).[26] Moreover, his plays typically demonstrate that divine justice lies behind the seemingly "natural" pattern in which tyranny leads to a rebellion that finally ends with the restoration of lawful, orderly government.

But as his description of the "Universally receiv'd" Christian doctrine of guardian angels would suggest (*Discourse concerning . . . Satire*, in *Works*, 4:19), there is also a special Providence that is intimately involved in the particularities of human affairs. This special Providence shapes the fate of individuals and nations. Dryden, like other royalists, saw God's hand behind the restoration of Charles,[27] and he continued to find evidence of divine intervention in England's history. In *Astraea Redux* he claims that "Providence design'd" (l. 151) General Monk to free England by negotiating Charles's return to the throne. *Annus Mirabilis* finds God responsible for the fire that scourged London as well as for the English victory over the Dutch. In *Britannia Rediviva*, celebrating the birth of King James II's son, Dryden looks back over the Civil War, the plague, the fire, and the Popish Plot and sees in all these things God's "avenging Angel" (l. 155) punishing England's crimes.[28] But if God is behind England's afflictions, He also takes special care of His monarchs (Charles I's fate notwithstanding). When Albion/Charles II, "the Care of Heav'n," is endangered by a rebellious faction, suddenly "Miracles are shown" as fires arise "To guard the Sacred Throne" (*Albion and Albanius*, III.i.154, 170–73).

Providence intervenes in remarkable ways. In *Conquest of Granada*, Part II, a "voice" "from above" (the ghost of Almanzor's mother) tells him to spare his father's life (V.iii.195) just as he is about to kill the duke of Arcos, who himself confesses that "Heav'n . . . did guid" his eyes to view the diamond cross and bloody heart on Almanzor's arm by which he recognizes his long-lost son (V.iii.187). Perhaps the most dramatic intervention occurs in *Tyrannick Love*, when St. Catherine's mother, about to be "Torn piece by piece" (V.i.300) on Maximus's rack of torture, is at the last minute rescued—not by her daughter (whose Christian virtue and modesty prevent her from giving in to Maximus's lust to save her mother) but by Catherine's guardian angel who *"descends swiftly with a flaming Sword, and strikes at the Wheel, which breaks in pieces; then he ascends again"* (stage directions at V.i.308).

The Christian providential view places all events within the framework of universal history extending from Creation to Judgment Day. Accordingly, Dryden often defines his poetic subject in relationship to both ends of this temporal spectrum. The "Song for St. Cecilia's Day" describes the contemporary festival and St. Cecilia's former musical accomplishments as both echoes of the heavenly music at Creation and anticipations of the trumpet's announcement of Judgment Day. Dryden's tendency to view contemporary subjects in terms of their apocalyptic implications reflects the eschatological concern of the providential view of history. Moreover, the Christian propensity to read all historical people and events in the context of the New Testament revelation fosters Dryden's typological treatment of the historical subjects of his poetry. Anne Killigrew and the duchess of Ormond as well as Charles II become types of Christ, and the suppression of ancient Jewish and contemporary English rebellions foreshadows God's final apocalyptic judgment.

Although the religious bias of this Christian interpretation of history led some people to reject everything non-Christian (Milton at times was drawn to this position), Dryden insists on recognizing the virtues and achievements of pagans as well as the inherent defects.[29] This tendency to discriminate strengths and weaknesses appears in his discussion of epic machinery in the *Discourse concerning . . . Satire*. Though Dryden criticizes the classical pagan epic for employing false gods as its machines, he defends its ability to provide standards for the modern Christian epic. In much the same way as Herrick senses a correspondence between pagan and Christian rituals and festivals, Dryden implies that there is a similarity between the pagan belief in divine intervention and the Christian notion of Providence.

Dryden's awareness of a partial harmony between Christian and pagan enables him, like Herrick, to combine the Christian, providential interpretation with the basically classical idea that history moves in cycles. He places his recurrent events and ages under the supreme control of Providence: "God is abroad, and wondrous in his ways,/ The Rise of Empires, and their Fall surveys" (*Britannia Rediviva*, ll. 75–76).[30] The development of Christian thought provides precedent for this combination of the providential and cyclical views of history. In its absorption of Hebraic and Greco-Roman elements, Christianity assimilated both the Jewish linear, eschatologically oriented conception of history and the classical, cyclical interpretation.[31] Moreover, both the Old and New Testaments at times reveal a preoccupation with paradigms of recurrence and reenactment that are at least partly cyclical.[32] Typology, as an outgrowth of the Christian providential view of history, furthered the merger of the linear and cyclical views of history. As we saw in Milton, typology can be thought of as embodying a progressive spirit. But while typology maintains a future, eschatological orientation and retains the historical concreteness of both type and antitype,[33] it also implies parallel relationships between the different types, which are all related to the same central figures and events of the New Testament. These parallels suggest the cycles of the classical view of history, but the Greco-Roman conception is sharply qualified by the notion of difference within similarity that is central to typology.[34]

For Dryden, typology provides an ideal way to combine the Christian and classical conceptions of history. Although the providential design of history is the main thrust of a typological interpretation, Dryden's typological treatment of his poetic subjects gives increased emphasis to the classical, cyclical idea of history. Characteristically he not only describes his subject as a type of a New Testament figure or event but also compares this subject to other figures and events that are capable of similar typological interpretation. His method thus focuses on the parallels between the different types, implying a cyclical conception of recurring people and events while simultaneously asserting the providential view of history. In this he differs sharply from Milton, for Milton's conception of typology reflects his ideal of progress and his aversion to the mere cyclical repetition of past experience. Thus he opposes the progressive aspect of typology to a static sense of cyclical repetition. Dryden, however, merges the providential and the cyclical as he explores typology's cyclical possibilities.

Absalom and Achitophel provides the consummate example of Dryden's technique of combining through typology the parallel recurrences of cyclical history with the eschatological direction of providential history.[35] David and Charles II are both types of Christ, and their victories over the rebels foreshadow Christ's final triumph over sin at Judgment Day. However, that both kings typify the same figures and events in the New Testament allows Dryden to construct the parallels between biblical and contemporary history, implying a cyclical conception of history in which the pattern of rebellion followed by judgment and punishment is repeated from the earliest revolt of the angels to God's final apocalyptic judgment.

It has often been remarked that Dryden was not alone in drawing parallels between England and Israel. Abraham Cowley and Milton also had in their different ways described England as recapitulating Israel's history. A particularly apt example is Peter Heylyn's sermon on the first anniversary of Charles II's restoration to the throne of England. Taking as his text Psalm 31:21, he observes at length the parallel between Charles's life and David's, between England's recent history and Israel's: "Who may not find the quality of our late afflictions, and our deliverance together in this present Psalm, and read the state of our affairs in the Story of *David;* and then draw down an easie and familiar parallel betwixt the Persons, and the mercies, and the places too? A parallel, right worthy of the pen of *Plutarch."* Heylyn's mention of Plutarch suggests that like Dryden his reading of the Bible is colored by an essentially classical cyclical view of history. Indeed, feeling no discomfort in using the methods of a classical historian to interpret the Holy Scriptures, Heylyn says he will follow Plutarch's method in examining the contemporary parallels: "we will observe the method which is used by *Plutarch,* in laying down the points in which they differ, or, those wherein one party seems to have preheminence above the other."[36] Heylyn sees the Bible as offering historical parallels in much the same way as secular histories do. The patterns of history are repeated throughout the ages, and thus the lessons the past offers, whether from secular or sacred history, are never outdated.

For Dryden, providential history can absorb the cyclical pattern of the classical view of history, but the providential design introduces the possibility of escaping the monotony of inevitably repetitive cycles. He parallels the Popish Plot with the history of the Holy League in France only to conclude with the hope that England's history will not follow the same disastrous course. In *Absalom and Achitophel* he refuses to pursue the parallel between Monmouth's and Absalom's rebellions to its end. If the pattern were inevitable and the former events were repeated, Monmouth would die as a punishment for his rebellion, but Dryden in his preface "To the Reader" holds out hope that Charles's rebellious son will repent and be reconciled to his father, thus avoiding Absalom's fate. Since even in the cycles of history "the event depends on the unsearchable providence of Almighty God" (dedication of *Duke of Guise*, in *S-S*, 7:16), the parallel patterns may eventually be broken by Providence, either directly through special divine intervention or indirectly through man's efforts. "The Deity . . . commonly works by second causes, and admits of our endeavours with his concurrence" (*S-S*, 7:16). Consequently, God may allow men to choose different actions that will produce different effects. Although Dryden does not share Milton's radical antagonism toward a cyclical pattern of history, he does share Milton's belief that by examining historical examples that parallel contemporary situations, men can learn to avoid past mistakes and to choose a better course of action, thereby escaping the inevitable repetition of the past. Dryden's faith in the efficacy of human action as well as in God thus leads him to reject the fatalistic cycles of the ancients and to imply the possibility of progress.

Progress and Politics

The idea of progress is part of a modern conception of history that began to emerge during the Renaissance. With increasing frequency historians rejected the miraculous and so were skeptical of fables and legends and sought to rely only on authentic sources.[37] They emphasized the natural rather than supernatural causes of events, and the concept of Providence became secularized into a "formulated theory of historical or social forces determining the rise of men and the outcome of events."[38] Universal histories were gradually replaced by a focus on the nation, the city, and eventually the individual; and biography became an increasingly important form of history.[39] One of the major consequences of these emergent views was the growth of a belief in progress.

Dryden's prose and poetry reveal that he assimilated the major characteristics of this modern interpretation of history. His *Life of Plutarch* insists that the historian concern himself with natural, human causes (*Works,* 17:271), rather than with supernatural, providential explanations. His critical essays frequently explain the literature of different ages in terms of the political forces that shaped it.[40] The Dedication of the *Aeneis,* for example, shows that different political situations made the moral of Virgil's epic quite unlike that of Homer's (Ker, 2:167ff.). Dryden's poems, moreover, reflect the increasingly specific focus of the modern historical perspective in their concern with contemporary English history.[41] Indeed, his absorption of the growing interest in biography seems responsible for his numerous panegyrics of historical figures as well as for his prose biographies.

Like Bacon and Milton before him, Dryden frequently expresses a belief in progress: "Something new in Philosophy and the Mechanicks is discover'd almost every Year: And the Science of Former Ages is improv'd by the Succeeding" (*Discourse concerning . . . Satire,* in *Works,* 4:19). He shares with Joseph Glanvill, Robert Boyle, and Thomas Sprat the recognition of England's recent scientific progress, and, like Sprat, he is excited by a sense that in literature, too, England is advancing. Several of Dryden's essays *"treat of the improvement of our Language since* Fletcher's *and* Johnson's *dayes, and consequently of our refining the Courtship, Raillery, and Conversation of Playes"* (preface to *An Evening's Love,* in *Works,* 10:202). For Dryden, progress usually assumes the form of gradual refinement or "perfecting" of language,[42] which must be "purg'd from the Dregs of Barbarism" (*Discourse concerning . . . Satire,* in *Works,* 4:44) before literature can improve: "By this graffing, as I may call it, on old words, has our Tongue been Beautified by . . . *Shakespear, Fletcher,* and *Jonson:* whose Excellencies I can never enough admire: and in this, they have been follow'd, especially by Sir *John Suckling* and Mr. *Waller,* who refin'd upon them; neither have they, who now succeed them, been wanting in their endeavours to adorn our Mother Tongue" ("Defence of the Epilogue," in *Works,* 11:212).

Even his poetry incorporates this historical optimism, for many poems conclude with a prophetic vision of England's secular progress.[43] *Astraea Redux* sees in Charles II's restoration to the throne not simply cyclical renewal but the beginning of England's expansion in empire and trade. Dryden's vision of the golden age that is beginning describes, not a static perfection, but continual growth and progress:

> Our Nation with united Int'rest blest
> Not now content to poize, shall sway the rest.
> Abroad your Empire shall no Limits know,
> But like the Sea in boundless Circles flow.
> Your much lov'd Fleet shall with a wide Command
> Besiege the petty Monarchs of the Land:
>
> .   .   .   .
>
> Their wealthy Trade from Pyrates Rapine free
> Our Merchants shall no more Advent'rers be. (ll. 296–305)

Similarly, *Annus Mirabilis* ends with Dryden predicting that England will surpass all other nations in glory and wealth, and *Threnodia Augustalis* foresees her "Conquering Navy proudly spread" (l. 511) to remote shores.[44]

Dryden shares Bacon's belief that progress is possible through the cumulative efforts of a succession of men: "no Art, or Science, is at once begun and perfected, but that it must pass first through many hands, and even through several Ages" (*Discourse concerning . . . Satire*, in *Works*, 4:73). As Juvenal could "surpass" Horace by "Building upon his Foundations" (*Works*, 4:73), so modern England can possibly produce satires superior to the classical ones. Like Jonson, Dryden transfers a Baconian sense of progress to the realm of literary endeavour. "One Age learning from another, the last (if we can suppose an equallity of wit in the writers) has the advantages of knowing more, and better than the former" ("Defence of the Epilogue," in *Works*, 11:204). Cumulative perfection in literature, as well as progress in the larger pattern of human history, is possible only because human beings have the capacity to avoid the faults of their predecessors.

In an important way Dryden's idea of progress diverges from both Bacon's and Milton's ideals. Although Bacon believed science could advance only if men worked together and if one generation's discoveries were improved on by the next, he insisted that people first had to abandon the corrupt traditions of the past and begin "anew" from the very foundation, since the intellectual edifice they had inherited was not fit to build on. Milton perhaps went even further in insisting on the necessity of breaking with the past. He saw the greatest obstacle to progress in people's tendency to rely on past experience as a pattern for future actions. Milton's heroes characteristically must break radically with the past before they can progress spiritually. Dryden's essential conservatism, however, leads him to insist on the importance of tradition — of building on the past — and he incorporates this conservatism into his idea of progress.[45] In his descriptions of progress he echoes Bacon's ideas about cumulative succession but not his insistence that people need to separate themselves from past traditions.

The difference between Dryden's and Milton's ideas of progress is reflected in their attitudes toward innovation. As we have seen, Milton's commitment to progress leads him to favor innovation, but Dryden like Donne fears it. As he argues in *Absalom and Achitophel,*

> All other Errors but disturb a State;
> But Innovation is the Blow of Fate. (ll. 799–800)

Donne's rejection of innovation is the consequence of his belief in decay. Dryden's, however, is based on his sense that present institutions have value mainly because they retain ties to the past that must not be severed.[46] Valuing continuity, Dryden traces origins and histories — of his hero Almanzor, of heroic plays, of satire. His interest in lines of succession in literature as well as in politics assumes that present accomplishments depend on the achievements of the past. From Ennius and Pacuvius to Lucilius to Horace to Juvenal, he finds a noticeable improvement in the art of satire, as each poet surpassed his predecessor by building on him. And Dryden suggests that in his own days Dorset continues this line. It would seem that poets as well as kings have their "lineal descents" ("Preface to the Fables," in Ker, 2:247).

A poet's dependence on his predecessors does not prevent his progressing beyond them. Dryden's belief that poets can surpass the achievements of the past recalls Jonson's idea that in imitating Horace and Martial he is perfecting his models. In the dedication of *Examen Poeticum* Dryden sees himself and his fellow poets as true successors, the "Lawful Issue," of Shakespeare and Jonson: "We Trayl our Plays under them," giving them all due honor, "so [that] we may lawfully advance our own, afterwards, to show that we succeed" (*Works,* 4:366). Dryden here carefully balances reverence for his predecessors' greatness with a desire to "advance . . . afterwards"—in the sense both of "going beyond" and of "following." Those critics who condemn modern poets actually wish to destroy this succession and usurp the rule themselves (*Works*, 4:366). Progress in England's literature as well as in her naval and mercantile power depends on maintaining the proper line of succession. Such a notion of succession implies both continuity—a strong sense of ties to the past that gives the present its value—and a Baconian ideal of progress as gradual, cumulative advancement.

To further the development of English literature, Dryden assumes the role of literary historian in his essays, advising what to choose or avoid on the basis of past literary examples. His skeptical approach discriminates the virtues and defects of past and present writers, so that his contemporaries and successors can "make use of the advantages we have receiv'd" ("An Essay of Dramatick Poesie," in *Works*, 17:22), for "to observe errours is a great step to the correcting of them" ("Defence of the Epilogue," in *Works*, 11:205). This historical perspective determines Dryden's method in the *Discourse concerning . . . Satire.* By defining the respective merits and defects of each of the great classical satirists, he enables future writers to surpass the ancients by producing a satire that combines all previous virtues. Even in writing the history of satire, Dryden employs the cumulative, progressive method, for he draws on "Casaubon, Heinsius, Regaltius, Dacier, and the Dauphin" yet "add[s] some Observations of [his] own" (*Works*, 4:28). The historically-oriented purpose that underlies Dryden's critical essays as a whole appears in the "Defence of the Epilogue": "I profess to have no other ambition in this Essay, than that Poetry may not go backward, when all other Arts and Sciences are advancing" ("Defence of the Epilogue," in *Works*, 11:203).

Dryden, however, is not a staunch progressionist. As his "progress-piece" on art in "To Sir Godfrey Kneller" reveals, the historical process of gradual perfection may include several relapses. From its "Rudiments" when "A Coal, or Chalk, first imitated Man" (11. 28–29), the art of painting advanced by degrees through the Greeks, but with the Romans it was "barely kept alive" (1. 45). Then with the barbarian invasion, the Muses were ruined. Only in Raphael's age did they again "rise" (1. 59).

Moreover, progress in one area need not be accompanied by progress in others. In the dedication of *Plutarch's Lives*, though

Dryden boasts that the English language has been polished and has attained such perfection that this translation of Plutarch surpasses previous ones, he sees no corresponding moral progress: his age is "only fit for Satyr" (*Works,* 17:229). "Since every Age has a kind of Universal Genius, which inclines those that live in it to some particular Studies" ("An Essay of Dramatick Poesie," in *Works,* 17:15), it is unlikely that any period would excel in everything. Even in the single field of literature we do not see progress in all areas. The moderns have perfected the rudimentary drama of the ancients, but they have not yet been able to equal Virgil's perfection in the epic. Though the Restoration has surpassed the previous age in "versification, and the Art of Numbers," in the drama we have not yet "arriv'd to the pitch of *Shakespear* and *Ben Johnson*" (dedication of *Examen Poeticum,* in *Works,* 4:374). Indeed, the late poem "To My Dear Friend Mr. Congreve" (1694) suggests that the progress made by refinement has been sharply qualified by a simultaneous loss of vigor: "what we gain'd in skill we lost in strength" (1. 12). Perhaps a similar sense of balance lies behind his comment that the Restoration has "better Poets" than Donne if "not so great Wits" (*Discourse concerning . . . Satire,* in *Works,* 4:78). Dryden's awareness of the inevitable imperfection of human nature produces a skeptical frame of the mind that prevents his believing that the course of progress could be constant or that any age could become an epitome of general perfection.[47] In this sense he differs from Bacon and Milton who, though they restricted the areas in which they hoped for progress (for Bacon it was science; for Milton, religious truth, freedom, and the life of the spirit), believed progress *could* be indefinite and continuous.

The limits of Dryden's faith in progress are implicit in his use of the "biological" metaphor. He frequently descibes progress as a natural process of development from a primitive to a mature state: "nothing is brought to perfection at the first. We must be children before we grow men" ("Preface to the Fables," in Ker, 2:259). Chaucer "lived in the infancy of our poetry" (Ker, 2:259); even in Shakespeare's time poetry was "if not in its infancy among us, at least not arriv'd to its vigor and maturity" ("Defence of the Epilogue," in *Works,* 11:206). Such a definition of progress in terms of natural growth not only suggests that gradual perfection may be part of the natural order but also implies that history is subject to the same limitations as nature. Dryden's optimistic assertion of progress is qualified by the implicit possibility that perfection will naturally be followed by decay and death. Just as Dryden modifies the classical, cyclical view of history by introducing the possibility of change and progress, so his skepticism prevents his wholehearted acceptance of a progressive view of history—not just by suggesting that progress in some areas may be balanced by decline in others but also by defining progress in terms of the natural cycle of life.

Dryden's awareness of the decay that naturally follows maturity has been underestimated.[48] His discussion of the refinement and maturation of language reveals quite clearly how the process of perfection can eventually become incorporated into a cyclical conception of history. The Latin language was gradually refined until it reached maturity during the times of Virgil and Horace ("Dedication of the Aeneis," in Ker, 2:214). Born only a few years after Horace, Ovid was one of the last to write while the "Roman tongue was in its meridian" ("Preface to the Fables," in Ker, 2:256). After his time, the "purity" of Latin suffered increasing corruption until the barbarian invasion brought about its final disintegration (*Discourse concerning . . . Satire,* in *Works,* 4:51; "An Essay of Dramatick Poesie," in *Works,* 17:70). In Dryden's reconstruction of the history of the Roman language, the period of gradual refinement is thus ultimately absorbed into the large cycle of birth, growth, maturity, decay, and death. It is hard to believe that Dryden forgot the second half of the pattern when he paralleled the gradual refinement of the English language with the development of Latin: "There was an Ennius, and in process of time a Lucilius, and a Lucretius, before Virgil and Horace; even after Chaucer there was a Spenser, a Harrington, a Fairfax, before Waller and Denham were in being; and our numbers were in their nonage till these last appeared" ("Preface to the Fables," in Ker, 2:259). In his effort to promote the improvement of English, Dryden focuses quite logically only on growth and improvement. Nevertheless, in the context of his historical view of Rome, his parallel implies that England may also witness a similar decline in the purity of its language once it has reached the apex. For all his apparently optimistic hope for progress in English language and literature, Dryden ultimately finds that the cyclical pattern of history may subsume the progressive.

Language and literature can be perfected only if the historical conditions of the times are favorable, for the quality of the arts is directly dependent upon the ambience of the age. Jonson had suggested that there is a relationship between literature (or, more properly, language) and the moral condition of the age when he noted that the degeneration of a people is reflected in the corruption of language. But Dryden has a far keener and more comprehensive sense that historical circumstances influence literature. His critical essays define the strengths and weaknesses of each author in terms of the historical condition of his age. Shakespeare's imperfections were really those of his unrefined age, and "*Horace* had the disadvantage of the Times in which he liv'd; they were better for the Man, but worse for the Satirist" (*Discourse concerning . . . Satire,* in *Works,* 4:65). The relationship between the age and its literary products becomes clearest in Dryden's explanation of the peculiarity of Plutarch's style: "in *Plutarchs* time, and long before it, the purity of the *Greek* Tongue was corrupted, and the native splendour of it had taken the tarnish of Barbarism, and contracted the filth and spots of degenerating Ages. For the fall of Empires always draws after it the language and Eloquence of the people: They, who labour under misfortunes or servitude, have little leisure to cultivate their mother Tongue" (*Life of Plutarch,* in *Works,* 17:279). Dryden's definitions of these historical conditions sometimes merely repeat set formulas, but his insistence on the relationship between the age and its literature reflects an important modern perspective emerging in the seventeenth century.

In general, the Renaissance lack of emphasis on the importance of historical knowledge of the past per se sometimes led to an uncritical glorification of classical times.[49] Bacon, however, implied a quite different historical awareness in questioning the authority of the ancients. His writings reveal a growing sense of the specific characteristics of the ancient times, as he indicates the effect that the historical environment had on scientific achievements.[50] Milton, too, recognized that the past is different from the present, that historical circumstances change, and he brings this recognition to his analysis of the Scriptures. In the *Doctrine and Discipline of Divorce* he argues that Jesus' prescriptions about divorce in the New Testament were conditioned by the excesses of the Pharisees, and thus that they may no longer be applicable.

This emerging historical perspective assumes even greater prominence in Dryden's conception of the relationship between the character of each age and its literature. In his suggestion that modern writers might be able to equal the classical epics, his emphasis on environmental influence sounds remarkably like Matthew Arnold's "The Function of Criticism at the Present Time" almost two centuries later: "in such an Age 'tis possible some Great Genius may arise, to equal any of the Antients. . . . For great Contemporaries whet and cultivate each other: And mutual Borrowing, and Commerce, makes the Common Riches of Learning, as it does of the Civil Government" (*Discourse concerning . . . Satire*, in *Works*, 4:12).

This modern awareness of the importance of the historical environment leads to Dryden's attempt to define the relationship between contemporary literary achievements and the character of his own age. He usually focuses on the political environment as the major historical influence. The "Defence of the Epilogue" praises the Restoration court's effect on the refinement of language since Shakespeare's "ignorant" times (in *Works*, 11:206): "Now, if any ask me, whence it is that our conversation is so much refin'd? I must freely, and without flattery, ascribe it to the Court: and, in it, particularly to the King; whose example gives a law to it" (p. 216). This passage does indeed flatter crown and court, despite Dryden's protest to the contrary, but it also presents Dryden's conviction that in order for literature to flourish it must be encouraged and supported by the aristocracy. The ancients produced great literature because "Poesie being then in more esteem than now it is, had greater Honours decreed to the Professors of it, and consequently the Rivalship was more high between them; they had judges ordain'd to decide their Merit, and Prizes to reward it. . . . Emulation is the Spur of Wit, and sometimes Envy, sometimes Admiration quickens our Endeavours" ("An Essay of Dramatick Poesie," in *Works*, 17:16). With his conviction that the quality of literature depends directly on the political environment, Dryden insists that the government's influence can be detrimental as well as beneficial. In *Threnodia Augustalis* he praises "the peaceful Triumphs" (l. 346) of Charles II's reign as propitious for the cultivation of the arts, but he fears that "Warlike" (l. 429) James's martial exploits will leave England no opportunity for literary achievement.

Dryden's view that literary progress is possible only under the influence of a favorable political environment is directly responsible for his unremitting efforts in his writing to improve contemporary political situations. If he can spur the king and nobles to greater encouragement of poets, then England's language may be further refined, and she may be able to produce epics that rival Virgil's. Much of what has been considered flattery in Dryden's dedicatory epistles is part of his attempt to procure government support for the improvement of literature. The private and the public combine, for he sees his plight as representative of the problems that the arts in general face.

Dryden's conviction that great literary achievements depend on the government's encouragement, specifically its financial endowment of poets, is anticipated in one of Jonson's late poems. Despite Jonson's Stoic insistence that the good poet, like the good man, must be superior and indifferent to material rewards, in the "Epistle Mendicant" he laments that without Charles I's money his Muse cannot "peep out." This idea that poetry will flourish only with the king's financial support becomes of cardinal importance for Dryden.

Since mere pleas for government patronage may not be sufficient to procure adequate encouragement for writers, Dryden must find other means of improving his political environment. He thus assumes the role of historian, giving political advice to those in office. As his dedication to the king admits, his purpose in translating Maimbourg's *History of the League* is not only to instruct the nation in the parallels between French and English history, but also to advise Charles II as to what action to take. In dealing with contemporary politics, many of his poems, such as *Astraea Redux, Absalom and Achitophel,* and *Britannia Rediviva,* contain implicit advice to the king. Even his heroic plays, with their analysis of the fall of empires and the vulnerability of kings who are ruled by passion, offer pointed, if tactful, admonitions to Charles.[51] Dryden's conviction that the course of literary history depends upon the pattern of political history influences the political nature of his writing and its rhetorical strategy of including advice within the framework of panegyric, satire, elegy, and drama. *Threnodia Augustalis* confirms Dryden's recognition of the close relationship between his role as a poet and the historian's role as counsellor, for he invokes Clio, the Muse of history.

Disillusion: Back to the Cycles

By the end of his career Dryden had become disillusioned about the possibility of creating a favorable political situation. As the payments for his positions as poet laureate and historiographer fell into arrears during Charles II's reign, he continued to insist on the importance of governmental support but he gradually lost hope of obtaining it. James's ascension to the throne only increased Dryden's fears about the fortunes of poetry, and after the revolution of 1688 his despair reached its nadir. Not only was the political environment generally antipathetic to the arts, but Dryden was also personally suffering from the government's indifference. In a letter to Mrs. Elizabeth Steward on November 7, 1699, he arraigns William's court for its neglect of "a man who has done my best to improve the language, and especially the poetry": "the court rather speaks kindly of me, than does any thing for me, though they promise largely; and perhaps they think I will advance as they go backward, in which they will be much deceiv'd; for I never go an inch beyond my conscience and my honour" (S-S, 18:160–61).

Dryden's growing despair about improving the political environment is reflected by his general shift from writing political poems containing advice to translating ancient writers. The *Discourse* prefacing his translations of Juvenal's and Persius's satires indicts the government as ultimately responsible for his failure to achieve his highest goal of creating a great English epic. With his knowledge of the requisites for an ideal epic, he "might perhaps have done as well as some of my Predecessors; or at least chalk'd out a way, for others to amend my Errors in a like Design. But being encourag'd only with fair Words, by King *Charles* II, my little Salary ill paid, and no prospect of a future Subsistence, I was then Discourag'd in the beginning of my Attempt; and now Age has overtaken me; and Want, a more insufferable Evil, through the Change of the Times, has wholly disenabl'd me" (*Discourse concerning . . . Satire,* in *Works,* 4:23).

"To Sir Godfrey Kneller" (1694), a late poem reflecting his disillusionment, perhaps best reveals the way in which Dryden's view of history influenced his evaluation of the state of the arts in England at the end of the century. The first part of the poem suggests the modern artist's ability to surpass the achievements of his predecessors through a cumulative assimilation of their virtues. Despite the setback resulting from the barbarian invasion, the history of art shows a general pattern of progress culminating in the "Genius" (l. 65) of Kneller, who unites the Roman perfection of color and the Lombard perfection of design. The rest of the poem, however, sharply qualifies Dryden's praise of Kneller. Kneller, in

241

fact, does not reach, let alone surpass, the excellencies of the earlier masters of the "*Roman,* and the *Lombard* Line" (l. 61). The poem rejects a progressive view of modern perfection in either painting or poetry. Dryden has retreated to Bacon's position at the beginning of the century, as he suggests that progress is possibility rather than actuality.

The political situation is as responsible for modern failures as it was for past successes. Raphael was amply rewarded with "*Leo's* Gold" (l. 98), but today's artists are not financially encouraged by the government to perfect their art. Although "Thou hadst thy *Charles* a while, and so had I" (l. 100), Dryden prefers to "pass . . . that unpleasing Image by" (l. 101), for the king's support was hardly liberal. The situation under William is even more discouraging, for "in a stupid Military State, / The Pen and Pencil find an equal Fate" (ll. 51–52). In England's present government the ideal order is inverted, for the king's "Reign" is dependent upon the "Subjects" who support him with "Taxes" (ll. 155–56). Similarly, the proper relationship is destroyed between the artist and the "Subjects" he immortalizes, for his life now depends on their financial generosity (l. 154). Because of this disorder in the arts produced by the political disorder, "thou sometimes art forc'd to draw a Fool" (l. 157). Ironically, the government's lack of financial support has reduced art to a mercenary level, forcing the artist to prostitute his talents to live. "Mean time, while just Incouragement you want, / You only Paint to Live, not Live to Paint" (ll. 164–65). Dryden and Kneller can be "the first of these Inferiour Times" (l. 118), but they cannot hope to "contend with Heroes Memory" (l. 119):

> Thy Genius bounded by the Times like mine,
> Drudges on petty Draughts, nor dare design
> A more Exalted Work, and more Divine. (ll. 147–49)

Their failure to produce truly heroic art is ultimately the failure of their government.

In his bitter disillusionment Dryden offers no hope for a change either in the government or in its policies toward artists, and consequently this poem makes no promises of glorious future achievement. The poem typically ends with a vision of the future, but it is a curiously limited consolation. The process of time will grant further "Beauties" (l. 181) to Kneller's paintings, but there is no suggestion that it will lead to England's perfection of the arts. Dryden's modern historical awareness of the relationship between the artist and his age, which earlier had fostered his hopes for England's progress in the arts, has led him to despair of any great artistic achievements in the present and to refrain from optimistic predictions about the future.[52]

Clearly his view of the pattern of England's history has changed since 1660, when he had celebrated the return of the golden age and looked forward to England's progress in the arts, in commerce, and in the expansion of her empire. He had hoped that her glorious advancement would be lasting. In *Astraea Redux,* as in Milton's early optimistic antiprelatical tracts, there is no hint that progress will be followed by cyclical decay.[53] Although in the next few years the Dutch War, the plague, and especially the London Fire might have seemed signs that England's renewed state of bliss was indeed vulnerable, nevertheless Dryden's final lines in *Annus Mirabilis* emphasize the constancy and security of her future happiness.

> Thus to the Eastern wealth through storms we go;
>   But now, the Cape once doubled, fear no more.
> A constant Trade-wind will securely blow,
>   And gently lay us on the Spicy shore. (ll. 1213–16)

But the Popish Plot and the Exclusion Crisis did much to alter Dryden's sense that Charles's reign signaled a new age of blessings and inviolable progress. With its parallel between the English in 1680 and the Israelites in David's time, *Absalom and Achitophel* suggests that history's cyclical course has persisted beyond the Restoration. Now Dryden has to adjust his scheme. Hoping that the resolution of these political turmoils will put an end to the periodic rebellions, he predicts that this second restoration of Charles's monarchy will initiate "a Series of new time," a "long Procession" of "mighty Years," unmarked by political vicissitudes (ll. 1028–29). But despite this desire, the final couplet underscores the cyclical pattern of history that pervades the poem:

> Once more the Godlike *David* was Restor'd,
> And willing Nations knew their Lawfull Lord. (ll. 1030–31).

By the 1680s Dryden is inclined to admit that the future may reveal, not England's progress, but a repetition of earlier rebellions.

With Charles II's death, the course of England's future seemed disturbingly uncertain. Dryden's funeral poem for Charles again invokes the idea that the restoration in 1660 had ushered in a golden age in which they "liv'd as unconcern'd and happily / As the first Age in Natures golden Scene" (*Threnodia Augustalis*, ll. 12–13). But with the death of Charles, who was "our *Atlas*" (l. 35), the nation he supported threatens to collapse. Though Dryden lauds James II as a Hercules, ready to uphold the state, behind this praise lurks Dryden's fear of sudden cyclical decline. Indeed, the poem suggests that even during Charles's reign England was in danger of falling, for Dryden calls Charles the

> . . . *Fabius* of a sinking State,
> Who didst by wise delays, divert our Fate,
> When Faction like a Tempest rose. (ll. 388–90)[54]

Not only does the allusion suggest that England may follow Rome's pattern in declining after reaching her greatest glories, but the lines also suggest that Dryden feared that the "Fate" of cyclical decline might be diverted or delayed but could not be avoided. Hercules/James may uphold England for a while. But just as Charles "escap'd the fatal blow / Of Faction and Conspiracy" only to have death "his promis'd hopes destroy" (ll. 406–8), so England may have escaped the fatal blow of Charles's death only to have to face destruction eventually. Like so many of the earlier poems, *Threnodia Augustalis* ends with Dryden foreseeing "The long Retinue of a Prosperous Reign, / A Series of Successful years" in which England's "Conquering Navy" will gain control of the ocean (ll. 507–8, 511). But the progress he predicts is conditional: it depends on James's repealing the loyalty oath. Moreover, the seeming optimism of the ending is qualified by the suggestion earlier in the poem that nations eventually decline—a view of history that, as we have seen, dominated Dryden's heroic plays of the 1660s and 1670s.

After the revolution of 1688, Dryden's view of history became decidedly more pessimistic, for once again England was ruled by what Dryden considered a usurper. Although perhaps he believed that the true succession would eventually be restored,[55] as the years passed it became increasingly less likely. There was very little now that could encourage the prophecies of progress, the celebration of a providential renewal of the golden age, and the conviction that God always restores lawful monarchy.[56]

In his late works, we occasionally find him suggesting that the pattern of history is one of decay. These "inferior times" in which the court goes "backward" are actually an iron age.[57] Whereas earlier he had praised the refinement and civilization of his age, in "To my Honour'd Kinsman, John Driden" he observes that the seeming process of refinement is actually a degeneration:

> By Chase our long-liv'd Fathers earn'd their Food;
> Toil strung the Nerves, and purifi'd the Blood:
> But we, their Sons, a pamper'd Race of Men,
> Are dwindl'd down to threescore Years and ten. (ll. 88–91)

Not only do these lines recall the sense in the poem "To Mr. Congreve" that our refinement has been accompanied by a loss of strength, but in the idea that man has degenerated ever since his primitive condition this passage also echoes Donne's anatomy in the *First Anniversary* of the historical process of decay.

But despite the occasional hint of a Donnean sense of continuous decay, Dryden at the end of his career settles into a firm sense of the cyclical pattern of history, in which decay is simply the final part of the cycle. Bodin and Louis Le Roy, while celebrating their age's achievements, had felt that their country would eventually decline just as others had in the past. Dryden, too, for all his attraction to the idea of progress, ultimately concludes that England will succumb to the same cyclical fate as other nations. He points out the disparity between the glories that England could achieve and the reality that she is already well on her way in the process of cyclical decline: "our Language is both Copious, Significant, and Majestical; and might be reduc'd into a more harmonious sound. But for want of Publick Encouragement, in this *Iron Age*, we are so far from making any progress in the improvement of our Tongue, that in few years, we shall Speak and Write as Barbarously as our Neighbours" (dedication of *Examen Poeticum*, in *Works*, 4:372). This prediction strongly suggests that he foresaw the fall of England, since as he remarks in the *Life of Plutarch*, "the fall of Empires always draws after it the language and Eloquence of the people" (*Works*, 17:279). "To Mr. *Granville*, on his Excellent Tragedy, call'd

Heroick Love" (1698) not only castigates the declining stage but draws an analogy between England and Rome that implies that England is repeating the same pattern of "decay" (ll. 33–36). No longer does Dryden hope for a political savior to avert the fall.

Whereas in 1660 Dryden could invoke the cyclical view of history to celebrate the return of order, the renewal of kingship, art, and religion, by the 1690s his idea of the cyclical pattern of history is cynical and grim. His attitude toward the cycles has gradually shifted from the view (reminiscent of Herrick's) that the cycles embody a reassuring providential order to a view (more akin to Milton's) that the cycles are a negation of progress, that they point to the unwillingness of the rulers (Milton blamed the people) to avoid repeating the errors of the past.

The bitter cyclical view that dominates the late works is evident in Dryden's dedication to *Don Sebastian* (1689). Here he suggests not only that history is cyclical, but also that the politicians themselves are sucked into this pattern of vicissitude as they "rise and fall in the variety of Revolutions." Ambitious for power, these men "have no sphere of their own, but . . . are whirl'd about by the motion of a greater Planet" — the great man (perhaps the ruler) on whom they sycophantically depend. "Ambitious Meteors! how willing they are to set themselves upon the Wing; and taking every occasion of drawing upward to the Sun: Not considering that they have no more time allow'd them for their mounting, than the short revolution of a day" (*Works*, 15:59–60).

Given the cyclical sense that pervades this dedication — and indeed the play itself, with its dizzying revolutions of fortune — it is not surprising that when Dryden compares Leicester to Atticus, he implies that England is repeating Rome's cycle. Both Leicester and Atticus lived in times when "their Countrymen . . . were just in the giddiness of their turning; when the ground was tottering under them at every moment; and none cou'd guess whether the next heave of the Earthquake, wou'd settle them on the first Foundation, or swallow it" (p. 61). Dryden raises the question of whether this recent political turmoil is a disruption that will lead to the restoration of the "first Foundation," the original order. Or is it that great earthquake that will precipitate the total collapse of the nation? Just as Atticus and Cicero could not be sure whether the political chaos they saw meant the destruction of the empire, so Dryden and Leicester live under a similar uncertainty. Though

Dryden holds out the possibility that order will be restored, by this time he is prepared for England's irreparable fall. Moreover, the parallel with Rome suggests that if not now, certainly in the future the fall will come. In this essay, Dryden's solution to these "revolutions"—the calamities of history that he no longer sees himself (or Leicester) capable of influencing—reminds us of Jonson's. Recalling Jonson's Stoic idea of withdrawal to the centered circle of virtue, Dryden praises Leicester, "who centring on himself, remains immovable, and smiles at the madness of the dance about him. He possesses the midst, which is the portion of safety and content" (p. 60).[58]

Ultimately all the revolutions of state force Dryden to conclude in the dedication of *Examen Poeticum* that "no Government has ever been, or ever can be, wherein Time-servers and Blockheads will not be uppermost. The persons are only chang'd, but the same jugglings in State, the same Hypocrisie in Religion, the same Self-Interest and Mis-mannagement, will remain for ever" (*Works*, 4:363). Here the uniformitarian idea that human nature is the same—an idea that could be used to argue that people in the present can perform deeds at least as great as those of the ancients—leads to the depressing conclusion that there is no hope for improvement. Perhaps most important, such a view of political history virtually deprives it of direction, meaning, and value.

The sense that human history seems pointless and futile emerges from "The Secular Masque," presumably Dryden's last verses. Standing at the end of the century, he surveys the past 100 years, charting first the age of Diana (the seemingly innocent pastoral time before the Civil War), the age of Mars (the period of the Puritan Revolution), and then the time of Venus (the age of love and pleasure that succeeded the war). Though Janus's description of the age of Diana when England was "in it's Prime" (l. 37) suggests the process of decline that we noted in "To . . . John Driden," the mocking figure of Momus eventually levels all the ages, insisting that there was neither progress nor decay. It's "All, all, of a piece throughout" (l. 86). Moreover, Dryden's description of these three ages presents his century as an epitome of mankind's history, thus implying that throughout history there has been neither perceivably meaningful direction nor value. Like the early poems, the masque ends with hope for the future: *"'Tis well an Old Age is out, / And time to begin a New"* (ll. 96–97). But Dryden refuses to say whether the new age will be better (or even just different) or whether it will simply be a repetition of the old.

Despite the hope that flickers at the end of "The Secular Masque," Dryden by the end of his life had lost most of his earlier faith in progress and had settled into a rather grim cyclical view of history. In an important sense this change parallels the one Milton experienced. Believing that progress was providentially ordained, Milton came to recognize that though man had the chance for progress, history would probably continue its cyclical course until the Apocalypse. Bacon, Milton, and Dryden were all attracted to the idea of progress that was developing during this time. But Bacon, writing at the beginning of the century, was the only one able to maintain his faith in progress. Perhaps it was because his hopes for the advancement of science did not depend on an idealistic conception of men or monarchs that long experience could undermine. The more that Milton and Dryden saw of contemporary history, the less they expected England's glorious advancement. At the end of their careers both men still believed that progress was possible, but neither thought it likely. Although in many ways Dryden points to future developments in the idea of history, like Janus in "The Secular Masque" he also looks back to the past, for he embraces the older interpretations of history's shape and finally rejects the optimistic reading of mankind's progress that was to dominate Western thought two centuries later.

Notes

1. *The Works of John Dryden,* gen. eds. E. N. Hooker and H. T. Swedenberg, Jr., 20 vols. in progress (Berkeley: University of California Press, 1956–), 17:270. I have used this edition (hereafter cited as *Works*) wherever possible. For the poems that have not yet been published in this edition, I have used *The Poems of John Dryden,* ed. James Kinsley, 4 vols. (Oxford: Clarendon Press, 1958); for the letters, *The Character of Polybius,* and the dedication of *Duke of Guise,* see *The Works of John Dryden,* ed. Sir Walter Scott, rev. George Saintsbury, 18 vols. (Edinburgh: William Paterson, 1882–93) (hereafter cited as *S-S*); for *Aureng-Zebe* and *All for Love,* see *John Dryden: Four Tragedies,* ed. L. A. Beaurline and Fredson Bowers (Chicago: University of Chicago Press, 1967); and for the dedication of the *Aeneis* and the preface to the *Fables,* see *Essays of John Dryden,* ed. W. P. Ker, 2 vols. (New York: Russell and Russell, 1961) (hereafter cited as Ker).

2. "An Account" of *Annus Mirabilis*, in *Works*, 1:50. For Dryden's comments about biography, see his discussion of history-writing in *Life of Plutarch* (*Works*, 17:271).

3. Bodin, *Method*, pp. 51, 53.

4. See Steven N. Zwicker, *Politics and Language in Dryden's Poetry: The Arts of Disguise* (Princeton: Princeton University Press, 1984).

5. Earl Miner, *Dryden's Poetry* (Bloomington: Indiana University Press, 1967), p. 9.

6. I use the term *skepticism* to refer, not to a philosophical position, but rather to the method of inquiry advocated by Bacon and the Royal Society. Phillip Harth, in *Contexts of Dryden's Thought* (Chicago: University of Chicago Press, 1968), ch. 1, has suggested the importance of this kind of skepticism in Dryden's role as poet and literary critic.

7. See, e.g., Abraham Cowley's *"Ode* Upon His Majesties Restoration and Return" and Edmund Waller's "To the King, upon his Majesty's happy return."

8. Thomas H. Fujimura, "John Dryden and the Myth of the Golden Age," *PLL* 11 (1975), 149–67, argues that this myth "dominates his poetry."

9. George de F. Lord, "'Absalom and Achitophel' and Dryden's Political Cosmos," in *Writers and Their Works: John Dryden*, ed. Earl Miner (London: G. Bell & Sons, 1972), pp. 156–90, discusses Dryden's preoccupation with "the restoration of royal authority after a period of rebellious disorder," and he links this concern to a cyclical view of history.

10. On Dryden's use of the analogy between literature and politics, see Alan Roper, *Dryden's Poetic Kingdoms* (London: Routledge and Kegan Paul, 1965), pp. 136–84.

11. Anne T. Barbeau, *The Intellectual Design of John Dryden's Heroic Plays* (New Haven: Yale University Press, 1970), has observed in passsing that the heroic plays deal with the rise and fall of kingdoms (p. 7 and ch. 3 passim), but the importance of the cyclical view of history in these plays has not received the attention it deserves.

12. Derek Hughes, *Dryden's Heroic Plays* (Lincoln: University of Nebraska Press, 1981), has argued that "Cortez is not a force of renewal but the reimbodiment of a bloody past," and thus we see in *Indian Emperour* "the cyclic repetition of history" (p. 58).

13. See Bodin, *Six Bookes*, p. 406, and Manuel, *Shapes of Philosophical History*, p. 59, who notes Bodin's concern with catastrophic falls.

14. John M. Wallace, "John Dryden's Plays and the Conception of a Heroic Society," in *Culture and Politics from Puritanism to the Enlightenment*, ed. Perez Zagorin (Berkeley: University of California Press, 1980), pp. 113–34, sees jealousy as "the single most disruptive passion in Dryden's plays" (p. 126). Hughes (*Dryden's Heroic Plays*) has emphasized that in these tragedies passion typically brings destruction, chaos, enslavement, and death. Though Hughes's focus is on the individual characters and their relationships, much the same should be said about the role of passion

in the large arena of history that the plays invoke as a framework for their actions.

15. Collingwood, *Idea of History,* finds the idea of history as a science incipient in Herodotus, but admits that the Greeks lacked a theory of causation (pp. 18, 23). Dryden's concept of history, however, incorporates the theory of causation developed by seventeenth-century science.

16. Rushworth, *Historical Collections,* 1 (1659), "The Epistle Dedicatory."

17. John M. Wallace, "Dryden and History: A Problem in Allegorical Reading," *ELH* 36 (1969), 265–90, discusses the similarity in Renaissance conceptions of exemplar poetry and exemplar history to illuminate Dryden's poetic use of historical examples and parallels from which the reader could infer contemporary applications. It is important, however, to recognize that history and poetry were considered exemplary precisely because the uniformity of human nature insured the cyclical, repetitive movement of history in which past examples could parallel present and future ones almost indefinitely.

18. Zwicker, *Politics and Language in Dryden's Poetry,* pp. 43, 45. Zwicker insists on the covertly polemical character of Dryden's poetry and rejects the idea that Dryden is a neutral observer of political events. On Dryden's polemical stance, see also Steven Zwicker and Derek Hirst, "Rhetoric and Disguise: Political Language and Political Argument in *Absalom and Achitophel*," *Journal of British Studies* 21 (1981), 39–55; and Elizabeth Duthie, "'A Memorial of My Own Principles': Dryden's 'To My Honour'd Kinsman,'" *ELH* 47 (1980), 682–704.

19. Bodin, *Method,* p. 44.

20. Rushworth, *Historical Collections,* 1:"The Epistle Dedicatory."

21. Clarendon, *History of the Rebellion,* 1:3.

22. Rushworth, *Historical Collections,* 1:"The Epistle Dedicatory." Zwicker offers fine readings of Dryden and does an excellent job discovering what he calls the "covert" meanings and arguments of the poems. However, he exaggerates the opposition between "overt" and "covert" meanings in Dryden when he typically characterizes the "overt" meaning (the rhetorical strategies, the claims for impartiality) as "disguise" (and thus the "false" meaning) and the "covert" meaning (the implicit political argument) as the real or "true" meaning.

23. Bodin, *Method,* pp. 51–55.

24. Wallace, "Dryden and History," pp. 271–79, notes that Dryden tends in his poetry to avoid reducing the implicit lessons of history to precepts, but Wallace overemphasizes "the historian-poet's neutrality" (p. 273) in omitting direct, topical application of history's lessons.

25. Patrides, *Grand Design of God,* pp. 2, 9.

26. Barbeau argues that the heroic plays, like *Annus Mirabilis* and *Astraea Redux,* suggest "that history, since the start of the Christian era, has been moving forward in an ever-increasing implementation of the Redemption in the secular sphere" (p. 10).

27. See, e.g., the conclusion of Clarendon's *History of the Rebellion* (end of Bk. XVI), 6:234.

28. Cf. *Albion and Albanius*, II.ii.83–88. Clarendon also saw in the "perplexities and distractions" of the Civil War "the immediate finger and wrath of God" (*History of the Rebellion*, 1:2), though he emphasized the natural causes that led to the war.

29. In the preface to *Religio Laici*, Dryden's assertion of his "natural" inclination to "skepticism" is followed by a "skeptical" discrimination of both strengths and limitations of the pagans.

30. Others also saw God behind the cycles. See, e.g., Raleigh's preface to *History of the World*, and Bodin's *Method*, pp. 16–17.

31. Manuel, *Shapes of Philosophical History*, p. 11.

32. See Trompf, *Idea of Historical Recurrence in Western Thought*, ch. 3.

33. Johan Chydenius, *The Typological Problem in Dante*, Commentationes Humanarum Litterarum, 25, no. 1 (Helsingfors: Societas Scientiarum Fennica, 1958), p. 23.

34. Jean Daniélou, S.J., *From Shadows to Reality: Studies in the Biblical Typology of the Fathers*, trans. Dom Wulstan Hibberd (London: Burns and Oates, 1960), pp. 12, 30. On the relationship between typology and a cyclical view of history, see Manuel, *Shapes of Philosophical History*, who suggests that typology became "a way of unconsciously assimilating the historical cyclicism of pagan thought" (p. 13); and Trompf, who notes that certain kinds of typology "constitute forms of recurrence thinking" (*Idea of Historical Recurrence*, p. 128). Trompf insists throughout his book that the classical historians did not, in fact, believe in *exact* recurrence.

35. Steven N. Zwicker, *Dryden's Political Poetry: The Typology of King and Nation* (Providence, R.I.: Brown University Press, 1972), discusses the importance of typology in Dryden's political poetry and suggests that through typology his poems unify "history past and present in an eternal paradigm" (p. 26).

36. Heylyn, *A Sermon Preached . . . on Wednesday May 29th 1661*, p. 25.

37. Patrides, *Grand Design of God*, pp. 57–59, 102–9, discusses the emergent modern conception of history.

38. Ruth Nevo, *The Dial of Virtue: A Study of Poems of Affairs of State in the Seventeenth Century* (Princeton: Princeton University Press, 1963).

39. Patrides, *Grand Design of God*, p. 58.

40. Miner, *Restoration Mode*, pp. 299–300, has observed that in *Essay of Dramatic Poesy* "the concept of historical periods of literature emerges . . . for the first time in English criticism, along with a sense of historical movement or development—and of a period of literature as something related to the other events of the time."

41. Miner, *Dryden's Poetry*, p. 34, significantly notes that Dryden is "the first really important English poet to bring contemporary history into poetry."

42. Robert D. Hume, *Dryden's Criticism* (Ithaca: Cornell University Press, 1970), p. 76.

43. Earl Miner, "Dryden and the Issue of Human Progress," *PQ* 40

(1961), 120–29, notes the frequency of "progress-pieces" in Dryden's poetry and prose.

44. Cf. Sprat's sense of England's military and commercial accomplishments and her future prospects for expansion: the *"English* name does manifestly get ground by the bravery of their *Arms,* the glory of their *Naval strength,* and the spreading of their *Commerce"* (*History of the Royal-Society,* p. 125).

45. In *Restoration Mode,* pp. 300–316, 353–54, Miner has argued that Dryden combines an essential conservatism and a commitment to progress. Such a combination, I believe, is evident in his version of the idea of progress.

46. Lord, "'Absalom and Achitophel,'" discusses Dryden's aversion to novelty and innovation. On Dryden's conservatism, see also Bernard Schilling's classic study, *Dryden and the Conservative Myth* (New Haven: Yale University Press, 1961).

47. Manuel, *Shapes of Philosophical History,* p. 67, suggests that there is no truly modern (nineteenth-century) idea of progress in the seventeenth century, which lacks the three essential elements that he finds characteristic of the modern idea: universality, inevitability, and infinity.

48. James W. Johnson, *The Formation of English Neo-Classical Thought* (Princeton: Princeton University Press, 1967), pp. 57–58, finds Dryden essentially unaware of the implications of eventual decline inherent in the "body-state" metaphor. Similarly Hume asserts, "He never really faces the cyclical nature of nations and their literatures, though such a view seems implicit in the biological metaphors he frequently employs" (*Dryden's Criticism,* p. 75).

49. Myron P. Gilmore, "The Renaissance Conception of the Lessons of History," in *Facets of the Renaissance,* ed. Wallace K. Ferguson et al. (New York: Harper and Row, 1963), pp. 73–103, has shown that the Renaissance, unlike the Middle Ages, had a sense of anachronism, a sense that the present culture and customs differed from those of classical antiquity. But Gilbert, "Renaissance Interest in History," emphasizes the limits of the Renaissance interest in historical knowledge of the past and connects this lack of interest with the glorification of classical times.

50. Bacon, *Valerius Terminus,* in *Works,* 3:225.

51. George McFadden, *Dryden the Public Writer, 1660–1685* (Princeton: Princeton University Press, 1978), has argued that Dryden was admonishing Charles through his portraits of weak kings in the heroic drama (pp. 92, 102, 193, 196).

52. Cedric D. Reverand II, "Dryden's 'Essay of Dramatic Poesie': The Poet and the World of Affairs," *SEL* 22 (1982), 375–93, claims that even in the late "apparently pessimistic poems" such as the Kneller poem Dryden still retains his belief in "poetry's ultimate efficacy" (p. 386). I would insist, though, that this belief in poetry's ultimate power is no longer tied to a progressive view of history.

53. McKeon, *Politics and Poetry in Restoration England,* has shown that although Dryden celebrates unity and the accord of prince and people

in *Annus Mirabilis,* England was actually troubled by divisions and plots that threatened to renew the chaos of the earlier rebellion against Charles I. Whether out of conviction or wishful thinking, however, Dryden predicts in the poems written during the early years of the Restoration that the golden age of peace and progress will last.

54. The phrase "sinking state" also occurs in the plays, where it refers to nations or empires that are falling. See, e.g. *Indian Emperour,* II.i.56, and *Aureng-Zebe,* where Dryden's description of Charles in *Threnodia Augustalis* is anticipated in Arimant's praise of Aureng-Zebe as an *"Atlas"* who "must our sinking State uphold" (I.104).

55. The poem "To My Dear Friend Mr. Congreve" sees William's violation of lawful succession reflected in the kingdom of letters. Dryden has been "Depos'd" and *"Tom* the Second" rules instead (ll. 42, 48). But at the end Dryden prophesies that after "some short parentheses" the true succession will be restored and Congreve (the only one "lineal to the Throne," l. 44) will be "High on the Throne of Wit" (l. 53). The parallel Dryden establishes between the kingdom of England and the kingdom of wit suggests that perhaps at this point he hoped a similar restoration would occur in England's government.

56. Zwicker, *Dryden's Political Poetry,* p. 103, has aptly observed that in the late poems England is no longer included in Dryden's "metaphors of sacred history."

57. For a reference to the iron age, see, e.g., Ker, 2:12. Fujimura, "John Dryden and the Myth of the Golden Age," has noted that "in the years following the Revolution of 1688 . . . the myth of the Iron Age embodied for Dryden his pessimistic feelings about the period he was living in" (p. 164), but he concludes that Dryden's temperament was basically "optimistic" and thus that the golden age myth is "the dominant one" (p. 166).

58. After 1688 Dryden found himself forced to withdraw from the "mad" political arena; his own position thus seems to have encouraged him to adopt this Stoic pose when he felt no longer able to affect his political environment. James D. Garrison has argued (*Dryden and the Tradition of Panegyric* [Berkeley: University of California Press, 1975]) that after 1688 Dryden gave up the traditional panegyric function of mediator between king and people (p. 191) and that in the 1690s his most characteristic poems are "epistles to private individuals, usually other artists" (p. 243).

CHAPTER VIII

Conclusion

THE PRECEDING CHAPTERS have explored the ways in which ideas of history affected six important seventeenth-century writers: Bacon, Donne, Jonson, Herrick, Milton, and Dryden. Several basic ideas of history's pattern were current during this period—the idea of decay, the cyclical view of history, and the idea of progress. Each of these six writers found certain of these paradigms particularly suitable to his temperament and adapted them in distinctive, personal ways. It is essential to recognize, however, that these writers' views of history are not simply a limited, isolatable part of their work but had a pervasive, wide-reaching influence: attitudes toward time and history informed their understanding of the entire range of human experience and endeavor. Ideas of history shaped these writers' characteristic structures of thought and language as well as their sense of purpose in writing.

Donne was most deeply affected by the idea of decay. His sense of history as a process of continuous degeneration and fragmentation lies behind his obsession with change; his interest in the source, "fountain," or "root" of things; his idealization of the most distant past as a time of wholeness and purity; his tendency to define both ideal love and God in terms of their opposition to decay; and his hope to find through love, memory, and religion some restoration of the original perfection. As poet and priest, Donne anatomizes the universal process of decay, reminds man of the lost perfection, and tries to reestablish the wholeness that has been lost.

The cyclical view of time predominates in Jonson and Herrick. Jonson's sense of cyclical vicissitude, very much part of the Stoic ethics that inform his work, affects his characteristic description of vice as involved in and thus subject to cyclical vicissitude; his repeated tendency to define virtue as a constancy that is unaffected by such temporal changes; and his belief that as a poet he stands in opposition to the times and raises his virtuous subjects above them. Jonson seems to have a stronger faith in the individual's ability to resist change than Donne, whose belief that human beings should counter the fragmenting force of time and history is frustrated by his recognition of man's seemingly inescapable disposition to change. Jonson's distrust of personae or masks reflects his sense that the good person must remain "one" and resist the changes that threaten to shake his constancy. In his nondramatic poetry he insists on speaking in his own voice, in marked contrast to Donne, who has multiple personae and who continuously shifts perspectives and arguments.

We often think of Metaphysical poetry as concerned with transcending the temporal and physical world, and of Jonson's poetry (and Cavalier poetry by extension) as more embracing of this world, less concerned with transcendence. But our understanding of Donne's and Jonson's attitudes toward history suggests that such distinctions may need to be revised or qualified. Both Jonson and Donne see time and change as an adversary that must be resisted. Jonson's sense of the need to transcend time is at least as strong as Donne's. Indeed, whereas Donne tends to idealize the earliest state at the beginning of time, Jonson's golden age, his transcendent ideal, is located not in the past but above time altogether.

Like Jonson, Herrick sees time as essentially cyclical, but he does not view the cyclical vicissitudes as the threat that Jonson does. Though these two poets share an essentially cyclical view of history, their *attitudes* toward these cycles are fundamentally different. Whereas Jonson sees cyclical vicissitude as a threat to the virtuous person and advises Lady Aubigny to pay no attention to "Times" and "occasions," Herrick tells his women to seize the moment, to gather the rosebuds while "time serves." The *carpe diem* theme, so important in Cavalier poetry, is not really congenial to Jonson. Herrick, unlike Jonson, even finds a certain comfort in the cycles and emphasizes the prospects of renewal that a cyclical view can offer. Thus the cycles of history give him consolation during the Civil War. Though Jonson seeks to escape or transcend the cycles, Herrick is concerned with ensuring their renewal, which he hopes to effect through ceremony and poetry.

These differences in historical attitudes between Jonson and Herrick should make us wary of assuming that Jonson and the Cavalier poets share a single view of history. Indeed, even among the Cavalier poets, there is no such uniformity. Richard Lovelace, for example, in poems such as "The Grasshopper," "Advice to My Best Brother, Colonel Francis Lovelace," and "The Snail," suggests that people need to find a refuge from or an alternative to the cyclical vicissitudes of history, that the self needs to withdraw, to protect itself from time, and to preserve its constancy amid the turmoils of life. His attitude toward history seems closer to Jonson's than to Herrick's.

Jonson's and Herrick's contrasting attitudes toward history foster quite different conceptions of the poet's function and of poetry's immortalizing powers. Jonson, with his conviction that cyclical vicissitude is something that one must rise above, tends to represent the poet's immortalizing power as a force that raises people above time, that holds them "up and even"; the poem offers, in a sense, a refuge from time. Herrick, on the other hand, with his affection for the seasonal cycle and his feeling for the renewals inherent in cyclical time, sees the immortality poetry provides as a "second Spring"—the poet "repullulates," gives a renewal to man that is analogous to the renewal of plants in the spring.

In their concern with providing immortality through poetry, Jonson and Herrick emphasize the importance of memory, but their conception of memory is quite different from Donne's, who also found in memory an antidote to time. For Donne, memory looks backward. It works against the degenerative course of history, taking a person back to purer, better times, reconnecting him with God. When Jonson and Herrick speak of memory, however, they look toward the future not the past, as they stress memory's ability to grant a person life that extends beyond death. The preservation of his memory in poetry offers Herrick continued life until the Apocalypse. For Jonson, the emphasis is on transcendence as well as on the perpetuation of life in the future—Morison, having "leap'd the present age," still "lives" with "memorie" (Cary-Morison Ode), while those who have lacked a poet to celebrate their fame "now lye lost in their forgotten dust" ("Epistle to Elizabeth, Countesse of Rutland").

If the idea of decay appears most clearly in Donne and the cyclical view in Jonson and Herrick, the idea of progress inspires Bacon, Milton, and, to a more limited extent, Dryden. Bacon sensed that he was living at a time when the pattern of history could be changed.

Though natural philosophy had degenerated throughout the past cycles of history, he was confident that the course of the future could be one of continuous progress in knowledge and power, if only men would begin anew and reform the method and goals of their knowledge. Bacon's commitment to progress and his dislike of the cyclical pattern of history are apparent not only in his definition of induction as an embodiment of the historical ideal of progress, but also in his characteristic tendency to describe error, sin, and the false philosophies in terms of cycles. Convinced that he was appointed to be a redeemer of mankind, he saw himself offering hope and salvation through science. Behind his writings lies an almost messianic desire to convince people that progress is possible.

Milton, too, felt that he was living at a time when the pattern of history could be radically changed, and his work was similarly impelled by his attempts to encourage this change. Others have noted that Milton shows some indebtedness to Bacon, especially in *Of Education,* but when one looks at their views of history, their similarities become striking. Though Bacon's concern was primarily with science and Milton's with religion and politics, both believed that history had been cyclical but that mankind was being given a providential opportunity to change its pattern. Both contrast the cyclical past with the progress they envision for the future. Milton's hopes for progress and his rejection of the cyclical pattern lie behind his tendency to define error as cyclical relapse, his characteristic contrast between cyclical and progressive patterns in his poetry as well as prose, and his insistent preference for linear, progressive movement. Milton's portrayal of man's Edenic state; his preference for the "new"; his tendency to define temptation as the lure of repeating the past; and his celebration of a God who incorporates the potential for growth into His creation and repeatedly engages in "new" creations—all reflect Milton's progressive view of history and his radical acceptance of change as positive.

For all the similarities in their views of history, Milton ultimately is more radical than Bacon in his commitment to change and progress. Both believe we must make a clean break with the past. But, like Donne and so many others during the Renaissance and seventeenth century, Bacon still tends to define the ideal in terms of an original perfection that has been lost in time. Bacon's science aims to restore Adam's condition before the Fall. Though Milton shares this sense of loss, he does not idealize the distant past as much as does Bacon. Neither does he see man's original state as the most perfect that could exist. Man's unfallen condition was one of potential for growth; it did not embody a perfection beyond which human beings could never advance. Milton, indeed, is unusual in that his ideal, his notion of the perfection for which mankind strives, is *not* something that existed in the past but a condition which has always been waiting to be fully realized in the future.

Both Bacon and Milton saw progress mainly as an ideal rather than actuality. The past was cyclical, but the present and future held the promise of change and progress. Dryden, however, in the early years after the restoration of Charles II felt that England had already made tremendous advances and would surely achieve greater heights in the future. His belief in progress not only informs his praise of England's achievements and the visions of the future that conclude so many of his poems, but it also leads him to defend the ability of the "moderns" to surpass the literary achievements of the ancients. Dryden's ideal of progress, however, differs markedly from Bacon's and Milton's, for he sees progress as contingent on tradition, continuity, and succession, rather than on a radical break with the past. In this he is far more conservative than these other two proponents of progress. Moreover, Dryden's progressive view of history is sharply qualified by an essentially cyclical reading of history. His sense of cyclical history is apparent in his fondness for biblical and historical parallels, in his interpretation of the Restoration as the renewal of a golden age, and in his attempts as poet-historian to advise England's leaders in the hope of averting cyclical decline. The cyclical view eventually came to dominate his thinking, especially after the ascension of William and Mary, when he even seemed occasionally attracted by the idea of decay, the sense that civilization entailed a loss of strength and virtue. In his later years he lost faith in England's progress and came to believe that his country had already embarked on her cyclical decline, much as Jonson had thought earlier in the century. With their knowledge of classical history, both writers felt that England was repeating the history of Rome, and like Cicero or Horace before them they recognized the virtue of trying to remain untouched by the corruption they could not reform. As Dryden moved from a progressive view of history to a firmly cyclical one, he gave witness at the end of the seventeenth century to the persistence and vitality of the cyclical view, which for many people continued to be the scheme that best explained history.

Ideas of history shaped these writers' interpretations of life, but in turn their ideas of history were sometimes altered by their experiences and the historical world they inhabited. Bacon's, Jonson's, Herrick's, and even Donne's views of history remained essentially the same throughout their work. Milton's and especially Dryden's views, however, went through major changes. Milton came to feel that though people have the opportunity to progress, it is unlikely that they will change. The degenerative cycles will probably continue until the end of the world. Dryden in his late years concluded that "Time-servers and Blockheads" always hold the greatest influence in government. Like Milton, he feared that history would prove inevitably cyclical because of human obstinacy. Both Milton and Dryden in quite different ways tied their hopes for progress to certain political conditions. Consequently, when these conditions changed, their views of history required modification and adjustment. The pressure of historical events and personal experiences could make a person who had expected progress finally conclude that history not only had been but would continue to be cyclical.

I have claimed that the three basic ideas of history had a more far-reaching effect on seventeenth-century literature than has been realized, and I would like now to mention some of the other writers in whom we see the shaping presence of these historical perspectives. My comments here can only be brief and suggestive; each of these writers really deserves a full study in his own right, for it is impossible to do justice to the complexity of their historical views in a few brief generalizations. Nevertheless, it is important to see that many of the ideas that I have been examining in Bacon, Donne, Jonson, Herrick, Milton, and Dryden were indeed widespread.

The idea of decay disturbed several writers whose works, like Donne's, are concerned with whether it is possible to remedy or reverse the degenerative effects of time. Robert Burton's *Anatomy of Melancholy*, defining melancholy as the postlapsarian human condition, implies that history reveals a process of continuous decay. Though man's first state was pure, perfect, and happy, with original sin he lost his health, and the course of time has seen a progressive falling away from his first state. Burton suggests that the only growth has been in human misery. We now have more diseases than the ancients did. Indeed, there are so many new varieties of madness and folly that were Democritus alive today, Burton suggests, he would have wept, not laughed.[1] Burton anatomizes melancholy partly to alleviate his own by keeping busy and partly in the hope that by understanding it people may be better able to endure it patiently. He frequently reminds us that as an effect and punishment of the Fall melancholy cannot be permanently cured by human efforts; nevertheless, in cataloging and describing numerous "remedies" he is trying to help people counter, even in a limited way, the degenerative effect of time and resist the forces that increase man's unhappiness.

The idea of decay also appears in George Herbert and Henry Vaughan, though we should be reluctant to conclude that the Metaphysical poets share a degenerative view of history since some were attracted by other views of history as well. Herbert's poem "Decay" reflects a nostalgia for a better state that existed in the days of Abraham and Moses. Like Donne in the *First Anniversary*, he realizes that man in the early days after the Fall had a closer, more intimate relationship with God than exists now, when "the world grows old" (l. 16):

> Sweet were the dayes, when thou didst lodge with Lot,
> Struggle with Jacob, sit with Gideon,
> Advise with Abraham, when thy power could not
> Encounter Moses strong complaints and mone:
>   Thy words were then, *Let me alone.*
>
> One might have sought and found thee presently
> At some fair oak, or bush, or cave, or well:
> Is my God this way? No, they would reply:
> He is to Sinai gone, as we heard tell:
>   List, ye may heare great Aarons bell. (ll. 1–10)[2]

Herbert's desire to recapture this lost intimacy lies behind the conversational style of his poetry. He directly addresses God, has conversations with Him, and receives "answers." In these poems or colloquies, he thus reverses the distancing effect of history as well as anticipates the state of the glorified soul in heaven, where (as "Love [III]" shows) he will be able to partake of God even more fully than Abraham was able to.

Although the idea of decay occasionally appears in Herbert's poetry, it shapes Vaughan's more radically. Vaughan laments that throughout the course of history man has progressively lost his glory and vision, his knowledge of the spiritual world.

> Sure, It was so. Man in those early days
>   Was not all stone, and Earth,
> He shin'd a little, and by those weak Rays
>   Had some glimpse of his birth.
>
> "Corruption," ll. 1–4[3]

These "early days" contrast with our present state in which "Sin triumphs" and we have "sunk" into a state of "deep sleep, and night" (ll. 35–37). The pattern of history is degenerative and is reenacted in the individual's life, as "The Retreate" makes clear, with its combination of the historical idea of continuous decay and the neo-Platonic idea of the soul's descent into the physical, material world.

> Happy those early dayes! when I
> Shin'd in my Angell-infancy.
> Before I understood this place
> Appointed for my second race,
> Or taught my soul to fancy ought
> But a white, Celestiall thought,
> When yet I had not walkt above
> A mile, or two, from my first love,
> And looking back (at that short space,)
> Could see a glimpse of his bright-face;
> When on some *gilded Cloud,* or *flowre*
> My gazing soul would dwell an houre,
> And in those weaker glories spy
> Some shadows of eternity;
> Before I taught my tongue to wound
> My Conscience with a sinfull sound,
> Or had the black art to dispence
> A sev'rall sinne to ev'ry sence,
> But felt through all this fleshly dresse
> Bright *shootes* of everlastingnesse.
>   O how I long to travell back
> And tread again that ancient track!

That I might once more reach that plaine
Where first I left my glorious traine,
From whence th'Inlightned spirit sees
That shady City of Palme trees;
But (ah!) my soul with too much stay
Is drunk, and staggers in the way.
Some men a forward motion love,
But I by backward steps would move,
And when this dust falls to the urn
In that state I came return.

Civilization is a process of decline, a loss of original purity and knowledge. When Vaughan suggests that the arts, even language, are a sign of degeneracy, it is clear how completely he rejects the view advanced by Bodin and others that human history shows a gradual advance from a barbarous to a civilized state. Vaughan idealizes man's original state and sees infancy or childhood as symbolic of this lost happiness. His idealization of childhood is similar to the glorification of an ancient golden age that so often accompanied the degenerative view of history, though Vaughan is unusual in believing that each individual, even in this degenerate age, automatically retains in his earliest days some of man's original glory.

Like Donne, Vaughan wants to reverse the pattern of history. His impulse to rise above the world of time and history, apparent in poems like "The World," may remind us of Jonson, but his nostalgic longing for the "Home" he left, his desire to move "by backward steps," and the emphasis on memory in poems such as "Silence, and stealth of dayes" all reflect a desire to remedy the degenerative course of history by returning to the purer time in the past. Vaughan's usual tone is one of frustrated, thwarted longing—unable to return, he is trapped in time. And his impulses are ultimately much more regressive than Donne's.

One final example of the influence of the idea of decay must serve. John Webster's *Duchess of Malfi* presents a grim picture of corruption and decay in the state and suggests that political corruption may be part of a larger, universal order in which all things decay. The virtuous Antonio as well as the evil Ferdinand comment on man's self-destructiveness in ways that remind us of Donne—people "strive / To bring [themselves] to nothing" and are "Like Diamonds . . . cut with our owne dust."[4] A similar self-destructiveness seems at work in the Italian society portrayed in the play. Antonio's fondness for "ruins" is based on his nostalgia for a better time, which existed in the past and from which his society has decayed.[5] We see in Ferdinand and the Cardinal the corruption of the law and religion, two pillars of society. Ultimately Antonio concludes that human institutions partake of the more general process of decay:

Churches, and Cities (which have diseases like to men)
Must have like death that we have. (V.iii.19–20)

The biological metaphor here, however, suggests that decay may in fact be part of a cyclical pattern. Indeed Webster's play, though deeply affected by the Jacobean preoccupation with universal, inevitable decay, raises the question of whether decay might in the cyclical nature of things be succeeded by renewal. Antonio's description at the opening of the play of the recent reformation of the French court implies that revival of Italy's moral and political health is possible, and the conclusion of the play reinforces this suggestion, since Antonio's eldest son survives, along with the virtuous Delio and Pescarra. But the darkness of the play threatens to overwhelm this hope. Webster does not provide a settled answer to the question of what the order of history is. Unsure whether fate, fortune, Providence, or chance shapes events and outcomes, uncertain whether decay and corruption can be reversed, we are, like so many of the characters in the play, left "in a mist" (V.v.118).

Like the idea of decay, the cyclical view of history shaped the way in which people interpreted intellectual and political history and the pattern of spiritual life. If Burton is affected by the idea of decay, he also at times seems to incline to a cyclical view of history. In Burton, as in many other writers we have looked at, several seemingly contradictory ideas of history coexist, but in his work in particular there seems a tension between these ideas of history, with their often quite different assumptions. Although sometimes he suggests that people are worse off now than in the past, at other times he shares Jonson's and Dryden's view that human nature is always the same. People have always been miserable, melancholy, and mad, subject to vicissitudes that overthrow their brief periods of felicity, and the best they can do is "scorn this transitory state" and exercise a kind of Stoic patience. Burton's amassing of quotations and his references to writers from many ages and countries reinforce this sense that mankind has always been the same, that experience is repetitive rather than degenerative. Solomon's words are as true now as they were in ancient Israel: there is still nothing new under the sun. Consequently Burton insists that the seemingly new astronomical theories of the late Renaissance are simply revivals of ancient ones. Copernicus's theory was actually "maintained of old" by Pythagoras and Democritus, and Bruno's idea that the universe is composed of "infinite Worlds in an infinite waste" was formerly held by Democritus, Epicurus, and Lecippus.[6] I am reminded of Sir Thomas Browne's remark that religious heresies enjoy cyclical revivals: "Heresies perish not with their Authors, but like the river *Arethusa*, though they lose their currents in one place, they rise up againe in another . . . opinions doe finde after certaine revolutions, men and mindes like those that first begat them."[7] Such a historical perspective lies behind Burton's sense that he is a second Democritus. His cyclical sense of history leads him to feel, like Jonson, Herrick, and Dryden, a special sense of community with others in the past.

Herbert's poetry, too, reflects a cyclical idea of time. The large pattern of history may be one of decay, but his own spiritual life reveals a somewhat different shape. Throughout the *Temple* he presents the continuing cyclical vicissitudes of his spiritual life, in which moments of grace and assurance are followed by rebellion, affliction, and doubt. Restlessness and flux rather than peace and stability characterize his life. Like Donne, Herbert sees inconstancy as the inescapable condition of human life, but his definition of these changes in terms of cyclical alteration rather than decay also suggests an affinity with Jonson and Herrick. Seeing God's hand behind the cycles of affliction and renewal, Herbert seems at times to derive a certain comfort from the orderliness of the cycles, much as Herrick does. There is a divine plan behind them. But often the cyclical vicissitudes seem not so much comforting as painful:

> Although there were some fourtie heav'ns, or more,
>   Sometimes I peere above them all;
> Sometimes I hardly reach a score,
>   Sometimes to hell I fall.
>
> "The Temper (I)," ll. 5–8

Though such tempering tunes as well as tortures, there is a sense of bewilderment at the rapid and continual changes, the alternations between joy and grief. God kills and quickens, "bringing down to hell / And up to heaven in an houre" ("The Flower," ll. 15–16). Like Herrick, Herbert finds in the natural cycle of the flower an analogy for the cyclical pattern of human life. But where Herrick laments that man has only one cycle, Herbert's complaint is that he has so many:

> Many a spring I shoot up fair,
> Offring at heav'n, growing and groning thither:
> Nor doth my flower
> Want a spring-showre,
> My sinnes and I joining together:
>
> But while I grow in a straight line,
> Still upwards bent, as if heav'n were mine own,
> Thy anger comes, and I decline:
> What frost to that?
>
> "The Flower," ll. 24–32

Though Herbert celebrates the renewals of God's grace, the "returns" of spring, he longs like Jonson for stasis, for an escape from the painful vicissitudes:

> O that I once past changing were,
> Fast in thy Paradise, where no flower can wither! (ll. 22–23)

Thomas Hobbes, whose concern with history extends well beyond his early translation of Thucydides or his history of the Civil War, offers a particularly interesting example of how political theory could be shaped by a cyclical view of history. *Leviathan* (1651), written in response to the chaos of the Civil War, is based on an interpretation of history that finds England repeating the cyclical pattern of other states in the past. When Hobbes speaks of the "generation" of the commonwealth, its "nutrition," "procreation," and "dissolution" or "death," he draws on the traditional biological analogy that suggests that the body politic, like the body human, goes through a cyclical process of growth and decay.[8] By forming or generating a commonwealth, men escape their original, natural condition, in which "every man [is] against every man,"[9] but eventually the commonwealth dies as it dissolves into war and returns to the state of chaos that existed in the beginning. Thus the growth of a civilization is always threatened by cyclical relapse into the natural state of war. England's recent Civil Wars confirmed Hobbes's theory, indeed probably helped mold it. Hobbes believed that the cyclical pattern would continue in England. He predicted that after the Civil War there would be a "return of peace," but that this peace would only continue until the "miseries" of war were "forgotten"; then England would once again return to the state of war.[10] He found this succession of cycles depressing, not reassuring.

Hobbes, however, presents a remedy for this rather discouraging pattern of history. On the assumption that it is within our power to stave off, at least for a time, the cyclical decline into war, he published his *Leviathan*, offering a set of rules, a pattern of government, whereby the death of the commonwealth could be postponed, if not prevented. Up until his time, Hobbes insists, states have never flourished for long. Lacking patience and the proper "art of making fit laws," people have always erected commonwealths that have "hardly last[ed] out their own time." But, like Bacon, Hobbes sees himself offering a plan that can change the course of history. Though nothing that "mortals" make can truly be "immortal," nevertheless if his "rules" are followed, "commonwealths might be secured, at least from perishing by internal diseases." They would still be subject to death by the "external violence" of foreign wars, but otherwise they would be "everlasting."[11]

Hobbes does not promise that civilization will progress if his rules are followed—he only offers the hope that decay will be postponed, and his rather grim assessment of human nature, of man's essential selfishness and inclination to war, makes him skeptical that men really will put his principles into practice. Nevertheless, he does share Bacon's sense that the course of the future can be different than the past, and he is affected by a Baconian sense that knowledge has been growing. "Time, and industry, produce every day new knowledge."[12] Distinguishing between the cyclical course of political history and the progressive advance of knowledge, he claims that his political philosophy is an important discovery. Echoing Bacon, he asserts that before him no one had the "leisure," "curiosity," and "method" to find out the "rules" for "maintaining commonwealths."[13]

As Hobbes shows, writers who thought that history was mainly cyclical or degenerative could still be affected by the newly emerging idea of progress. Bacon, Milton, and Dryden (at least in the early years after the restoration of Charles II) are the seventeenth-century writers most influenced by the idea of progress, but we do see in other writers the attraction of this new historical perspective, though none is as wholeheartedly committed to it as are Bacon and Milton.

Burton, with his cyclical and degenerative views of history, is hardly a proponent of the idea of progress, but we do occasionally see in him a glimmer of the belief that the moderns can advance beyond the ancients. Though he is a second Democritus reviving the work of the first, he claims not only that he will complete what his predecessor left unfinished but also that his treatise may surpass all previous works on melancholy simply by its accumulation of the knowledge of others: "As a good house-wife out of divers fleeces weaves one piece of cloth, a bee gathers wax and honey out of many flowers, and makes a new bundle of all." Burton repeats the analogy that was commonly invoked throughout the century to argue for the superior advantages of the "moderns": "A dwarf standing on the shoulders of a Giant may see farther than a Giant himself; I may likely add, alter, and see farther than my predecessors."[14] Unlike Bacon and Milton, however, he does not suggest that a radical break with past traditions is necessary for progress. Indeed, his *Anatomy* with its numerous quotations from others creates a sense that Burton feels a real collegiality, even intimacy, with his predecessors. His conception of progress is more like Dryden's than Bacon's—one of succession, of adding to what others have done.

Like Burton, Sir Thomas Browne's historical perspective is eclectic, combining cyclical and decay theories with hints that in the history of knowledge the pattern might be progressive. He feels that he is contributing to the progressive discovery of truth by examining popular beliefs and myths in his *Pseudodoxia Epidemica*, though it is typical of his skeptical temperament that he often finds it impossible to determine conclusively whether these opinions are false or not. Even *Hydriotaphia*, so much concerned with decay, corruption, and the tendency of all earthly things to resolve to dust, reveals his sense that he is living in an age of discovery. This treatise on mortality, on the inability of man to find any earthly remedies for Time the Destroyer, paradoxically opens with Browne's celebration of Time the Revealer: "Time hath endless rarities, and shows of all varieties; which reveals old things in heaven, makes new discoveries in earth, and even earth it self a discovery. That great Antiquity *America* lay buried for thousands of years; and a large part of the earth is still in the Urne unto us."[15] Much of the paradox in this work turns on these two conflicting views of time, for the newly discovered urns reveal our ignorance about the past, and human ignorance and vanity more generally.

Cowley embraced the progressive view of knowledge more firmly than either Burton or Browne. Although works such as his *Discourse By Way of Vision, Concerning the Government of Oliver Cromwell* offered a decidedly cyclical interpretation of the Civil War period, his interest in science led him to embrace a Baconian ideal of progress. Soon after the Restoration he published *A Proposition for the Advancement of Experimental Philosophy* (1661), proposing that a college be established that would "study the improvement and advantage of all other Professions."[16] Though at the time he felt it was probably "hopeless" to raise the necessary money "out of those few dead Reliques of Human Charity and Publick Generosity which are yet remaining in the World," by 1667 the Royal Society had been firmly established for five years (though begun in 1660, it was not incorporated until 1662), and Cowley's "Ode" prefacing Thomas Sprat's *History* of the society could enthusiastically praise the progress science had made. His poem praises Bacon as a heroic man who liberated philosophy and began a new course of progress in learning. Like Bacon and Milton, Cowley reveals a strong preference for linear movement and a tendency to associate error with "wandering." "Our wandring Predecessors" in philosophy were like "th'old *Hebrews*" who "did stray" for years in "Desarts" and "barren Wilderness" (st. 5). The analogy between science and religion reminds us of Bacon, and Cowley's tendency to read contemporary English history in terms of its typological parallels with biblical history also recalls Milton and Dryden. Although Cowley in his emphasis on historical parallels suggests, like Dryden, that there is a repetitive pattern to human experience, his sense of the linear, decidedly progressive movement of history is clear as he describes Bacon as a Moses who "led us forth" from the Egyptian bondage and brought us to "the very Border . . . Of the blest promis'd Land" (st. 5). Bacon, like Moses, could not enter this Canaan, but Cowley envisions the Royal Society actually conquering "these spacious Countries" (st. 6), and he ends the poem by predicting that having begun its "bold work" the society will now move on to new discoveries and advances.

Cowley saw in the Israelites' progress from Egypt to the promised land the pattern of philosophy's history; Bunyan saw in the biblical journey a type for mankind's (and the individual's) spiritual life, its journey from the bondage of sin to salvation.[17] Clearly the idea of man's life as a journey was a conventional Christian metaphor, with deep roots in the Bible and in Judaeo-Christian traditions. But this basic metaphor could be adapted in different ways depending on one's attitude toward history. Whereas Vaughan longed to move by "backward steps," reversing the degenerative pattern of time, Milton, with his radical commitment to progress, believed that people should move continually forward. Turning back is precisely the error to avoid. John Bunyan's *Pilgrim's Progress* similarly stresses the necessity of advancing and the evil temptation of stopping, turning aside, or going back. Bunyan, like Bacon and Milton, insists on the necessity of making a break with the corrupt past. Christian must sever his ties with his past, even leaving his family, to journey to the Celestial City. He realizes that "to go back is nothing but death, to go forward is fear of death, and life everlasting beyond it."[18] Mistrust and Timorous tempt him to "return" to the City of Destruction, Demas to "turn aside" from the path. The monument of Lot's wife that Christian meets vividly reminds him that she was turned into a Pillar of Salt simply for "looking behind her."[19] For Bunyan as for Milton, the Bible encourages a progressive ideal and an acceptance of the "new" as better than the old. Whereas Vaughan with his regressive tendencies finds congenial the biblical notion that one must again become as a child to enter the kingdom of heaven, Bunyan insists that salvation depends on a "New birth," that the danger is in "backsliding."[20] The journey to the Celestial City has its ups and down — evident in the hills and valleys Christian encounters, and in the vicissitudes in the long process of conversion that Bunyan traces in *Grace Abounding* (like Herbert, he was "sometimes up and down twenty times in an hour"[21]) — but it is insistently linear, progressive, and forward-moving.

Milton believed that political history could assume a progressive pattern if people were willing, but Bunyan, long imprisoned for preaching as a Nonconformist, harbored few hopes for an enlightened, reformed England. It was, he believed, the saint's lot to be persecuted. He thus assumes a fundamental split between the pattern of the good Christian's spiritual life and that of the world at large. As his *Life and Death of Mr. Badman* clearly suggests, he believed that England was well on its way to ruin. "Wickedness like a flood is like to drown our English world," indeed perhaps the entire world.[22] But though England is "sinking" in sin, Bunyan proclaims he will "deliver [himself] from the ruins of them that perish,"[23] much as Christian does in *Pilgrim's Progress*. Like the disillusioned Milton at the end of his career, Bunyan contrasts the pattern of England's history with the pattern of spiritual progress that the individual can achieve.

Writers could find progress in science and the arts and in spiritual life, but few saw it in political history. Milton's hopes for England were frustrated by events and by what he saw as his countrymen's obstinate preference for bondage. Dryden for a while believed that England was advancing, but by the time of the supposedly Glorious Revolution of 1688 he had had to revise his assessment of history's pattern. Andrew Marvell, too, for a time seemed to possess a vision of England progressing. In "The First Anniversary of the Government under O.C.," Marvell praises Oliver Cromwell for working to perfect England. Cromwell "tune[s] this lower to that higher Sphere" of heaven (l. 48) as, Amphion-like, he builds the commonwealth.[24] Cromwell is exceptional in his powerful control over history. Whereas other men, including monarchs, are victims of time, disappearing "In the weak Circles of increasing Years" (l. 4), "*Cromwell* alone" rules it, progressing with ever "greater vigour" (l. 7):

> 'Tis he the force of scatter'd Time contracts,
> And in one Year the work of Ages acts. (ll. 13–14)

Marvell even speculates that

> . . . if in some happy Hour
> High Grace should meet in one with highest Pow'r,
> And then a seasonable People still
> Should bend to his, as he to Heavens will. (ll. 131–34)

perhaps the "*Course*" of history could be "Fore-shortned" (l. 139) and the end of time arrive. One is reminded of Bacon's hopes that people through their own efforts, but blessed by Providence, might accelerate history and bring mankind to salvation earlier. Marvell's vision of progress, however, is qualified and conditional. And it was short-lived. Nevertheless, it attests to an optimistic hope that man can mold history.

Marvell's praise of Cromwell addressed the problem of man's relationship to history that concerned these seventeenth-century writers: can human beings control the course of time? To my mind, this is one of the most important issues of this study, and its significance is clearly not limited to the seventeenth century.

As we have seen, several writers believed that people are the makers of history and that they can alter the course of time for the better. Marvell's sense of man's control was limited. For him, only the exceptional individual—a Cromwell, or a Thomas Fairfax[25]—has the power to shape history; the rest are its slaves or victims. Dryden thought that this power was more widely held. Devoting much of his energy as poet-historian to offering political advice, he believed that people could learn from the past and that England's rulers could avert cyclical decline and even encourage progress. Still, the fate of a nation, he believed, depends on its rulers, not on its masses, and if monarchs refuse to learn the lessons of history, there is not much the private individual can do to affect its course. It is Bacon and Milton, however, who were the most revolutionary, for both refused to limit the potential to shape history to the special few, and both argued that the course of history could be radically different in the future than it had been in the past. Though both men believed that England had been given a special providential opportunity, their belief in Providence did not diminish their faith in man's ability to determine the course of history.

Hobbes might seem odd company for Milton, but he too believed that men were responsible for history. In *Leviathan* not only does he blame human weakness and errors in judgment for the Civil War, but he asserts that if the people as well as leaders would accept his rules for preserving commonwealths, cyclical decline could be postponed. Unlike Bacon and Milton, Hobbes does not offer the prospect of a radical change in history from cycles to progress, and there is an element of determinism implicit in his view of human nature, but he does share their sense that people have the power to alter the pattern of history.

Some of these writers lost faith that people would change the course of history for the better—indeed, Hobbes never seems to have had much faith that they would—but they all believed that history is in people's control, and thus that they can alter it. Other writers, however, were convinced that the pattern of time was fixed, essentially unalterable. For them, the question was what people's response to history should be.

A few seemed to find a certain comfort or security in the fact that there was a rational, predictable, stable order to time. Herrick, and Herbert to a lesser extent, saw in the cyclical pattern a reassuring, divinely ordained order. Browne felt that the cycles of history revealed the perfection of God; the balance of light and darkness, generation and corruption, in its symmetry, suggested to him a beautiful order.

More often, however, the pattern of time seemed disappointing or even threatening. Even if they accepted a providential view of history, most writers felt that history presented a less than perfect pattern, which needed to be remedied in some way. Those who assumed that the forces of history were beyond the individual's control, and thus that the shape of history could not be reformed, sought other solutions. Some felt that even if it could not be changed, the course of history must somehow be resisted by the individual. Both Vaughan and Donne suggest that the individual must work against the degenerative pattern of time. One might counter it through memory or perhaps through love or through an imaginative retreat into the past. Herbert tried to recapture the lost intimacy of God through poetry; Burton offered remedies that the individual might try to cure his melancholy, even though madness as a result of the Fall will always be with us. For Herbert and Burton as for Donne and Vaughan, God was ultimately the only perfect remedy for the destructive or painful effects of time. God could prevent Donne from sinking and raise him to heaven; He could take Vaughan home and clear his vision, transplant Herbert to an eternal paradise where there are no cyclical vicissitudes, and permanently cure Burton's melancholy. Nevertheless, the individual's attempts to reverse or resist the course and effects of time anticipated God's final remedies.

If one could not remedy or resist history, he could withdraw. This solution seems to have been of great appeal, judging from the proliferation of "retirement" literature in the seventeenth century. Perhaps when an individual feels powerless to affect the forces of history, the best he can do is retire, protect himself from the storms of time, try to become indifferent to them, and thus in a sense remain untouched. We find this impulse not just in Jonson—with his emphasis on Stoic constancy, on the good man who withdraws from or tries to remain above the threatening vicissitudes of Fortune—but also, for example, in Lovelace, whose poem "The Grasshopper" celebrates self-sufficient friendship as a stable and enduring refuge from the calamities of the Civil War. As is clear in the case of Lovelace, such withdrawal need not be narrowly escapist but may rather be an attempt to create an enduring alternative, more real than the supposedly "real" historical world we live in. Marvell, too, for all his belief that the special individual can shape history, was clearly attracted to the virtues and pleasures of retirement, of withdrawal from active involvement in history, as "Upon Appleton House," "The Garden," and "On a Drop of Dew" attest. There is a fundamental tension in Marvell between the insistence on the necessity of controlling or shaping time—evident not only in the Cromwell poems but also in the admonition "To his Coy Mistress" that it is better to "Rather at once our Time devour, / Than languish in his slow-chapt pow'er" (ll. 39–40)—and the feeling that one should instead retreat from the heated, dusty race of time. Indeed, in *Rehearsal Transpros'd* (1672), Marvell could look back at the Civil War and conclude that "the Cause was too good to have been fought for." At least as important as this famous statement are the sentences immediately following, which suggest that people should not bother to try changing or controlling the course of history. "Men ought to have trusted God; they ought and might have trusted the King, with that whole matter. The *Arms of The Church are Prayers and Tears,* The Arms of the subject are Patience and Petitions. The King himself being of so accurate and piercing a judgment, would soon have felt where it stuck. For men may spare the pains where Nature is at work, and *The world will not go the faster for our driving* [italics mine]. Even as his present Majesties happy Restauration did it self, so all Things else happen in their best and proper time, without any need of our officiousness."[26] We are far here from the sense in Marvell's "First Anniversary . . ." that history's course can be "fore-shortned." Even Dryden at the end of his career seemed to wonder whether people could control history. If, as his late plays *Amphitryon* and *Don Sebastian* suggest, decent individuals are victims of large, impersonal, uncontrollable forces, then perhaps the only thing one can do is withdraw and try to keep one's virtue as best one can, hoping that the revolution of time may bring something better.

For all their varied views and responses, all of these writers felt the need to define the shape of history and to discover in it an order that would make sense of the otherwise bewildering complexity of experience, and all confronted the problem of whether man can control history or is simply victimized by it. Such concerns are by no means restricted to the seventeenth century. They are universal and are still urgent in our own day when we wonder if our civilization is continuously advancing or is bringing about its own destruction. And if it is indeed moving toward its dissolution, is there anything one can do to arrest the process and prevent a catastrophic end? The questions about the shape and purpose of time, and about our relationship to history, persist. Assumptions about time are fundamental. They are embedded in our language and affect our thinking in ways we are only beginning to understand.

Notes

1. Robert Burton, *The Anatomy of Melancholy*, ed. Floyd Dell and Paul Jordan-Smith (New York: Tudor Publishing Co., 1927), pp. 119, 42–43, 48.

2. *The English Poems of George Herbert*, ed. C. A. Patrides (Totowa, N.J.: Rowman and Littlefield, 1974). Subsequent quotations of Herbert's poetry are from this edition.

3. *The Complete Poetry of Henry Vaughan*, ed. French Fogle (New York: Norton, 1964). Subsequent quotations of Vaughan's poetry are from this edition.

4. John Webster, *The Duchess of Malfi*, in *The Complete Works*, ed. F. L. Lucas, 2 (New York: Gordian Press, 1966). See III.v.97–98; V.v.92.

5. See Antonio's speech, V.iii.10–20.

6. Burton, *Anatomy of Melancholy*, pp. 422–23, 11.

7. Browne, *Religio Medici*, in *Works*, 1:16.

8. Thomas Hobbes, *Leviathan*, ed. Michael Oakeshott (Oxford: Basil Blackwell, 1946). See, e.g., pp. 5, 112, 126, 160, 209.

9. Ibid., p. 82.

10. Ibid., p. 119.

11. Ibid., pp. 209–10, 220.

12. Ibid., p. 220.

13. Ibid., p. 136.

14. Burton, *Anatomy of Melancholy,* pp. 19–20.

15. Browne, *Works,* 1:135.

16. Abraham Cowley, "A Proposition for the Advancement of Experimental Philosophy," in *Works,* p. 51.

17. See John Bunyan's preface to *Grace Abounding to the Chief of Sinners,* ed. Roger Sharrock (Oxford: Clarendon Press, 1962), pp. 1–4.

18. John Bunyan, *Pilgrim's Progress,* ed. James Blanton Wharey, 2d ed., rev. by Roger Sharrock (Oxford: Clarendon Press, 1960), p. 43.

19. Ibid., pp. 43, 106, 109.

20. See Bunyan, *Grace Abounding,* p. 15, and Bunyan, *Pilgrim's Progress,* p. 152.

21. Bunyan, *Grace Abounding,* p. 60.

22. Bunyan, "The Author to the Reader," in *The Life and Death of Mr. Badman* (London: Oxford University Press, 1929), p. 13.

23. Bunyan, *Life of . . . Badman,* p. 14.

24. *The Poems and Letters of Andrew Marvell,* ed. H. M. Margoliouth, 3d ed., 1 (Oxford: Clarendon Press, 1971).

25. See "Upon Appleton House," st. 41–45.

26. Andrew Marvell, *"The Rehearsal Transpros'd"* and *"The Rehearsal Transpros'd, The Second Part,"* ed. D. I. B. Smith (Oxford: Clarendon Press, 1971), p. 135. In a different context, Annabel M. Patterson has suggested that throughout Marvell's work there is "a pattern of alternating commitment and retreat, of rash involvement followed by self-doubt or apology" (*Marvell and The Civic Crown* [Princeton: Princeton University Press, 1978], p. 10). Indeed, Marvell's sense of the futility of much human action in *Rehearsal Transpros'd* did not prevent him from himself continuing to defend the "English Liberties." Not long before his death he published his *Account of The Growth of Popery and Arbitrary Government in England* (1678) in an attempt to stir his countrymen to action. At the end of the *Account* Marvell clearly reveals his frustration at his countrymen's unwillingness to act for their own preservation: "It is now come to the fourth act, and the next scene that opens may be Rome or Paris, yet men sit by, like idle spectators, and still give money towards their own tragedy" (*Account . . . ,* in *The Complete Works of Andrew Marvell,* ed. A. B. Grosart [1875; rpt. New York: AMS Press, 1966], 4:412).

Index

Horace, 116, 119, 120, 126, 131n

Idealization of the past: and idea of decay, 6, 74-85; rejected, 23-26, 186. *See also* Donne, John
Innovation: Church of Rome accused of, 14, 77; Hooker's view of, 24. *See also* Bacon, Francis; Donne, John; Dryden, John; Jonson, Ben; Milton, John

Jonson, Ben, 105-29; interest in classical historians, 105, 108; and Stoicism, 106, 116-25; antihistorical attitude, 106, 119-20, 121-24; on parallels between England and Rome, 108-9, 126; on novelty and "news," 110-11; on inconstancy, 111-13; on masks, roles, disguise, 111-12, 117; on fortune, 112-20 *passim*, 125, 128; attitude toward drama, 112, 127-28; on constancy, 116-18, 121; and idea of progress, 119; on poetic immortality, 119-20, 128-29; on golden age, 126; mentioned, 4, 17, 31, 32, 138-57 *passim*, 178, 184, 191, 205, 233, 237-38, 255-60 *passim*, 265, 266, 274
— *The Alchemist*, 110, 111, 113-15, 117, 130n
— *Bartholomew Fair*, 130n
— *The Case is Altered*, 114, 116
— *Catiline*, 105-9 *passim*, 124-25, 127
— *Cynthia's Revels*, 106, 109, 110, 111, 117, 118, 127
— *Eastward Ho*, 109
— "An Epigram. To K. Charles for A 100. Pounds He Sent Me in My Sicknesse" (*Und.* 64), 127
— "An Epistle Answering to One That Asked to be Sealed of the Tribe of Ben" (*Und.* 49), 121-22
— "Epistle to Elizabeth Countesse of Rutland" (*For.* XII), 120, 131n, 156, 257
— "An Epistle to a Friend, to Persuade Him to the Warres" (*Und.* 17), 116
— "Epistle to Katherine, Lady Aubigny" (*For.* XIII), 105, 117, 122, 126

— "An Epistle to Master, John Selden" (*Und.* 16), 105
— "Epithalamion" (*Und.* 77), 120
— "Eupheme; or, the Faire Fame. Left to Posteritie. Elegie on my Muse" (*Und.* 86, 9), 117
— "Eupheme; or, the Faire Fame. Left to Posteritie. The Dedication of her Cradle" (*Und.* 86, 1), 120
— *Every Man in His Humour*, 128
— *Every Man out of His Humour*, 111, 112
— *Golden Age Restored*, 126
— *Hymenae*, 126
— *Love Restored*, 126
— *Magnetic Lady*, 110
— *Masque of Queens*, 119, 126
— "The Mind of the Frontispice to a Booke" (*Und.* 26), 105
— *News from the New World Discovered in the Moon*, 130n
— *Oberon*, 118
— "An Ode. To Himselfe" (*Und.* 25), 125, 127, 128
— "Ode to Himselfe" (*Uncol.*, 53), 128
— *Sejanus*, 105-11 *passim*, 115, 123-24, 125, 214, 219-20
— *The Staple of News*, 106, 109, 111, 114, 130n, 131n
— *Timber*, 109, 118, 125
— "To Clement Edmonds, on his Caesars Commentaries observed, and translated" (*Epig.* CX), 105
— "To Edward Allen" (*Epig.* LXXXIX), 119
— "To Mary Lady Wroth" (*Epig.* CV), 119
— "To My Chosen Friend, the *Learned Translator* of Lucan, Thomas May, *Esquire*" (*Uncol.*, 47), 105
— "To Penshurst" (*For.* II), 118
— "To Sir Henrie Savile" (*Epig.* XCV), 105
— "To Sir Henry Goodyere" (*Epig.* LXXXV), 127
— "To Sir Thomas Roe" (*Epig.* XCVIII), 118
— "To the Immortall Memorie . . . of Sir Lucius Cary, and Sir H. Morison" (*Und.* 72), 123, 129, 257

A NOTE ON THE AUTHOR

ACHSAH GUIBBORY is a member of the department of English at the University of Illinois at Urbana-Champaign. She received her bachelor's degree from Indiana University and her master's and doctorate from the University of California at Los Angeles. Her previous publications include articles in such journals as *Clio,* the *John Donne Journal,* the *Journal of English and Germanic Philology,* and *Huntington Library Quarterly.*